At Home *in the* Kitchen

At Home
in the
Kitchen

The Art of Preparing the Foods
You Love to Eat

Jorj Morgan

CUMBERLAND HOUSE
NASHVILLE, TENNESSEE

Published by
CUMBERLAND HOUSE PUBLISHING, INC.
431 Harding Industrial Drive
Nashville, TN 37211

Cover design by Karen Phillips
Text design by Julie Pitkin

Library of Congress Cataloging-in-Publication Data

Morgan, Jorj, 1953–
    At home in the kitchen : the art of preparing the foods you love to eat / Jorj Morgan.
        p. cm.
    ISBN 1-58182-170-0 (pbk. : alk. paper)
    1. Cookery. I. Title.
    TX652.M568 2001
    641.5—dc21

                                                                2001017242

Printed in Canada
2 3 4 5 6 7 8 — 06 05 04 03

To Morgo, with unending love and gratitude,
for choosing me to share your life.
And to my babies, Trey, Chris, and Jon,
for making me work hard to be the mom you guys deserve.

In loving memory of my Dad
for his everlasting encouragement.

Table of Contents

Foreword

My mom hated to cook. Don't get me wrong—she was a great mom. It's just that the kitchen was foreign territory in terms of her expertise. We even had a mural of a Parisian café painted on the wall. Somehow, it symbolized mom's desire to dine out. She avoided home cooking by employing a wonderful nanny and living close to my grandparents. In fact, my earliest memories of warm, cozy ovens and savory smells are rooted in my two grandmothers' kitchens. I was lucky that they each lived on the same small street only a few houses apart. At the north end of a gravel road lived my robust Irish grandmother and grandfather. Gram was very adept at cooking from huge steaming pots for her ever-enlarging family, of which my dad was one of five children. The south end of the same road was home to my petite Polish grandmother and courtly Jewish grandfather. Grammy was at her best when she crafted dainty morsels for the children of her only child—my mom. I learned to cook from both of my grandmothers. Gram in a uniform of a starched white apron over everything she ever wore, cooking ten apple pies or making griddlecakes from three skillets at once and Grammy offering chicken soup with tiny matzo balls alongside her tangy stuffed cabbage no bigger than her finger. Their varied backgrounds and totally different styles of cooking merged to create my diverse palate.

Spending time with my grandmothers and cousins led me to love kitchen cooking. The impression that cooking is an event that is meant to be shared with others was instilled in me as a youngster. One of my earliest attempts at entertaining took place after my brother's first little league winning season. The entire team found its way to our back porch to celebrate their final victory. Dad found his way to the grill with the hot dogs. We iced the sodas in our aluminum red wagon. I raced to the kitchen to decorate the hastily purchased store-bought cake with M&Ms and whipped cream. Pleased with the finished product, I moved on to peanut butter and jelly sandwiches cut into circles—my tribute to the baseball. In need of entertainment, I turned on my phonograph and played the Beatles current hit, "I Want to Hold Your Hand." The boys ate and goofed around and I danced with the star pitcher. I am certain that this was the day that I decided that I liked to "cook" for parties!

Out on my own and living in a new city far away from my grandmas, I found that cooking meals and sharing them with others was a wonderful way to create and build new friendships. Soups and stews are meant to be communal. On my first Christmas, in my own apartment, I decided to have a fondue party. The menu featured fresh vegetables and pieces of cubed meat cooked in hot oil served with an assortment of terrific sauces. The food was set on a square glass cocktail table (my first piece of furniture) and we sat on the floor—because I didn't have chairs. Seating aside, it turned out to be a fun party. I repeated it for years adding more guests and chocolate fondue for dessert.

For my mother's surprise forty-fifth birthday party, I served Lobster Newburg, her favorite dish, to 35 people in that same tiny one bedroom apartment. The party spilled out into the hall, but no one seemed to mind. The Newburg recipe called for lobster meat, but it didn't specify whether the meat should be raw or cooked. I had only my own instincts to go on and chose to purchase eight pounds of ridiculously expensive frozen lobster. The defrosting alone took hours, not to mention all that shelling! But the sauce was divine and the party was a huge hit.

After I was married and started my family, my husband and I would often invite new friends to our home for dinner parties. I would plan a festive menu at the beginning of the week and set the table the night before with my best china or wildest paper plates. Our small children made planning ahead a necessity. I always allowed some extra time for unforeseen problems. For example, to allow for inevitable child emergencies that might interfere with the timing of dinner, I prepared simmering braised lamb shanks and wild rice instead of a last minute entrée like grilled steaks. Lamb shanks become tender with additional cooking, while steaks are best served directly from the grill. Not to mention that grilling steaks while wiping running noses has a way of subduing any guest's appetite.

My children matriculated to pre-school and I found myself enrolled in the PTA. Parent groups led to charitable organizations and my assignment to the hospitality committee. I found it easy to be creative with breads and cakes for last minute bake sales. In just a few short years I found myself chairing even larger fundraising events, including luncheons, shipboard galas, festivals, and hotel balls. No matter what the venue, the affair centered on great food. Elaborately presented entrées or interesting finger food appetizers could make or break an otherwise uneventful soiree. I discovered that the backbone of a successful event is delicious food designed by talented chefs.

I spent hours organizing menus and tasting meals for all of these fantastic parties. I copied every menu or meal that I enjoyed and carefully watched every food presentation. At home I would try out the dishes on my family and friends. I wrote down every experiment and filed my personal notes in a huge box for later use at future dinner parties. I had very responsible critics, my three growing sons, who took their recipe tasting duties extremely seriously. If they spit it out—I started over. The day they all agreed on a dish that they loved was the day that I became a recipe writer.

With all of this early family and entertaining experience, and the bonus of some free time when the boys began full days of school, my two best friends and I embarked on a catering career. We had previously worked together on several successful charity events, and we envisioned a party-planning company that would do three or four functions a year. We grossly underestimated the demand for new and creative caterers. Our first job fell into our laps, while the ink was still drying on our freshly printed stationery. We agreed to serve a luncheon for three hundred people in the early fall of the new social season. The event was held at the waterfront home of one of the most prominent hostesses in South Florida.

To accommodate the large number of guests, we hired a carpenter to build the world's largest salad bar station. It sat atop two large tables and allowed service from both sides. It looked like a giant toolbox, painted white, with large cut out circles. The ice sat in pans underneath this display, to chill the large bowls that fit snugly into the sides—although resting at a precariously delicate angle. We filled the bowls with fresh seasonal salads that merged the flavors of roasted chicken with fresh dill, tangy lemon and garlic marinated vegetables, and tortellini pasta tossed with a jalapeño-spiked vinaigrette. Every vacant surface on the "tool box" was covered with fresh whole green and red peppers, yellow squash and bunches of herbs. At the ends of the station, we placed wicker baskets lined with colorful linen napkins filled with corn, zucchini, and apple streusel muffins. Waitresses passed trays of bite size key lime squares and loaded chocolate brownies for dessert. The event was a huge success and we were exhausted. Before we could blink an eye, the jobs started pouring in and our party planning company was launched. This was the day I became a caterer.

Those were fun and totally hectic years. Our parties were creative and expansive. We catered a corporate party for seventy aboard a cruise ship. We brought aboard all of the supplies hours in advance and prepared the food in a small galley two decks below the open-air party area. Individual platters of hors d'oeuvres, featuring skewered marinated tortellini, spicy baked shrimp, and new potatoes stuffed with caramelized salmon salad, were painstakingly assembled in very close quarters. Only when we were an hour out to sea did we realize that two out of three of us were not immune to seasickness!

Soon thereafter, we orchestrated a groundbreaking ceremony for the development of a new shopping center. We handled every detail. The invitations were written with calligraphy, sealed with wax and delivered by tuxedoed messengers, who presented each one on a silver tray. We erected a gleaming white tent on the empty lot and surrounded it with truckloads of potted shrubs and trees. Since there was no kitchen, we opted for a cold, gourmet picnic supper as our theme. Each guest was seated at a table for eight served by their personal waiter. At each place setting there was a green lacquered picnic basket containing a china plate, utensils, linen napkin, wine glass and a blooming white rose sitting in a single stem crystal vase. The centerpieces were created from larger vases filled with crisp wafers and bread sticks. The picnic theme continued with bowls of fresh garden salad, tossed at each table, and served with crisp tarragon vinaigrette poured from rustic pitchers. Each server offered the seated guests at his or her table a large platter of cold chicken medallions smothered in tuna and lemon caper sauce, chilled fresh asparagus, and wild rice pilaf. Dessert choices included strawberry layer cake with cream cheese frosting, lemon sunshine cake with butter cream frosting and decadent chocolate mahogany cake. The party was a huge success and the requests for corporate events kept coming.

Within a few years, my friends and I found that the needs of our children, now ranging in age from infants to adolescents, took precedence over our growing and demanding business. One by one, we exited our party-planning and catering adventures. I continued to be involved with many social and charitable functions, particularly those events that included food, cooking, and entertaining. One of my favorites was a spectacular dinner party held in our home for forty-five loyal patrons of the county public library system. The guests of honor were authors Jeremiah Healy, Carol Higgins Clark, Steven Alten, and rhythm and blues singer Darlene Love. Patrons contributed to the charity anticipating an intimate evening with celebrity authors, while dining on fabulous food. No pressure! The authors moved from table to table in order to get to know and talk to all of the guests. Out of necessity, I planned five distinct courses to accommodate the table switching. Musical chairs turned out to be great fun and I found ways to use this idea at many of my home parties. My menu featured a salad showstopper of portabella mushrooms stuffed with goat cheese and sun-dried tomatoes on fresh greens. The star of the meal was grilled pork tenderloin medallions with Jack Daniels sauce, and mashed sweet potatoes garnished with sprigs of rosemary. I offered desserts that included fresh berries with sabayon and chocolate Amaretto cheesecake. The weather was gorgeous. We sat poolside with flickering candlelight, pastel-colored tablecloths and bowls of fresh-cut flowers. This was the evening when I became an established hostess.

Through all of the fantastic parties I never lost sight of the real value of cooking at home. I sometimes fuss as much with a Wednesday night quesadilla or a Sunday football supper as I do with any party that I host. My boys are always bringing friends over and there is always a meal to be shared. I spend the minutes before dinner chopping and slicing as my personal relaxation technique after a stressful day. This quiet time is often interrupted by boyish conversation, beginning with, "Hey mom, you'll never guess...."

It wasn't until my oldest son left for college that the idea of writing a cookbook began to take form. Many of my peers have children that are out on their own for the first time. During this period, our careers are established and our families are self-supporting which creates previously unthinkable free time. I found a common bond between young adults that are setting up housekeeping for the first time and their parents that have recently found a few extra minutes in each day. Both groups want to spend more time cooking at home. As I am never bashful about my love of cooking and entertaining, I often receive telephone calls about the most basic cooking questions. These calls come from my large circle of friends and even their sons and daughters. What is the difference between sautéing and frying? How do I cook a steak if I don't have a grill? There are no fresh herbs in the winter—can I substitute dried herbs? This recipe for chicken is getting old—how do I make a new sauce? I lost the directions for lasagna, do I bake it at 350 degrees? Mom, I miss your grilled chicken Caesar salads! Jorj, can you give me the recipe for your easy meat loaf with eggplant? Now is the time that I have decided to become a cookbook writer.

I realized as I began assembling my recipes that I had developed a unique philosophy about food. For me, cooking and entertaining are synonymous with sharing and growing. The sociality of food solidifies our everyday family life as well as opens the door to new relationships. The calming sameness of stirring and cutting is a tension reducer that decreases the stress of the day and invites shared experience with family and friends. I discovered that you don't have to be cooking for guests to enjoy preparing a midweek meal.

Now I want to share with you the simple fact that you can cook the foods that you love at home. All you need is the desire to create a wonderful meal, fresh ingredients, a stocked pantry, a few kitchen gadgets, and a basic knowledge of cooking terms.

I want to encourage the everyday cook so that we do not become obsolete in today's hectic society. I believe that we can add daily family meals to our numerous activities like little league games, dancing lessons, and business meetings. If we can schedule our lives using computer chips and pagers, we can utilize this same technology to incorporate menu planning into our schedule. We owe it to ourselves and to our families to find the time to enjoy cooking and pass down the rituals of a shared existence.

We begin by occasionally passing the convenient-drive through restaurant on the nearest street corner. Try looking away from the easily purchased, scientifically created, microwave meals that imitate real food. Let's not allow a generation of children to be raised thinking that a sit-down dinner only occurs on holidays and in restaurants. A get-together after work does not have to be held in a restaurant and could involve a gathering at someone's home or apartment.

We can re-create the days of joining together to set tables and helping to prepare the meal. This in turn will spark the fun and creativity of entertaining. The simplest concepts of cooking need not loom as unknown territory and block the way to more sophisticated culinary skills.

I'm going to challenge you to believe that you can create a different cooking environment. You have already taken the first step. This cookbook takes the mystique out of cooking with simple, easy-to-read recipes. I begin with basic kitchen setup. The first chapter includes a listing of the foods that you want to keep on hand, a guide to the gadgets and small appliances that you need in the kitchen, and an explanation of basic cooking terms.

In each recipe you will find Helpful Hints that give you insight to the specific recipe. I have included Simple Substitutions to alert you to ingredient options. Technique tips discuss various cooking processes and the All About tips tell you more than you will ever need to know. Setting the Scene helps you to uniquely present a dish and is my favorite tip.

Every recipe, cooking tip and entertainment style comes from my personal experience. This knowledge is crafted from dining in wonderful restaurants, collecting articles from beautifully pictured magazines, deciphering grandma's hand-written notes, watching television food chefs, thumbing through turned-down pages of my most worn cookbooks, and dozens of other influences. I have perfected these recipes and techniques over many years and assembled them in a way that will allow you to make them yours. Share your cooking experiences and get answers to your questions by visiting my website at www.jorj.com. There you will find supplemental information that will further your ability to liberate yourself from traditional recipes and gain the inspiration to create your own favorite dishes.

My expertise in the culinary field includes 25 years of entertaining and 22 years of being a mom. I have made plenty of errors and been surprised on more than one occasion with compliments. All the while I have built self-confidence in my own ability to be creative in the kitchen and share that creativity with friends and family. My hope is that this book will give you the same confidence to enter the kitchen and begin the adventure. Today is the day that you become a cook!

Acknowledgments

One doesn't embark on a project of this size unless someone else influences or prods them along—even a little. I had a huge push from my son, Trey. Getting ready to leave home for college—afraid that I would miss him too much (I did)—he suggested that I write down some of my recipes for him to share with pals out on their own for the first time. Little did we know that his little push would develop into this cookbook and supporting website. I hope you will join me in saying, "Thanks, Treysers."

Thanks also to my husband, the editor. My first group of recipes and articles needed some serious help! He taught me a lot that I had managed to ignore in high school grammar class. Morgo also gets the Ultimate Taster award for twenty-four years of sampling my experiments and constantly giving me his thumbs up.

Thank you to my best gal pals Cindy Greenberg, Doreen Koenig, and Sharon Stiles, and their husbands for all the recipe sharing, dinners out, and tons of love, friendship, and support.

The Internet component for this project grew out of conversations and information from my special friends Linda and Mike O'Bryon. You guys are the best.

From my Memorable Occasions catering days, thank you to Mary Mullen and Robin Schmidt for teaching me everything from bathing broccoli in a bath tub to creating hundreds of gourmet baskets. We had a blast!

To my "executive mom" friends at BlueSuitMom.com, Maria Bailey and Rachael Bender, thanks for the opportunity to share my cooking-at-home philosophy with thousands of busy, working moms. Thanks also to Jill Kasky at Money.net for the chance to write holiday articles for stock-watching cooks.

Now, on to my email recipe testers who dedicated weeks and weeks to testing recipes on their family and friends. I am eternally thankful for every comment, suggestion, and criticism. You have made this book so much better than it would have been without you. The readers can look forward to meeting you on the website and interacting with you about recipes, menus, party plans, and fun kitchen tips. Thank you to Gail Jordan, Nellie Shelton, PJ Forbes, Susie Belt, Suzy Caldwell, Linda O'Bryon, Lucy Weber, Susan Holden, Kathy Guerke, Rose Dreyfus, Patty Echarte, Lisa Scott Founds, Sharron Jackson, Micki Lindemann, Judy Zimmer, Beth Park, Lisa Woods, Rita Case, Jan Crocker, Susan Arch, Gail and Lanny Kalik, Melodie Monberg, Lynn Frasier, Eileen Lank, and Beth and John Trombino.

To Ron and Julie Pitkin and everyone at Cumberland House Publishing, thank you for allowing me to realize my dream.

And most importantly, thank you from the bottom of my heart to the women who shaped my life with their strength, caring, warmth, laughter, and loving kitchens—Marie Skoronik Cohen, Mary Daugherty Magner, Mary Jane Morgan and Re Re Da Silva Cohen Magner. I love you all and know that you are with me every day.

"Come on guys—just one more little taste...please?"

—Glenda's urgent plea to taste the chicken pepperoni sauce one more time before the governor arrives for dinner in Neil Simon's play *Seems Like Old Times.*

Getting Started

FOOD TO KEEP ON HAND

Stocking your kitchen with some basic food stuffs is the first step to becoming a relaxed and organized cook. Stocked shelves are necessary for three reasons. First, keeping some essential items on hand prepares you for the arrival of unexpected guests. Second, weekly meal preparation becomes easier, faster, and smoother. Third, grocery shopping is better organized and reduced to finding fresh ingredients and specialty items required for specific menus.

You definitely do not have to fill your pantry with all of the items at one time. Your tastes, budget, and culinary talents will differentiate between the items you constantly depend upon and those you only need once in a while. Here is a list of basics that will work well with the recipes in this book.

OILS, VINEGAR AND WINES

Vegetable cooking oil is used for sautéing, frying, and in baking. Choose one that fits your dietary requirements.

Good quality olive oil is used when making salad dressings or to toss in with a spur-of-the moment pasta sauce. When you sauté with a small amount of olive oil be aware of its higher smoking point.

Sesame oil is not used as often as the others, but is nice to have available when adding an Asian flavor to marinades and sautéed vegetables.

Vegetable oil cooking spray is excellent to use in preparing baking pans, casserole dishes, sauté and grill pans so that the food does not stick. A beneficial side effect is the reduction in the amount of fat used in preparing the dish.

Vinegar comes in many flavors. I keep a large bottle of red wine vinegar in the pantry. I also keep balsamic, tarragon, raspberry, champagne, and rice wine vinegars because they are basically interchangeable when preparing a salad dressing or marinade.

Good quality white and red wines are used in many sauces. You do not need to purchase the most expensive wines to cook well. However, the wine must be good tasting. My rule of thumb for purchasing wine that will be used in a sauce is that if the wine is good enough to drink, then it is good enough to use in your sauce. A wine that has turned to vinegar will make the sauce taste bitter. *Sherry* is bottled either dry or sweet and sometimes is called cocktail sherry. *Cooking sherry* is found with cooking wines in the grocery store. I prefer to use an inexpensive bottle of dry sherry when flavoring soups.

CANNED GOODS

Chicken and beef broth can be purchased in canned, boxed, or soup-base form. Homemade stocks are the most desirable when making soups and sauces. Check out the recipe for

Chicken Stock with Roasted Vegetables (page 58). The canned alternative is important to keep on hand for the times when homemade stock is not available. Choose a product that meets the sodium requirements in your diet. I prefer a low sodium broth, so that I can control the seasonings of the finished meal.

Chopped tomatoes also come in varying sizes of cans or boxes. I prefer to use a chopped plum tomato product rather than a stewed or puréed product. This also gives you the luxury of creating a fresh dish like salsa or a crostini topping. *Tomato paste* comes in various can sizes. I keep several small cans in the pantry because most recipes call for only a small amount of tomato paste when flavoring or thickening a sauce.

Canned black beans are a staple because the beans can be used in many ways. They are a great addition when mixed with rice, perfect when rinsed and tossed into a salsa, and flavorful when sautéed with onions and puréed into a smooth, thick sauce. *Refried beans,* although not quite as diverse as black beans, are easily made into quick appetizers in both nachos and layered dips. (See the recipe for Super Nachos Two Ways on page 260.)

Canned corn and *peas* are the basic vegetables that I keep on hand in the pantry. Sweet peas work well in soups and creamy pasta sauces. Corn is used in salsa or served in fresh grilled quesadilla. If you have more freezer space than room in your pantry, frozen vegetables work just as well. Add a package of frozen spinach for dishes like Vegetable Lasagna (page 178).

Tuna and *salmon* can be used interchangeably in appetizer dips with vegetables or spread onto crackers. You can create a rich sauce by blending either with mayonnaise, capers, lemon, and anchovies to serve over cooked chicken, fish, or vegetables. (Take a look at the Vegetable Party Platter with Tuna Sauce recipe on page 100).

Black olives, whether sliced or whole, act as a great last minute garnish for a party platter, a colorful addition to a tossed salad, or a robust ingredient in a lemon and wine sauce.

JARS AND SUCH

A jar of *sun-dried tomatoes* packed in olive oil is the most expensive way to purchase this product, but it is a must in the pantry. A less expensive alternative is to buy packaged dried tomatoes and reconstitute them in warm water or olive oil as needed. I love the jar option because the tomatoes are tender and you can use the flavored olive oil in pasta sauce or to top a homemade pizza.

Capers are small, salty flower buds that usually require rinsing before use. They are excellent in white wine and lemon sauces over fish and chicken. (See the recipe for Sole with Parsley, Butter, and Caper Sauce on page 221.)

Bottled *spaghetti sauce* and *pizza sauce* are useful as starters when making a large amount of red sauce for pasta. You can substitute either when making a quick meal. Take a look at the recipe for Chicken Pepperoni (page 186) for a good example.

Bottled *Italian salad dressing* can be a great substitute for a meat, fish, or poultry marinade when dinner preparation time is short. It works equally well as a flavoring for sautéed or grilled fresh vegetables.

Anchovies are a crucial ingredient in Spicy Caesar Salad (page 116), which makes terrific mid week meal. I usually buy the flat fillets in the tin and keep several in the pantry.

Roasted red peppers are precooked, sliced, bottled in liquid, and presented in a jar. Although this is not nearly as desirable as fresh roasted peppers, it can be a good substitute in certain recipes when time is limited. They are listed as an ingredient in Grilled Stuffed Veal Chops (page 126).

CONDIMENTS

Mustard, mayonnaise, and ketchup are stocked for all the typical reasons. However, combining ketchup and mayonnaise with fresh dill creates a sensational sauce (see the recipe for Salmon Cakes with Sauce Remoulade on page 230).

Barbecue sauce is terrific when time does not permit cooking one of your own. Brush a small amount on a fresh fish fillet while it sizzles in the grill pan for a new twist on fish.

Hot pepper sauce, although best known for its addition to tasty chicken wings, is also used to flavor soups and sauces and spice up salsa.

Worcestershire sauce is used in salad dressings and marinades.

Chili sauce and chutney have very different tastes, but can be used similarly. For a quick appetizer, pour the chutney over a spreadable sharp or Swiss cheese product and serve with crackers. The same is true for chili sauce served over goat cheese or cream cheese.

Salsa from the jar is great for chip dipping. It is also used in flavoring chicken and fish, or topping vegetables like cold asparagus.

Soy sauce is an Asian flavoring used mostly in marinades and vinaigrettes.

PASTA, RICE, & DRIED BREAD PRODUCTS

Pasta in its dried form comes in dozens of shapes and sizes and has a very long shelf life. I keep at least two boxes on hand at all times. A flat noodle (such as linguini or vermicelli) and a tube shape (like Penne or ziti) allows me to match the pasta to the sauce that I have prepared.

Rice comes in quick cook versions and premixed packages. As a staple, I keep one box of white rice and one box of brown rice . Arborio rice is a real treat to keep in the pantry for making risotto when time permits.

Crackers should always be kept in stock to accompany quick dips and spreads, and *tortilla chips* for salsa dips, nachos from the microwave, and in creating a delicious sauce (See the recipe for Rustic Cinnamon Roasted Chicken on page 190.)

Bread crumbs and corn flake crumbs can be used together for crusty coatings when frying chicken or separately when used to top a casserole. I keep a box of both on hand. I use the unseasoned (plain) bread crumbs in many of the recipes because I prefer to season the crumbs myself. *Croutons* and *packaged stuffing cubes* are used as the packages suggest or as an alternative to bread crumbs when crushed and flavored.

Dried beans are not necessary to keep on hand since they generally require more preparation than other staples. However, they will last for a long while in the pantry, and are great to have when making soups with leftovers like ham or turkey.

BAKING NEEDS

Flour is used in baked goods and to thicken sauces and gravy. If you are planning to bake bread using a bread machine, then include bread flour and whole wheat flour on this list.

Oats are a wonderful addition to cookies, breads, and cobbler toppings. (See the recipe for Apple Strawberry Cobbler on page 302.)

Cornmeal lasts forever and is necessary when making corn muffins.

Granulated sugar, confectioners' sugar (also known as *powdered sugar),* and *brown sugar* are required in most baking recipes. Keep a box of each, knowing that you can sometimes interchange them if you run out of one or the other.

Cocoa powder is an unsweetened cooking ingredient and not a hot chocolate drink. A tin will last for a long time in the pantry.

Honey and molasses are used in many baking recipes. Molasses comes in dark and light forms and although they can be interchanged, it is better to follow the specifics of the recipe. Store the remainder in a tightly sealed bottle and it will last until the next time you need it.

Unsweetened chocolate squares, semisweet chocolate, and white chocolate are used in many different forms when baking cookies, cakes, and breads. The shelf life is not quite as long as with other staples, but we tend to use chocolate a bit more often than some other ingredients, so it rarely goes to waste.

Nut pieces are used in toppings, cookies, and snack cakes. Depending on your preference keep one or two packages of chopped walnuts or pecans in the pantry.

Cornstarch is used to thicken and smooth sauces or gravy and as the basis of a fluffy cookie batter. (See the recipe for Iced Orange Treats on page 284.)

Baking powder and baking soda are two very different ingredients that are often used in the same recipe. Keep a tin of baking powder and a box of baking soda, making sure that you do not mix them up.

Yeast comes prepackaged in rapid rising or standard forms. I prefer the jar version for allowing accurate measurements when using the bread machine.

Coffee, sweetened condensed milk, and evaporated milk are used in some recipes. I prefer to keep a can on hand, rather than to run out to the store for the few times that I need either evaporated or sweetened condensed milk. I keep a jar of *instant coffee* to mix with boiling water when a recipe requires brewed coffee. (See the recipe for Loaded Chocolate Brownies on page 296.)

Vanilla extract is kept in my pantry rather than with the spices, because it is used much more in baking than in cooking. I buy a large bottle of good quality vanilla, and store it well sealed.

INSTANT FIXERS

Gravy browning sauce adds a dark color to your most flavorful gravy without adding any taste.

Instant mashed potatoes are great for those times when you have added too much milk to the boiled potatoes. A small amount of the instant mixed into the bowl will change runny potatoes into creamy ones.

Instant onion soup mix is very rarely used to make soup in my kitchen, but it is a good tool to spice up dips and ground beef.

Packaged *ranch or Italian dressing mix* can be used to flavor dips or as a rub on meats when the spice cabinet is running low.

Spices

Salt and pepper are used to your individual taste in most recipes. I choose freshly ground pepper and coarse salt. Keep both on hand as well as *ground white pepper*.

Dried basil, oregano, tarragon, dill, and cilantro are used interchangeably in most recipes. I prefer to use fresh herbs, but many times the dried version will work as a good substitution. Use a lesser amount of dried herbs than fresh in recipes. *Old Bay Seasoning* is a specialty spice that I like to use for chicken and fish. One tin will last a very long time. *Bay leaves* are whole dried leaves used to season soups and stews. Remember to remove the leaves before you serve the dish.

Chili powder adds a uniquely rich and spicy flavor to many dishes. Keep plenty available as you will use more of this than you think. (See the recipe for Chicken Chili with Veggies on page 142.)

Dried red pepper flakes are a hot spice and should be used sparingly.

Ground ginger, ground cinnamon, and ground nutmeg are spices that are most used in baking. However, ginger and cinnamon can also flavor cooked sauces. Nutmeg flavors a creamy white sauce called béchamel.

Lemon and lime juice are found in concentrated form, packaged in bottles or frozen in cans. Although fresh is best, either of these alternatives will work in a pinch.

Dairy Staples

Milk, butter, and eggs will be a weekly addition to your shopping list. Remember to check the freshness dates on each. *Sour cream* and *cream cheese* are staples for making quick appetizers or sauces and in baking.

Grated Parmesan cheese and other cheeses will keep for several weeks in the refrigerator. Crumbled cheeses like *Gorgonzola, blue,* and *Feta* are great additions to a fresh, tossed salad. *Goat cheese* is terrific especially when combined with sun-dried tomatoes. Packaged shredded *sharp* and *mozzarella* cheeses are excellent in casseroles.

Jars of *prepared horseradish* and *chopped garlic* are used in sauces and when cooking. Both will keep for a long time in the refrigerator.

To share your thoughts on must-have pantry food visit www.jorj.com.

FOODS TO KEEP ON HAND

Oils, Vinegar, and Wines
Vegetable cooking oil
Good quality olive oil
Vegetable oil spray
Vinegar
Red and white wines

Jars and Such
Roasted red peppers
Sun-dried tomatoes
Capers
Spaghetti sauce
Pizza sauce
Italian salad dressing
Anchovies

Pasta, Rice and Beans
Pasta
Brown and white rice
Crackers
Tortilla chips
Bread crumbs
Corn flake crumbs
Croutons
Packaged stuffing cubes
Dried beans

Instant Fixers
Gravy browning sauce
Instant mashed potatoes
Instant onion soup
Packaged salad dressing

Spices
Salt and pepper
Dried basil
Dried oregano
Dried tarragon
Dried dill

Dried cilantro
Old Bay Seasoning
Bay leaves
Chili powder
Dried red pepper flakes
Ground ginger
Ground cinnamon
Ground nutmeg
Lemon juice
Lime juice

Canned Goods
Chicken broth
Beef broth
Cream soups
Canned tomatoes
Canned beans
Canned corn and peas
Tuna and salmon
Black olives

Condiments
Ketchup
Mustard
Mayonnaise
Soy sauce
Barbecue sauce
Chutney
Hot pepper sauce
Worcestershire sauce
Salsa
Chili sauce

Baking Needs
All-purpose, bread, and whole wheat flour
Oats
Cornmeal
Granulated and confectioners' sugar
Good quality vanilla extract

Cocoa powder

Honey

Molasses

Unsweetened chocolate squares

Semisweet chocolate

White chocolate

Evaporated milk

Nuts

Baking powder

Baking soda

Yeast

Instant coffee

Sweetened condensed milk

Cornstarch

Dairy Staples

Milk

Butter

Eggs

Sour cream

Cream cheese

Grated Parmesan cheese

Gorgonzola, blue, and feta cheese

Goat, mozzarella, and sharp cheese

Horseradish

Chopped garlic

GADGETS IN THE KITCHEN

The bricklayer must have a trowel to spread cement. The painter requires a brush to transfer his art to canvas. The lion tamer keeps a chair nearby as he places his head into the lion's mouth. Likewise, the aspiring cook must possess the right tool to prepare a worthwhile dish.

Technology and inventiveness provide a wide array of appliances and gadgets designed for kitchen use. Entire stores are devoted to pots and pans of all sizes, colors, coatings and materials. Catalogues boast warehouses full of timesaving tools and utensils. Television personalities devote segments of their shows to the newest and coolest prototypes of culinary machines.

While all of this can be overwhelming, it's really quite easy to pare down the list to basic kitchen essentials. The following is a brief description of utensils, gadgets, and appliances that are necessary tools to use with the recipes in this book.

UTENSILS

Long-handled spoons are essential kitchen utensils. The *wooden spoon* is perfect for stirring soups, scraping the brown bits from the bottom of a pan, and stirring batters. A *slotted spoon* removes vegetables from boiling water. A *pasta fork* has several tines that both stir and gently lift the pasta from the cooking water.

Spatulas come in many sizes and styles. They are basically long handled flat utensils used to flip pancakes, turn sautéing foods and lift cooked foods from the pan. Choose a flat spatula that works well with your pan. A slotted one is useful for lifting foods from oil. I keep a narrow, flat spatula on hand for transferring cookies from the baking tray to the rack. Use a rubber spatula for scraping down the sides of mixing bowls.

Tongs are useful for picking up the food from the hot surface, as one would do when removing a hot dog from a grill.

A *long-handled ladle* is great for serving soup from the pot to the bowl.

A good set of *kitchen knives* is an essential component of the well-equipped kitchen. The set must include a wide knife for carving, a serrated knife for slicing bread, and at least one paring knife for chopping and cutting. Beyond the basics you may want to add a *knife sharpener,* a pair of *kitchen shears,* and a large *cleaver.* An easily cleaned *cutting board* will protect your countertops from scratches.

A *meat mallet* is used to pound certain cuts of meat and chicken to tenderize them.

A *rolling pin* is used to roll out dough for cookies and breads. If your kitchen does not include a meat mallet, the gentle use of a rolling pin is a good substitution.

Whisks come in sizes ranging from small to large, round or flat, and can be made of plastic or wire. Choose one that feels comfortable to your hand and fits into your bowls and pots.

GADGETS

The *garlic press* is used to crush whole, peeled or not peeled, cloves of garlic into tiny, minced pieces.

Measuring cups and measuring spoons are required for accurate measurements. Choose functional pieces rather than decorative ones.

A *turkey baster* has a round rubber bulb on one end. It is used to withdraw the liquid from the bottom of a roasting pan in order to baste the meat or poultry.

The *pastry brush* is used to paint food with butter, oil, or egg.

Hand-held grating tools come in many sizes and shapes. Because I do most of the grating in a food processor, I only keep a small, flat grating tool in order to grate fresh ginger or small amounts of Parmesan cheese.

A *funnel* is necessary when pouring liquids into a container with a small opening, such as transferring olive oil to a cruet.

Use a *meat thermometer,* inserted into the fleshiest part of the meat or poultry to determine its doneness. (See the recipe for Roasted Chicken and Vegetables on page 184.)

Choose either an *electric* or *hand-held can opener.*

Steamer baskets are made in a collapsible form or as one pot that fits into a larger one. You can also use a small wire mesh colander sitting in a pot of boiling water with a fairly tight lid to accomplish the steaming task.

A *wire mesh colander* comes in many sizes. I suggest one that fits easily into your pot in order to double its use.

A *vegetable peeler* is used on everything from potatoes to apples. Make note of your preference as they offer right- and left-handed peelers.

POTS, PANS, AND SUCH

A *two-piece broiler pan* comes sized to your oven in most cases. Use it to broil foods under high heat. The shallow bottom piece can be used as a baking pan if necessary. *Sauté and frying pans* (also called skillets) come in many sizes and depths. Technically a frying pan has sides that are deeper and more perpendicular than a sauté pan. But the two are really interchangeable. I prefer a good quality pan with a nonstick surface. In order to make soups, stews, and deep fried foods, you need a large *stockpot* with lid.

Choose a standard size *saucepan* with lid to boil water for veggies and pasta, cook sauces, and warm canned food.

A *cookie baking sheet* and *wire racks* for cooling are necessary to bake cookies. The baking sheet can also be used for roasting sliced vegetables such as eggplant.

A *double boiler* is a pot that comes equipped with an insert that sits inside and does not touch the bottom of the pan. Therefore the food in the inserted piece does not come in direct contact with the heat source. A double boiler is mostly used for melting chocolate and making sauces. (See the recipe for Chocolate Shortcake with Strawberries and Chocolate Sauce on page 300.)

The hottest pan in town is the *grill pan*. Foods that are prepared using this pan are seared over high heat using a small amount of oil. (Check out Seared Tuna in Oriental Marinade on page 220 and Big Juicy Hamburger with Grilled Onions on page 109 to see what I mean.) Choose one with a nonstick surface for easy cleanup.

A note about *casserole dishes* and *mixing bowls:* choose those that fit your decor and drawer space. Casserole dishes tend to be decorative as well as functional. Mixing bowls should offer at least three sizes and be easily stackable for storing. The basics of baking pans (or dishes) include a *pie pan*, two or more *cake pans, muffin tins, loaf pans*, and a *springform pan* for cheesecakes.

APPLIANCES

A *food processor*, with its many attachments, is the one absolutely essential small appliance that a well-equipped kitchen demands. Chopping, grating, puréeing, mixing, kneading, and whipping are all tasks that are made easy with this tool. A *mini food processor* is also a great addition to the small appliance list. While not as essential as its larger counterpart, it will make easy work of chopping fresh herbs and blending salad dressings.

A *heavy-duty electric mixer* is a must for all types of baking, from making cake batters to mixing cookie dough. If the budget permits, choose one that has attachments for making pasta and grinding meats.

An *electric blender* is useful for emulsifying soup ingredients, creating juice drinks, and blending sauces.

The *hand-held blender* I prefer for the above tasks is called an *immersion blender*. It is placed directly into a soup pot, thereby eliminating the step of puréeing in small batches. See the recipes for "Creamy" Asparagus Soup (page 63) and Sweet Pea Soup with Mint (page 64) to see what I mean.

A *bread machine* simplifies the complicated process of baking bread and preparing bread dough to an absolutely basic task. I consider it a must for your kitchen. Take a look at the recipes for Ricotta Bread (page 236) and Herb and Cheese Bread (page 237) for two mouth watering suggestions.

EXTRAS

Although not essential, I find that the time savings of a *salad spinner* when cleaning lettuce is worth the minimal investment. Likewise, an *upright roasting rack* used to hold chicken and turkey in a roasting pan makes for an evenly cooked bird.

The completely organized cook has a computer in the kitchen installed with any one of the newest software packages that have been created to keep track of personal recipes. Twenty years ago, a prepared cook made notes in cookbook margins and entered her favorite recipes on index cards, in files, that were sorted by categories. Today's cook can input recipes into a database, change the ingredients and refigure the number of servings. Weekly shopping lists are automatically prepared, nutritional information disseminated, and substitutions noted. Recipes can be shared with friends over the Internet and modified for use in your particular kitchen. Today's cook has many tools at his or her disposal to create an interesting, creative meal.

To share your favorite kitchen gadget visit www.jorj.com.

GADGETS IN THE KITCHEN

Utensils
spoons (wooden and slotted)
pasta fork
spatulas (wide, narrow, and rubber)
tongs
ladle
knives
cutting board
whisk
meat mallet
rolling pin

Pots, Pans & Such
broiler pan
skillet
stockpot with lid
saucepan with lid
cookie baking sheet
wire rack
double boiler (insert)
grill pan
casserole dish

mixing bowls
Items for baking: pie pan, cake pans, muffin tin, loaf pan, and springform pan

Gadgets
Garlic press
Measuring cups
Measuring spoons
Turkey baster
Pastry brush
Hand-held grater
Funnel
Meat thermometer
Can opener
Steamer basket
Colander
Vegetable peeler

Appliances
Food processor
Mini food processor
Heavy duty electric mixer

Electric blender

Bread machine

Hand-held blender(immersion)

Extras

Salad spinner

Upright roasting rack

TERMS TO LEARN

Driving a car without understanding posted speed symbols might find you speeding through a school zone or rambling down an expressway. While the first will most probably yield a traffic ticket, the second will certainly make you unpopular. Although you may arrive at your destination unscathed, flowing with traffic would have made the trip a much more pleasant one.

Just as speed symbols direct you down the road, instructions in a recipe guide you through a process. For example, the process of steaming green beans achieves an amount of doneness necessary for perfecting the dish. If you are unfamiliar with the term, you may end up with beans that are undercooked (blanched) or overcooked (stewed). The green beans will still be intact, but the integrity of the recipe is not quite the same.

There are recipes that require you first to blanch and then to sauté a food. In this case, you need to understand that blanching produces a crispy texture and enhances the color of a vegetable. Sautéing it after the veggie has been blanched and refreshed will not cause it to be overcooked. Listed below are some cooking terms that will let you better understand the recipes in this (and other) cookbooks.

CUTTING TERMS

A food is *cut into pieces* using a knife or kitchen scissors. A whole chicken breast is cut into two halves. A food is *chopped* into pieces either *finely* (small segments) or *roughly* (larger sections). A potato is *diced* by cutting it into small squares. The smaller the squares the finer the dice. A stack of sliced bread, cut into 1-inch square pieces produces *cubes* of bread.

A vegetable is *julienned* to produce thin, match-like strips. This can be accomplished in a food processor, or by cutting (see Julienne Zucchini, Yellow Squash, and Carrots in Rosemary Butter on page 92.)

By pushing a clove of garlic through a garlic press, it becomes *minced*. Very small sections (almost a paste) are produced using this tool. A cooked potato is *mashed* using an electric mixer. Vegetables that cook in liquid for a soup are *puréed* using a food processor or an immersion blender to produce a thick, consistent texture. A hard cheese or fresh herb like ginger or nutmeg is *grated* by rubbing it against a hand-held grater in order to shave it into very small pieces.

COOKING TERMS

Hot liquid in a pot or pan *simmers* over low heat. It bubbles slowly. That same liquid, when cooked over high heat, rapidly bubbling, is being *boiled*. When the liquid begins to boil away, it is *reduced* and you are left with a more refined and concentrated mixture. Some recipes require you to *scald* milk. In this instance, the milk is warmed in a pan until it just begins to boil.

You *sauté* food by cooking it in a skillet in a small amount of fat (usually oil or butter). Increasing the amount of fat *fries* that same food. Meats that are simmered in liquid, over low to medium heat, for a long period of time are *braised*. By cooking fish or chicken in boiling liquid for a short period of time and then removing it, the food is *poached*.

Vegetables briefly placed into boiling water to retain color and crispness are *blanched*. These vegetables are then immediately placed into ice water in order to *refresh* them and stop the cooking process. A *steamed* vegetable is cooked in a basket placed in a pan with a small amount of liquid in the bottom, covered, and brought to a boil. The trapped steam cooks the food. Steaming can also be accomplished using a microwave oven.

In order to break down a vegetable to its sweetest point, it is *caramelized*. This occurs by cooking it in a skillet in fat until it has a syrupy consistency and turns a rich dark color but does not burn. You would *deglaze* this skillet by removing the vegetable and adding a liquid (usually stock or wine) to the pan. Stirring the brown bits from the bottom of the pan while cooking over medium high heat usually signals the beginning of a delicious sauce.

MIXING TERMS

An ingredient in a recipe is *added* to those ingredients listed before it, as in "add the chopped herbs to the soup." You *blend* and *combine* ingredients together by *stirring* with a spoon or *mixing* in a the bowl of an electric mixer.

Ingredients, as in a salad, are *tossed* using a light, lifting motion. You *fold* whipped cream into a cake batter by gently sliding the spatula across the bottom of the bowl and then upward, repeating until the batter is just blended. This is done so as not to release the air that has been incorporated into the whipped ingredient.

In the mixing bowl of an electric mixer, sugar and butter are *creamed* together to form a well-blended consistency. The mixer then *beats* the eggs into the batter.

You can *whip* heavy cream by first pouring it into the bowl of an electric mixer and whipping on high speed to soft peaks. Overwhipping cream will produce butter.

BAKING TERMS

An oven is *preheated* to the temperature required for cooking before the food is placed inside. Food is *baked* either covered or uncovered in an oven using dry heat. If this food is meat or poultry, this same process is termed *roasting*. A food is *broiled*, in an oven, by placing it directly under the heating source set on the highest temperature designation. A roasted food is *basted* during the cooking process, by lifting the juices collected at the bottom of the pan and spooning them over top of the meat or fowl.

OTHER STUFF

An *egg wash* is made by beating an egg with a small amount of liquid (usually water). It is used to adhere a coating onto chicken, seal the edges of pasta, or brush a shine onto a pie crust. If you wish to *dredge* an item through flour, it is coated on all sides without first using an egg wash. *Breading* a food is achieved by dipping it into egg wash and rolling it through a flour mixture.

A *marinade* is made of spices, herbs, and liquid. A food is *marinated* by allowing it to sit in a marinade for a period of time in order to increase flavor and tenderize. While marinating, the food is kept chilled in the refrigerator.

A *roux* is made by cooking flour and butter over medium heat until the mixture begins to brown and bubble. A liquid is then added to produce a sauce. A small amount of a hot ingredient is stirred into a cold ingredient in order to *temper* the mixture before the entire amount is added. This is done in order to prevent a sauce from breaking. (See the recipe for Dilled Beef Stroganoff on page 203.)

When presenting a dish, you use various types of *garnish* (traditionally thought of as parsley or lemon wedges). In many of the recipes in this book you are instructed to *sprinkle* a platter with finely chopped herbs. This is done for eye appeal, as desirable to the palate as taste and smell. When asked to place a *dollop* of sour cream on top of soup, the amount is less than a tablespoon, and should be in proportion to the size of the serving. A thin stream of liquid (usually a sauce) is *drizzled* decoratively over the top of the food for an interesting presentation.

FRESH TALK

A *fresh* fruit or vegetable is found in the produce department of the grocery store or at a road side stand. Foods like lobster or seafood are sometimes fresh-frozen, for shipping purposes. The term "fresh" in the recipes in this book refers to foods that are not canned or frozen.

An *organic* fruit or vegetable is one that has been grown without the use of pesticides. *All-natural* is a term that pertains to the ingredients in food packages. Some dairy products claim all-natural ingredients, as does licorice. It always pays to read the ingredient labels before purchasing a product.

To learn more about cooking terms visit www.jorj.com.

TERMS TO LEARN

Cutting Terms	Mixing Terms
cut	add
dice	blend
cube	combine
julienne	stir
chop	mix
mince	toss
mash	fold
puree	cream
grate	beat
	whip

Other Stuff

egg wash

dredge

bread

marinade

marinate

roux

temper

garnish

sprinkle

dollop

drizzle

Cooking Terms

simmer

boil

reduce

scald

sauté

fry

braise

poach

blanch

refresh

steam

caramelize

deglaze

Baking Terms

preheat

bake

roast

broil

baste

Fresh Talk

fresh

organic

all natural

The Salad Bar

SLICING, CHOPPING, AND DICING

Many days during the week, dinner doesn't begin until after work, errands, homework, the gym, and whatever else has been crammed into the hours after five. The temptation is to grab something on the run and settle in for the evening. However, by claiming just a few minutes, you can prepare a scrumptious dish and discover that you actually wind down in the process. Imagine yourself in line at your favorite salad bar. All of the yummy, fresh vegetables and colorful salad dressings are at your fingertips. You can order up a salad bar at home by purchasing fresh produce, sharpening your knife, and using the items that are stocked in your pantry.

Read about cutting terms in the first chapter, Getting Started. Terms that are put to use in The Salad Bar recipes are *chop, rough chop,* medium and fine *dice, cut* into florets, and *snip.* A vegetable is chopped by using a sharp knife and cutting it into pieces. The word *chop* implies that the pieces are not necessarily the same size. *Rough chop* indicates large pieces. This is usually done in preparation for the vegetable to be used in a food processor or to be cooked in a soup that will later be emulsified. A medium size dice is larger than a fine dice. A finely diced onion will produce very small squares to toss into a salad whereas a medium-diced potato offers bite-sized pieces that are perfect for potato salad. Broccoli and cauliflower are two vegetables that are cut into small pieces or florets instead of cubes. In many salads, the idea is to match the size of the florets to the dice of the remaining ingredients. Kitchen shears may be used to snip small pieces of herbs directly into the dish.

A food processor is a terrific gadget to use for creating vinaigrette dressing. Place all of the ingredients for your vinaigrette except the oil into the bowl of the machine. Use the cutting blade to chop the contents by pulsing briefly. Pour the oil through the feed tube of the processor with the blade running. The oil will emulsify into the dressing, producing a flavorful vinaigrette. If a food processor is not available, a whisk, a large bowl, and a little wrist action will accomplish the same result.

Practice with the recipes in this chapter to learn about making sumptuously fresh salads, then use the skills that you have mastered to create your own favorites.

Find more information about the recipes in The Salad Bar chapter at www.jorj.com.

Sweet Cucumber and Mandarin Orange Salad

Very thinly sliced cucumbers, tiny oranges pieces, and a hint of sweet onion produce a delicate tasting salad that comes together in moments.

1	medium cucumber, peeled and sliced into very thin rounds (about 2 cups)
1	11-ounce can mandarin oranges, drained (about 1¼ cups)
1	medium Vidalia onion, sliced into very thin rings (about 1 cup)
2	teaspoons granulated sugar
⅓	cup distilled white vinegar
1	teaspoon chopped fresh tarragon
	Salt and freshly ground pepper

1. In a serving bowl combine the cucumbers, oranges, and onion rings.
2. In a small bowl stir together the sugar and vinegar until the sugar dissolves.
3. Pour the vinegar sugar mixture over the cucumber salad. Toss well.
4. Add the chopped tarragon. Season with salt and freshly ground pepper.
5. Chill the salad before serving.

Serves 4
Preparation time about 15 minutes

SIMPLE SUBSTITUTION:
Feel free to experiment with any fresh herb such as snipped dill or slivered mint. Either will add a wonderful flavor and aroma to this easy salad.

ALL ABOUT ONIONS:
The produce section of the grocery store is filled with varieties of onions. In most cases they are interchangeable in recipes. There are some subtle differences in flavor and texture. A Vidalia onion has a sweet taste. A red onion is also referred to as a Spanish onion and has more bite to it. Green onions come in bunches of 6 to 8. These are sometimes also called scallions or Spring onions. A yellow onion is the most common and can range in size from small to large. You choose the perfect onion for your recipe. And don't be afraid to substitute the onion you have on hand!

Greek Style Salad with Garlic Lemon Dressing

The dressing for this salad offers a combination of tastes not ordinarily found on a traditional Greek salad.

1	head iceberg lettuce, chopped (about 6 cups)
1	medium white onion, finely sliced (about ½ cup)
1	cup pitted black olives
4	ounces crumbled feta cheese

¼	cup olive oil
2	tablespoons lemon juice
1	tablespoon fresh parsley
1	clove garlic, minced (about ½ teaspoon)
1	tablespoon honey mustard
	Salt and freshly ground pepper

1. In a large bowl combine the lettuce, onion rings, olives, and feta cheese.
2. In a small bowl stir together the olive oil, lemon juice, parsley, minced garlic, and honey mustard.
3. Season with salt and pepper.
4. Pour the dressing over the salad and toss well.

Serves 4 to 6
Preparation time 15 minutes

SIMPLE SUBSTITUTION:
Feel free to experiment with the choice of mustard and the amount of garlic.

EASY WEEKDAY MENU

Greek Style Salad
with Garlic Lemon Dressing
❧
Island Spiced Flank Steak
❧
Baked Cauliflower

Fresh Vegetable Salad with Tarragon Vinaigrette

During the heat of the summer there is nothing quite as satisfying as a chilled salad. Use as many fresh vegetables as you can find and accent with cheese and meat.

1	head iceberg lettuce, roughly chopped (about 5 to 6 cups)
2	large carrots, sliced into rounds (about 1 cup)
2	ribs celery, sliced (about 1 cup)
1	large green bell pepper, medium diced (about 1 cup)
1	pint cherry tomatoes, halved (about 2 cups)
1	bunch green onions including tops, sliced (about 1 cup)
1	stalk broccoli, cut into florets (about 1 cup)
⅓	head cauliflower, cut into florets (about 1 cup)
½	cup cubed turkey breast
½	cup cubed Swiss cheese
2	hard boiled eggs, chopped
⅓	cup pitted and sliced black olives
	Freshly ground pepper

½	cup tarragon vinegar
1	teaspoon prepared mustard
2	tablespoons chopped fresh tarragon
2	tablespoons chopped fresh dill weed
½	cup olive oil

1. In a large salad bowl combine all of the vegetables with any combination or all of the meat, cheese, egg and olives. Toss and season with freshly ground pepper.
2. In a food processor combine the vinegar, mustard, and herbs.
3. Add the olive oil with the motor running.
4. Toss the salad with just enough of the dressing to lightly coat the ingredients.

Serves 4 for supper
Preparation time about 20 minutes

ALL ABOUT VINAIGRETTE:
You can follow this simple formula to create your own favorite vinaigrette. Mix one half oil to one half vinegar. Classic vinaigrettes require three-fourths oil to one-fourth vinegar, but I like mine on the tangy side. Oil is olive oil, vegetable oil, or sometimes mayonnaise. Vinegar includes all types of vinegar (balsamic, tarragon, raspberry, etc.) or a combination of vinegar and citrus juices (lemon, orange, and lime). Season the vinaigrette with fresh herbs, condiments, and vegetables to create your own fabulous salad dressing. Whisk the vinegar, herbs, and condiments in a bowl. Continue whisking while you slowly pour the oil into the mixture. You may use a food processor to accomplish this task. The oil will be emulsified into the vinegar forming a richly flavored vinaigrette.

HELPFUL HINT:
Cover the salad with plastic wrap and refrigerate until you are ready to serve. Add the vinaigrette and toss at the last minute so that the vegetables remain crisp.

SETTING THE SCENE:
For an interesting presentation of a fresh veggie salad, chill large margarita glasses in the freezer for at least 30 minutes. Serve the salad in the chilled glasses. Garnish the rim of the glass with a round slice of cucumber. A pitcher of vinaigrette placed next to the salad completes the festive appearance.

Mixed Greens with Goat Cheese, Walnuts, and Chili Vinaigrette

You can purchase bags full of mixed greens in the produce section of the grocery store. Better yet, prepare your own using romaine, red leaf, arugula and Bibb lettuces.

4	cups mixed greens
2	ounces goat cheese, sliced into 4 ¼-inch medallions
½	cup chopped walnut pieces
¼	cup champagne vinegar
¼	cup orange juice
1	tablespoon prepared chili sauce
1	tablespoon fresh tarragon leaves
½	cup olive oil
	Salt and freshly ground pepper

1. In a large bowl place the mixed greens, goat cheese, and walnuts.
2. In a food processor combine the vinegar, orange juice, chili sauce, and tarragon. Pulse until well combined.
3. Add the olive oil with the blade running.
4. Season with salt and freshly ground pepper.

Serves 4
Preparation time about 15 minutes

ALL ABOUT MIXED GREENS:
You can avoid the expensive prepared bag of gourmet greens by combining your own special selection of lettuces. Purchase heads of your favorite lettuces such as Bibb, red leaf, and romaine. Wash and dry the leaves. Combine them in a large bowl. Add a few leaves of basil or arugula. Toss to mix. Divide the greens among several plastic bags and seal. Pierce the bags with the tines of a fork to allow the air to circulate. Your bag of fresh gourmet greens is available when you need it.

SETTING THE SCENE:
Chill salad plates in the freezer while you prepare the dish. Toss the salad with just enough of the dressing to moisten the leaves. Garnish each plate with a goat cheese medallion.

Plum Tomatoes with Basil

Here is a very simple recipe that guarantees a great tasting tomato. A spoon full of this dish goes well with every entrée. You can also use it as a topping for any fresh garden salad.

6	**to 8 medium plum tomatoes, sliced into quarters (about 2 cups)**
½	**teaspoon granulated sugar**
8	**fresh basil leaves**
¼	**cup olive oil**
	Salt and freshly ground pepper

1. In a small bowl place the quartered tomatoes.
2. Sprinkle the sugar over the top.
3. Place the basil leaves in the bowl.
4. Drizzle the olive oil over all and toss. Season with salt and pepper.
5. Cover the bowl with plastic wrap and chill for at least 30 minutes or as long as overnight.

Serves 4
Preparation time about 10 minutes

SIMPLE SUBSTITUTION:
Choose the ripest tomatoes available. You can easily substitute roma, cherry, or even the sweet grape tomatoes for this dish.

SETTING THE SCENE:
The luscious red color of marinated tomatoes goes well with almost everything. Serve the tomatoes in a glass bowl placed in a larger bowl filled with crush ice for a dramatic presentation. Garnish with whole basil leaves. The leftovers are terrific over fresh pasta.

Tri-Color Tomatoes with Basil and Mozzarella Cheese

Make use of the freshest seasonal ingredients when planning a buffet menu. Ripe veggies have enough flavor to stand alone without a lot of fuss. This dish is an example of what you can create when you shop at the market before you plan your meal.

4	red tomatoes, sliced
4	yellow tomatoes, sliced
4	orange tomatoes, sliced
1	pound mozzarella cheese, sliced
1	bunch fresh basil leaves
2	tablespoons olive oil
	Freshly ground pepper

1. On a large platter layer the tomatoes, cheese and basil leaves, alternately.
2. Drizzle with olive oil and season with freshly ground pepper.
3. Serve chilled or at room temperature.

Serves a crowd
Preparation time 15 minutes

OUTDOOR ALFRESCO SUPPER

Tri-Color Tomatoes with Basil
and Mozzarella Cheese

Grilled Florida Lobster Tails
with Garlicky Tomato Sauce

Vermicelli with Olive Oil
and Fresh Parsley

Sautéed Fruit with Walnut
Shortbread

Panzanella

Stale bread is the inspiration for this Italian salad. Some recipes call for the bread to be first soaked in water and then mixed into the salad. I prefer to toast the bread cubes, combine them with the flavorful dressing, and allow to stand for a while to soak up the flavors.

6	to 8 cups crusty bread, cut into cubes
1	medium red onion, finely sliced (about ½ cup)
1	cup pitted Niçoise olives
1	bunch fresh basil leaves, chopped (about 1 cup)
12	to 16 medium plum tomatoes, chopped (about 4 cups)
½	cup olive oil
⅓	cup balsamic vinegar
1	clove garlic, minced (about ½ tablespoon)
	Salt and freshly ground pepper

Preheat the oven to 350°.

1. Place the bread cubes on a baking sheet and toast for 5 to 10 minutes.
2. Place the toasted bread cubes in a large bowl. Add the red onion, olive, basil, and tomatoes.
3. In a small bowl whisk together the olive oil, balsamic vinegar, and minced garlic. Season with salt and pepper.
4. Pour the dressing over the salad and toss well.
5. Cover and let stand for 15 to 30 minutes. Serve at room temperature.

Serves 4 to 6
Preparation time 15 minutes

HELPFUL HINT:
To remove the pits from Niçoise olives, place them on a cutting board. Press down on the olives with the flat side of a broad knife. The pits will squirt out.

EASY WEEKDAY SUPPER

Panzanella

Stuffed Chicken Breasts with Ham and Swiss Cheese

Broccoli with Garlic and Lemon

Fresh Fruit Salad with Raspberry Yogurt Sauce

Presentation is the most important factor in this dish. Choose fruit that is ripe, sweet and in season. Display the bite size pieces in a beautiful crystal bowl or on an elegant china platter. The tangy yogurt sauce can be served from an ornamental pitcher, or drizzled over the fruit.

1	pint ripe strawberries, sliced in half (about 2¼ cups)
½	medium cantaloupe, cut into 1 inch pieces (about 2 cups)
¼	medium watermelon, cut into 1 inch pieces (about 3 cups)
2	medium apples, peeled and cut into ½ inch pieces (about 2 cups)
½	medium pineapple, cut into 1 inch pieces (about 1½ cups)

⅓	pound fresh raspberries (about 1 cup)
1	cup plain yogurt
1	teaspoon vanilla extract
2	tablespoons honey

1. Prepare all of the fruit by washing, peeling, and then slicing into similar sized pieces.
2. In a bowl combine all of the fruit except the raspberries. Cover with plastic wrap and chill.
3. In a food processor pulse the raspberries until the fruit becomes emulsified.
4. Add the yogurt, vanilla, and honey, and mix well. The sauce will be fairly thick.
5. Chill the yogurt sauce for at least 30 minutes.

Serves 6 to 8
Preparation time about 30 minutes

SIMPLE SHORTCUT:
You can prepare the salad with any fruit that is in season. The secret is to have a colorful blend of similar size pieces. Delicate fruit like banana is prone to browning and must be added just before serving.

HELPFUL HINT:
Drizzle some lemon juice on the apples to prevent browning.

SETTING THE SCENE:
Present the fruit salad in a beautiful bowl that has been chilled in the refrigerator. Garnish with fresh mint leaves and candied orange zest prepared by simmering thin strips of orange peel in equal parts of water, sugar, and grenadine syrup.

Classic Caesar Salad

An authentic Caesar salad is made tableside at some of the best restaurants in the world. The salad dressing ingredients are whisked by hand in a wooden salad bowl where they are emulsified. Large leaves of Romaine lettuce are tossed in the dressing and garnished with wide shavings of Parmesan cheese and cubed croutons made from day old bread. Try this version at home!

1	large head romaine lettuce, torn (about 6 cups)
1	2-ounce can anchovy fillets (about 6 to 8)
2	cloves garlic, minced (about 1 tablespoon)
1	teaspoon Worcestershire sauce
1	tablespoon Dijon style mustard
1	large egg, optional
	Juice of 1 medium lemon (about 2 to 3 tablespoons)
1	tablespoon red wine vinegar
1	tablespoon balsamic vinegar
¼	cup olive oil
½	cup prepared croutons
¼	pound Parmesan cheese, shaved (about ½ cup)
	Freshly ground pepper

1. Wash the lettuce leaves and pat dry. Tear each leaf into large pieces. Wrap the leaves in paper towels and place in the refrigerator to chill.
2. In a large wooden salad bowl place the anchovy fillets, garlic, Worcestershire, and mustard. Use the back of a wooden spoon to mix the ingredients together.
3. Add the egg and stir to emulsify the ingredients.
4. Add the lemon juice and both vinegars and stir again.
5. Pour in the olive oil slowly and continue to stir.
6. Toss the lettuce leaves into the salad bowl.
7. Toss the croutons and cheese into the salad.

Serves 4
Preparation time about 20 minutes

ALL ABOUT CROUTONS:
Prepare homemade croutons by using day old bread. Cut the bread into 1-inch squares. Place the bread squares on a baking sheet. Spray with a vegetable oil spray and sprinkle with garlic powder. Toss gently. Bake at 350° for 10 to 15 minutes until golden brown.

HELPFUL HINT:
A raw egg is a part of the traditional Caesar Salad. It is not a necessary ingredient. You may eliminate it and nevertheless be assured of a great result.

SETTING THE SCENE:
Serve the salad from the bowl and offer freshly ground pepper for each plate.

RECIPE UPDATE:
Check out the Spicy Caesar Salad with Sliced Grilled Chicken Breasts recipe (page 116) to learn how to prepare an updated version of the Classic Caesar Salad topped with grilled chicken.

Deviled Eggs

Deviled eggs have a special place on a salad bar. Chilled and tangy, they are the perfect size to pick up and nibble on while you are when perusing the other choices.

6	large eggs, hard boiled
2	tablespoons mayonnaise
1	teaspoon Dijon mustard
	Salt and freshly ground pepper
	Fresh dill sprigs

1. Peel the eggs and slice each one in half lengthwise. Transfer the yellow yolk to a bowl. Place the white part of the egg on a decorative platter.
2. Mash the yolks in the bowl, using the back of a fork.
3. Add the mayonnaise and mustard. Continue blending with the fork.
4. Season with salt and freshly ground pepper.
5. Fill the eggs with the yolk mixture.
6. Place a small sprig of dill on top of each.

Makes 12 deviled eggs
Preparation time about 10 minutes plus cooking

HELPFUL HINT:
To boil eggs that peel easily, purchase the freshest eggs possible. Place the eggs in a pan and cover them with water. Place the pan on the stove and bring the water to a boil. Continue boiling for 10 to 12 minutes over medium high heat. Remove the pan from the heat. Drain the hot water from the pan and immediately cover the eggs with ice water until they are cool.

SETTING THE SCENE:
Deviled eggs make a great addition to an appetizer platter. There are several variations that enhance the end result. For example, in place of the fresh dill, top each egg with a dollop of sour cream topped with a hint of caviar. Or place one half of a cook shrimp on top and dot with a drop of prepared cocktail sauce. Experiment with your own deviled egg toppings.

To share your favorite deviled egg recipe visit www.jorj.com.

Dilled Potato and Egg Salad

Feel free to make this potato salad at least one day in advance as it gets better and better. It won't last longer than two days—because there is usually none left!

6	medium potatoes, peeled and diced (about 4 cups)
6	large eggs, hard-boiled and diced
2	medium celery ribs, sliced (about 1 cup)
1	bunch green onions including tops (about 1 cup)
4	tablespoons snipped garlic chives
⅔	cup sour cream
⅔	cup mayonnaise
2	tablespoons chopped fresh dill weed
	Salt and freshly ground pepper

1. Boil the potatoes for about 10 to 15 minutes until they are soft but not mushy.
2. Drain the potatoes and place in a large bowl to cool.
3. Add the chopped eggs, sliced celery, chopped onions, and garlic chives to the bowl.
4. In a small bowl or large measuring cup combine the sour cream, mayonnaise, and chopped dill.
5. Pour the mixture over the potato salad and stir gently but thoroughly.
7. Season with salt and freshly ground pepper. Cover and chill for several hours or overnight.

Serves 6 to 8
Preparation time about 30 minutes plus cooking

TECHNIQUE:
To boil the potatoes place them in a medium pot. Cover the potatoes with water. Cook over high heat until the water begins to boil. Continue cooking until the potato is done. The time will vary depending on the size of the potato piece. Test the potatoes with a fork while they are boiling. If the fork enters the potato piece with little resistance it is done.

HELPFUL HINT:
Skip ahead to New Potato Salad with Salmon and Green Beans (page 44) to see how to turn potato salad into an entire meal!

Southern Style Slaw

Here is an excellent opportunity to add crisp veggies to your diet. Traditional coleslaw is made from white and/or red cabbages. Today's produce packaging allows you to add already shredded veggies like carrots and broccoli by just opening up a bag.

½	head medium cabbage, shredded (about 3 to 4 cups)
½	head red cabbage, shredded (about 3 to 4 cups)
2	large carrots, shredded (about 1 cup)
1	broccoli stalk, shredded (about 1 cup)

1½	cups mayonnaise
3	to 4 green onions, chopped (about ½ cup)
2	tablespoons white wine vinegar
1	teaspoon Worcestershire sauce
1	tablespoon prepared yellow mustard
1	tablespoon prepared chili sauce
1	to 2 teaspoons sugar
	Salt and freshly ground pepper

1. In a large bowl place the shredded vegetables.
2. In a medium bowl stir together the mayonnaise, green onion, vinegar, Worcestershire sauce, mustard, and chili sauce.
3. Stir in sugar to taste. Season with salt and pepper.
4. Pour the dressing over the vegetables and toss well.

Serves 6 to 8
Preparation time 15 minutes

SUNDAY SUPPER MENU

Southern Style Slaw

Dilled Potato and Egg Salad

Grilled Corn with Thyme Infused Butter

Spicy Fried Chicken

Loaded Chocolate Brownies

New Potato Salad with Salmon and Green Beans

This recipe for potato salad is inspired by the French version that incorporates a vinaigrette based dressing in place of the traditional American version that relies on mayonnaise. Make it a day ahead to let it absorb all of the yummy flavors. The next day, spruce it up a bit with the salmon and green beans so that you can easily incorporate the entire dish into a buffet menu. You can also serve smaller portions for a flavorful one-dish supper.

2	pounds small new potatoes, cut into quarters
1	bunch green onions including tops, chopped (about 1 cup)
4	medium celery ribs, sliced (about 2 cups)
6	tablespoons dry white wine
5	tablespoons tarragon vinegar
2	tablespoons chopped fresh tarragon
2	tablespoons chopped fresh dill
1	tablespoon Dijon style mustard
1	clove garlic, minced
1	teaspoon salt
¾	cup olive oil
	Freshly ground pepper
1	8- to 10-ounce salmon fillet
1	tablespoon olive oil
1	tablespoon chopped fresh dill
2	cups petite green beans
6	hard boiled eggs, quartered

1. Cook the potatoes in boiling water for about 20 minutes until just soft.
2. Drain the potatoes, cool, and place in a large bowl.
3. Toss in the green onions and sliced celery.
4. In a small bowl combine the white wine, vinegar, tarragon, dill, mustard, garlic, and 1 teaspoon of salt. Whisk in the olive oil. Reserve one-fourth of the

SIMPLE SUBSTITUTION:
Substitute purchased potato salad in place of homemade, canned tuna in place of salmon, or canned garbanzo beans in place of blanched green beans for a quick version of this simple dish.

SETTING THE SCENE:
Assemble the dish by mounting the potato salad in the center of a large platter. Use a fork to flake the salmon into bite size chunks. Pile the flaked salmon on the side of the platter. Line the green beans on two sides of the potato salad. Layer the quartered eggs on both ends. Season the eggs and beans with salt.

dressing for later use. Pour the remaining three-fourths of the dressing into the potatoes and toss. Season with freshly ground pepper.

5. Place the salmon on a baking sheet.

6. Drizzle with olive oil and dill.

7. Bake at 350° for about 10 minutes until the salmon is firm to the touch. Cool and refrigerate until ready to serve.

8. Blanch the beans in boiling water for several minutes. Plunge into a bowl of ice water to stop the cooking process. Drain and refrigerate until ready to serve.

Serves a crowd
Preparation time 30 to 60 minutes

EASY BUFFET MENU

Tri Color Tomatoes with Basil and
Mozzarella Cheese

New Potato Salad with Salmon
and Green Beans

Whole Wheat Baguettes

My Favorite Cheesecake

Chilled Green Bean Salad with Mustard Shallot Vinaigrette

Cool, crisp green beans are flavored with a mustard vinai-grette and garnished with egg salad and crumbled bacon in this colorful salad.

1	**pound fresh green beans, chopped into 1-inch pieces (about 3 cups)**
1	**medium head romaine lettuce, cut into 1 inch strips (about 4 cups)**
½	**cup red wine vinegar**
3	**tablespoons Dijon mustard**
1	**tablespoon honey**
2	**large shallots, peeled**
1	**teaspoon chopped fresh mint**
½	**cup olive oil**
	Salt and freshly ground pepper
2	**large eggs, hard boiled, diced**
1	**tablespoons mayonnaise**
1	**teaspoon mustard**
1	**teaspoon chopped fresh parsley**
4	**slices bacon, cooked and crumbled**

1. Blanch the beans in boiling water for 1 to 2 minutes. Immediately remove to a bowl of ice water. Drain the beans when they have cooled completely.
2. Place the romaine lettuce in a large bowl.
3. In a food processor combine the red wine vinegar, mustard, honey, shallots, and mint. Pulse to combine.
4. Add the olive oil through the feed tube with the blade running.
5. Season the vinaigrette with salt and pepper.
6. In a small bowl mix together the chopped egg, may-onnaise, mustard, and fresh parsley. Season with salt and freshly ground pepper.

TECHNIQUE:

To blanche green beans bring a pot of water to boil over high heat. Place the beans in the water and cook for 2 to 3 minutes. They beans will turn a vivid green color. Remove them from the boiling water. Immediately plunge the beans into a bowl of ice water. The cold water will refresh the beans and prevent further cooking. Remove the beans from the cold water and pat dry. The blanched beans retain some crispness along with their appealing color.

7. Assemble the salad by tossing the green beans with the lettuce and the vinaigrette in the salad bowl. Place the egg salad mixture in the center, on top of the greens. Sprinkle the crumbled bacon on top of the egg salad.

Serves 6
Preparation time about 45 minutes

LADIES WHO LUNCH MENU

Chilled Green Bean Salad with
Mustard Shallot Vinaigrette

Roasted Salmon in the Grass with
Cucumber Mint Sauce

Mixed Fresh Berries with Zabaglione
Sauce

Pasta Salad with Southwestern Vinaigrette

Serve this pasta salad as a light supper or as a satisfying side dish. The easy preparation allows for all of the ingredients to be tossed with the vinaigrette and chilled until you are ready to serve.

1	pound cheese-filled tri-colored tortellini

½	pound salami, cut into ½-inch pieces (about 1 cup)
½	pound sharp white Cheddar cheese, cut into ½-inch pieces (about 1 cup)
1	7-ounce jar roasted red peppers, drained
1	pint grape tomatoes (about 2 cups)

¼	cup red wine vinegar
	Juice of 1 medium lime (about 2 tablespoons)
¼	medium red onion, chopped (about ¼ cup)
1	clove garlic
1	teaspoon honey
1	tablespoon fresh cilantro
½	cup fresh spinach leaves
½	cup olive oil
	Salt and freshly ground pepper

1. Prepare the tortellini according to the package directions. Rinse in cold water and set aside to cool.
2. Prepare the salami and cheese by cutting into pieces. Place in a large bowl.
3. Slice the roasted pepper into strips and add to the bowl.
4. Add the grape tomatoes and tortellini to the bowl and toss.
5. In a food processor place the red wine vinegar, lime juice, red onion, garlic, honey, cilantro, and spinach leaves. Pulse to combine.
6. Add the olive oil through the feed tube with the motor running.

SIMPLE SUBSTITUTION:
A good quality bottled salad dressing is easily substituted for the vinaigrette recipe. For a lighter twist substitute low fat mozzarella for the sharp white cheese and cubed turkey breast for the salami.

HELPFUL HINTS:
1. Purchase the salami and cheese from the deli department of your grocery store. Request that it be purchased in one piece rather than sliced. This will allow you to cut it into cubes.

2. This fast salad actually gets better the day after it is prepared. Pack leftovers in individual containers for an easy grab-and-go lunch or snack.

SETTING THE SCENE:
Serve the pasta salad in a clear glass bowl garnished with fresh basil leaves.

7. Season the vinaigrette with salt and freshly ground pepper.
8. Pour the dressing over the salad. Toss, cover, and chill for 30 minutes. Drain any extra dressing from the bowl before serving.

Serves 6 to 8
Preparation time about 45 minutes

Chopped Salad with Gorgonzola and Sun-Dried Tomato Thousand Island Dressing

Whether you are planning for a party or just want a quick and yummy supper, this salad is a perfect dish for the busy family. The crisp veggies are chopped into bite size pieces. The rich Thousand Island salad dressing takes on a new twist with sun-dried tomatoes and fresh parsley.

1	medium head iceberg lettuce, chopped into 1-inch pieces (about 6 cups)
1	medium cucumber, diced into ½-inch pieces (about 2 cups)
½	medium head red cabbage, chopped into 1-inch pieces (about 2 cups)
2	large carrots, peeled and grated (about 1 cup)
⅔	pound fresh green beans, cut into ½-inch pieces, blanched (about 2 cups)
1	bunch green onions including tops, cut into ¼-inch pieces (about 1 cup)
½	pound bacon, cooked, drained, cut into ½-inch pieces
6	ounces Gorgonzola cheese, crumbled
1	cup mayonnaise
1	7-ounce jar sun-dried tomatoes in oil
2	tablespoons sweet pickle relish
2	tablespoons fresh parsley
⅓	cup tarragon vinegar

1. In a large salad bowl combine all of the vegetables, bacon, and cheese. Chill until ready to serve.
2. In a food processor combine the mayonnaise and sun-dried tomatoes (including the oil). Pulse until smooth.
3. Add the relish and parsley. Pulse until blended.
4. Add the vinegar. Pulse again.
5. Toss the salad with enough of the dressing to just moisten each piece.

Serves 4 to 6
Preparation time 30 minutes

TECHNIQUE:
To grate a carrot you may use either a hand-held grater or the grating blade of a food processor. The result is very thin long strips of carrot.

HELPFUL HINT:
This salad dressing is rich and thick. To accommodate your tastes you can thin it by adding a little water. Store extra dressing in an airtight container in the refrigerator for several days.

SIMPLE SUBSTITUTION:
Reduce the preparation time by purchasing packaged pre-shredded carrots and cabbage.

SETTING THE SCENE:
For a dramatic presentation, prepare salad plates by chilling them in the freezer. Holding a cucumber from stem to stem, cut long, thin strips. Place two or three strips on each salad plate. Top each strip with a spoonful of the salad. Drizzle the dressing across the plate. Sprinkle fresh chopped parsley over all.

Spinach, Apple and Pecan Salad with Citrus Vinaigrette

Toasted pecans add an interesting flavor to tart fresh spinach leaves in this easy salad recipe. The sweetness of the apple is offset by the tartness of the vinaigrette.

1	cup whole pecans, toasted
1	pound fresh spinach leaves (about 4 cups)
1	medium apple, peeled and diced

¼	cup fresh orange juice
2	tablespoons fresh grapefruit juice
1	tablespoon fresh lime juice
1	tablespoon olive oil
1	teaspoon honey
1	teaspoon Dijon mustard
1	teaspoon soy sauce
1	teaspoon minced fresh ginger
	Salt and freshly ground pepper

1. Spray a nonstick skillet with vegetable oil spray. Heat over medium high heat.
2. Add the pecans and cook for 5 minutes, stirring frequently. Remove from the pan and cool.
3. In a large bowl place the spinach leaves, diced apple, and pecans.
4. In a small bowl whisk together the orange juice, grapefruit juice, lime juice, olive oil, honey, mustard, soy sauce and fresh ginger.
5. Pour the dressing over the salad and toss well.
6. Season the salad with salt and freshly ground pepper.

Serves 4 to 6
Preparation time about 15 minutes

FRIENDS FOR DINNER MENU

Spinach, Apple, and Pecan Salad
with Citrus Vinaigrette
❧
Grilled Stuffed Veal Chops
❧
Pumpkin Brownies with Cream
Cheese Frosting

Salad Niçoise

A Niçoise salad can be found in all of the best French restaurants. Traditionally it is served with Dijon vinaigrette. This salad celebrates seasonal veggies and pairs them with freshly seared tuna and steamed artichoke hearts.

4	**6-ounce tuna steaks**

10	**to 12 small new potatoes (about 3 cups)**
1	**pound fresh green beans (about 3 cups)**
2	**large artichokes, outer leaves removed, trimmed**

1	**10 ounce bag mixed lettuce leaves (about 4 cups)**
1	**pint cherry tomatoes, sliced in half (about 2 cups)**
2	**hard boiled eggs, quartered**
1	**4¼-ounce can sliced black olives (about ⅔ cup)**
	Freshly ground pepper
	Dijon Vinaigrette (recipe follows)

1. Marinate the fresh tuna steaks.
2. Boil the potatoes until just tender. Rinse in cold water. Slice in half. Place them in the refrigerator to cool.
3. Steam the green beans for several minutes until just crisp tender. Remove to a bowl of ice water to stop the cooking process. Drain well and set aside.
4. Trim the outer leaves from the artichokes. Slice off the top and peel the stems. Steam the artichokes for 30 to 45 minutes until tender. Cool. Remove the spiny choke from the center and the remaining outer leaves to reveal the tender hearts and stem. Slice each one into quarters.
5. Warm a grill pan over high heat, and spray it with a vegetable oil spray.
6. Remove the tuna from the marinade. Lay the steaks onto the grill pan and sear both sides of the steak. Sear the tuna, turning once, for about 2 to 4 minutes per side.

SIMPLE SUBSTITUTION:
If fresh tuna is not available, feel free to use canned tuna on the platter.

TECHNIQUE:
For a simple yet yummy tuna marinade skip ahead to the Fresh From the Sea chapter and read the recipe for Seared Tuna in Oriental Marinade on page 220.

7. Assemble the salad by lining a large platter with the lettuce leaves. Top the leaves with sections of green beans, potatoes, tomatoes, egg quarters, and black olives. Slice the tuna into medallions and place on both sides of the platter. Garnish the salad with the quartered artichoke hearts. Season with freshly ground pepper. Serve with a pitcher of Dijon vinaigrette on the side.

Serves 6 to 8
Preparation time about 45 minutes

Dijon Vinaigrette

2   tablespoons white wine vinegar
1   teaspoon Dijon mustard
2   teaspoons finely chopped fresh dill
2   teaspoons honey
     Salt and white pepper
½   cup olive oil

SIMPLE SUBSTITUTION:
Feel free to substitute your favorite herbs, spices, and flavored oils to create a different vinaigrette for every salad you prepare.

1. In a small bowl combine the vinegar, Dijon mustard, fresh dill, honey, salt, and freshly ground pepper.
2. Slowly whisk in the olive oil.

Makes ½ cup
Preparation time about 5 minutes

Grilled Lime Chicken Salad

This recipe is a snap to make ahead for a luncheon or out-door summer supper. Marinate the chicken in the morn-ing, before you leave for work or errands, then assemble the salad when you return home.

4	6-ounce skinless, boneless chicken breast halves
½	cup fresh lime juice (about 3 to 4 limes)
½	cup olive oil
1	tablespoon chopped fresh rosemary
	Salt and freshly ground pepper
1	pound fresh asparagus (about 2 cups)
1	red bell pepper, cut into thin strips (about 1 cup)
1	yellow bell pepper, cut into thin strips (about 1 cup)
1	green bell pepper, cut into thin strips (about 1 cup)
¼	cup olive oil
¼	cup fresh lime juice (about 1 to 2 limes)

1. Pound the chicken breasts between sheets of waxed paper.
2. In a small bowl whisk together the lime juice, olive oil, rosemary, salt, and pepper.
3. In a shallow dish marinate the chicken in the lime mixture for at least 1 hour or overnight.
4. Grill the chicken breasts until just done, about 5 min-utes per side. Remove to a platter to cool. Cut diago-nally into thin strips.
5. Blanch the asparagus in boiling water for 5 minutes. Drain and plunge into ice water to stop the cooking process. Drain again.
6. In a large bowl place the pepper strips, asparagus, and chicken slices.
7. Add the olive oil and lime juice and toss. Season with salt and freshly ground pepper. Serve cold or at room temperature.

Serves 4 to 6
Preparation time about 20 minutes plus marinating

OUTDOOR SUMMER SUPPER MENU

Grilled Lime Chicken Salad
❧
Foccacia Bread
❧
Lemon Coconut Macaroons

Get more information on this and other Salad Bar recipes at www.jorj.com.

Fresh Garden Salad Dressings

When you have the time, whip up your own fresh salad dressing and store for use during a busy work week. Use the following recipes as guideline. Add your own favorite herbs and spices to create interesting flavors for fresh vegetable salads.

GARLIC BUTTERMILK DRESSING
1   cup sour cream
¾   cup buttermilk
¼   cup mayonnaise
2   tablespoons white wine vinegar
2   teaspoons sugar
2   cloves garlic, minced (about ½ tablespoon)
2   tablespoons snipped fresh garlic chives
    Salt and freshly ground pepper

RANCH DRESSING
1   cup buttermilk
½   cup prepared salsa
3   tablespoons mayonnaise
3   tablespoons chopped fresh cilantro
1   tablespoon fresh lime juice
1   teaspoon honey
1   teaspoon prepared yellow mustard
    Salt and freshly ground pepper

BLUE CHEESE DRESSING
4   ounces blue cheese, crumbled
1   cup sour cream
1   tablespoon white wine vinegar
1   tablespoon minced fresh garlic chives
    Salt and freshly ground pepper

1. For each dressing, use a food processor or whisk to combine all ingredients.
2. Store in an air tight container until ready to serve.

Makes about 1 to 1 ½ cups dressing each
Preparation time about 15 minutes

HELPFUL HINT:
Feel free to spice up the flavor of your favorite mile-high sandwiches with a spoonful of your freshest salad dressing. Skip ahead to Super Sandwiches (page 81) to see what I mean.

To share your favorite salad dressing recipe visit www.jorj.com.

The Soup and Sandwich Deli

SAUTÉING, SIMMERING, AND PURÉEING

The richest tasting soups are easily made in just a few minutes using fresh ingredients, simple techniques, and a few time saving gadgets. Your favorite fresh breads, starring savory ingredients, become the foundation for the biggest, most overstuffed sandwiches found anywhere. Together the combination is as comforting as mom's kitchen.

To create your Soup and Sandwich Deli at home, review the terms *sauté, simmer,* and *purée* in the first chapter, Getting Started. Soup recipes in this chapter will also use the term *cook*; "in a large pot cook the onions in olive oil over medium high heat." In this way the terms *cook* and *sauté* are interchangeable. Several of the soup recipes require that you purée the ingredients to achieve a thick, rich, and smooth consistency. There are two kitchen gadgets that produce great results. A food processor will purée soup ingredients in batches. Remove the vegetables from the liquid with a slotted spoon. Place them into the processor. Add a portion of the liquid and pulse until the ingredients merge together. Pour the contents into a large bowl. Continue to do this until all of the ingredients are combined. Add the batches back to the pot and continue the recipe. An immersion blender is a hand-held blender that produces similar results when puréeing soup ingredients. The blender is placed directly into the pot and turned on. The blade is on the bottom of the appliance. The ingredients are blended together in the same pot that they are cooked.

While fresh herbs are best, there are often times when fresh herbs are not readily available or are not the best choice for the recipe. My rule of thumb is that you use fresh herbs when they are easily added at the end of the recipe. By using them in this way, the delicate flavor and aroma is not broken down by prolonged cooking. For example, in soups or sauces, I add fresh herbs at the last moment, cooking only a few minutes more and then serving immediately. Dried herbs work well in soups, stews, and sauces that are simmered for a long period of time. Even with this guideline, fresh and dried herbs are easily interchanged. Use less of the dried herb than you would the fresh. One tablespoon of chopped fresh herbs is equal to one teaspoon of crushed or dried herbs. Introduce the herbs in small amounts. You can always add more depending on your tastes.

Use the soup recipes in this chapter as an inspiration to create your own favorites alternating between what you have on hand and the season's freshest ingredients. Soup is made to share. Cook a big batch and freeze the extra. When you see a friend or coworker in need of a smile, offer a sip of your homemade soup. Enjoy the grin that you get in response.

Find more information about the recipes in The Soup and Sandwich Deli chapter at www.jorj.com.

Chicken Stock with Roasted Vegetables

Make this stock on a day that you plan to hang around the house. It doesn't require much effort and it yields a richly flavored stock that you can use for soups and sauces.

4	**chicken back pieces**
4	**chicken breast halves with ribs**
3	**whole onions, quartered**
6	**cloves garlic**
3	**large carrots, cut into thirds**
1	**large green bell pepper, quartered**
3	**celery stalks, cut into thirds**
2	**tablespoons fresh thyme**
2	**tablespoons fresh rosemary**
1	**bunch parsley, washed and patted dry**

Preheat the oven to 350°.

1. Place the chicken backs, chicken breasts, onions, garlic, carrots, green pepper and celery into a large roasting pan. Bake uncovered for 1 hour.
2. Remove the pan from the oven.
3. Remove the skin and cut the breast meat from the bone and set it aside.
4. Place all of the vegetables and chicken bones into an 8-quart stockpot. Cover with water.
5. Add the thyme, rosemary, and parsley to the pot.
6. Cover the pot with a lid. Simmer for at least 2 hours over very low heat.
7. Strain the stock by pouring the contents of the pot through a colander. You may season the stock with salt and pepper at this point or wait until you use it in a soup or sauce.

HELPFUL HINT:
The stock may be kept in an airtight container in the refrigerator for several days or frozen for several weeks. Rich, flavorful stock is used for sauces, as a poaching liquid, and as the base for many terrific soups. Check out Feel Good Chicken Soup on the next page.

HELPFUL HINT:
Don't worry about peeling or trimming the vegetables. The stock is strained before use.

HELPFUL HINT:
Use the breast meat to add to chicken soup or for a cold chicken salad.

HELPFUL HINT:
If the liquid reduces too rapidly, add more and make sure that the stovetop burner is set on the lowest temperature.

Feel Good Chicken Soup

In the old world tradition this soup really does work for almost anything that needs fixing. It is guaranteed to remedy morning sickness, stuffy noses, sub-par report cards, broken hearts, skinned knees, and bad hair days. It must be made to share but freezes well for emergencies.

4	medium celery ribs, sliced (about 2 cups)
4	large carrots, sliced (about 2 cups)
2	medium onions, chopped (about 1 cup)
1	tablespoon olive oil
4	cloves garlic, minced (about 2 tablespoons)
3	quarts Chicken Stock with Roasted Vegetables (page 58)
4	chicken breast halves with ribs, cooked, chopped into ½-inch pieces
2	tablespoons chopped fresh dill weed
½	cup dry sherry
2	cups uncooked long-grain white rice
	Salt and freshly ground pepper

1. In the bottom of a large pot cook the celery, carrots, and onions in the olive oil until soft and beginning to brown.
2. Add the garlic and cook for 5 minutes.
3. Pour the chicken stock into the pot. Simmer for 20 to 30 minutes.
4. Add the cooked chicken pieces to the pot.
5. Add the dill, sherry, and rice to the pot. Cover and cook for 15 to 20 minutes more.
6. Season generously with salt and pepper.

Serves 6 to 8
Preparation time about 45 minutes

SIMPLE SUBSTITUTION:
This is a terrific home-cooked soup to use as the base for experiments. For example, try diced fennel or sliced cabbage as an addition to the carrots and celery. Or, substitute pasta such as macaroni or shells instead of rice. Give it a try and create your own special batch of "T.L.C."

SETTING THE SCENE:
Serve each bowl of soup with a huge smile and a great big bear hug.

Tortilla Soup

The garnish is the fun part of this soup. Lightly fried thin strips of tortilla are clumped on top of the soup for a terrific presentation.

2	**6-ounce skinless, boneless chicken breast halves**
	Salt and freshly ground pepper
1	**tablespoon olive oil**
1	**medium yellow onion, diced (about ½ cup)**
1	**large carrots, diced (about ½ cup)**
1	**red bell pepper, diced (about 1 cup)**
2	**stalks celery, diced (about 1 cup)**
1½	**cups corn kernels**
6	**cups chicken broth**
¼	**cup tomato paste**
1	**cup crushed tortilla chips**
2	**tablespoons chopped fresh cilantro**
4	**to 6 corn tortillas, cut into ⅛-inch strips**
⅓	**cup olive oil**
1	**cup shredded Monterey Jack cheese**
½	**avocado, thinly sliced**

1. Season the chicken breasts with salt and pepper. Place in a baking pan. Bake at 350° for 20 minutes. Cool. Cut into bite size pieces.
2. In a soup pot heat 1 tablespoon of olive oil over medium high heat.
3. Add the carrot, onion, pepper, celery, and corn, and cook for about 5 minutes until just beginning to brown.
4. Pour in the chicken stock and tomato paste and simmer for about 20 minutes until the vegetables are soft.
5. Add the crushed tortilla chips and cilantro to the soup. Cook for 10 minutes more.
6. In a medium skillet heat ⅓ cup of olive oil over medium high heat. Cook one-third of the tortilla strips in the hot oil until just golden (very quickly). Remove the

MEXICAN MIDWEEK SUPPER

Tortilla Soup

Dolphin Fajitas

Key Lime Squares

strips and drain on a paper towel. Continue until all of the strips are fried.

7. Strain the soup so that only the tomato vegetable broth remains. Return the broth to the soup pot.

8. Add the chicken pieces to the broth. Season the soup with salt and freshly ground pepper. Heat for 5 minutes.

9. Ladle the soup into bowls. Top each bowl with a handful of shredded cheese, slices of avocado, and a mound of fried tortilla strips.

Serves 4
Preparation time 30 minutes

Caramelized Onion Soup

This soup is made in the tradition of the classic French onion soup. It is updated by adding a touch of brown sugar while caramelizing the onions to guarantee the sweetest flavor.

2   **tablespoons butter**
1   **tablespoon olive oil**
4   **large Vidalia onions, halved and thinly sliced (about 8 cups)**
¼   **cup firmly packed brown sugar**
¼   **cup dry white wine**
½   **cup port wine**
2   **quarts chicken stock**
2   **teaspoons chopped fresh thyme**
    Salt and freshly ground pepper

    Croutons
    Parmesan cheese

1. In a large pot melt the olive oil and butter together over high heat.
2. In a large bowl toss together the sliced onions with the brown sugar.
3. Place the onions in the pot and cook, stirring constantly, for about 20 minutes until they begin to brown.
4. Add the white wine to the pot and stir.
5. Reduce the heat to medium low and stir in the port wine.
6. Add the chicken stock to the pot. Cover and simmer for 20 minutes more.
7. Add the fresh thyme and season with salt and freshly ground pepper. Cover the pot and simmer for 5 minutes more.
8. Ladle a generous portion of soup into a bowl and top with warm croutons and shaved Parmesan cheese.

Serves 6 to 8
Preparation time about 45 minutes

SIMPLE SHORTCUT:
Feel free to use any variety or combination of varieties of onions for this soup.

HELPFUL HINT:
As the onions cook they will become very brown and syrupy. This process caramelizes the onions, which means the sugar in the vegetable is released. Continue stirring while the onions cook to prevent burning.

TECHNIQUE:
The white wine is used to deglaze the pan allowing the bits of onion that are sticking to the bottom of the pan to merge with the liquid to begin the soup.

TECHNIQUE:
Make your own croutons by toasting cubes of day-old bread in a 350° oven. Sprinkle the warm croutons with a combination of salt, pepper, Parmesan cheese, and a dash of chili powder!

"Creamy" Asparagus Soup

By adding potato you can create a creamy soup without using milk or cream. The crunchy texture comes from the fresh asparagus tips tossed into the pot at the last minute. Serve the soup as a first course with any entree or by itself with a small salad and fresh bread for a great quick supper.

1	medium onion, chopped (about ½ cup)
2	tablespoons olive oil
2	pounds fresh asparagus, chopped, tips reserved (about 5 cups)
3	medium potatoes, peeled and diced (about 2 cups)
2	quarts chicken stock
½	pound fresh spinach leaves (about 2 cups)
½	cup fresh dill
½	teaspoon ground nutmeg
½	teaspoon ground cayenne pepper
	Salt and freshly ground pepper
½	cup dry sherry (optional)

1. In a large pot cook the onion in the olive oil over medium high heat until soft.
2. Add the chopped asparagus stems, potato, and chicken stock to the pot. Bring to a boil.
3. Reduce the heat, cover, and continue to cook for at least 25 minutes.
4. Add the spinach, dill, nutmeg, and cayenne pepper. Cover and cook for an additional 5 to 10 minutes.
5. Process the soup in batches in a food processor and return to the pot (or use an immersion blender).
6. Add the asparagus tips to the soup and season to taste with salt and freshly ground pepper.

Serves 6 to 8

Preparation time about 45 minutes

HELPFUL HINT:
The taste and aroma of sherry is a savory addition in many types of soups. I have included it in this recipe. However, it is not necessary.

TECHNIQUE:
There are two ways to purée soup that transforms it from a liquid based soup with chunky pieces to a thicker, smoother consistency. The first technique is to ladle some of the hot soup with chunky pieces into the bowl of a food processor. Pulse until the soup is puréed. Pour the mixture into a large bowl. Continue until all of the soup has been puréed. Return the puréed soup to the pot and continue with the recipe. A more convenient technique uses an immersion blender. This hand-held blender is placed directly into the soup pot to purée the ingredients. Remember to turn off the heat while you are doing this step!

A bowl of soup and a loaf of fresh bread are the perfect combination for a warm supper on a chilly evening. Skip ahead to take a look at the recipe for Ricotta Bread (page 236).

Try this potato secret to add creaminess to your favorite soup. To share your new creamy soup recipe visit www.jorj.com.

Sweet Pea Soup with Mint

A delicious springtime vegetable, peas have a distinctively sweet taste. This soup incorporates their sweetness with an abundance of fresh vegetables to produce a vibrantly full flavor.

2	**tablespoons butter (¼ stick)**
2	**tablespoons olive oil**
1	**medium head Savoy cabbage, sliced into thin strips (about 2 cups)**
2	**large leeks, sliced (about 2 cups)**
2	**medium celery ribs, sliced (about 1 cup)**
4	**(or more) cups chicken stock**
2	**tablespoons chopped fresh watercress**
2	**tablespoons chopped fresh mint**
1	**pound frozen peas (about 4 cups), reserving 1 cup** **Salt and freshly ground pepper**

French bread croutons (optional)

1. In a large pot melt the butter and olive oil over medium high heat.
2. Add the cabbage, leeks, and celery. Cook about 10 minutes until soft.
3. Pour in 4 cups of the chicken stock.
4. Add the watercress, fresh mint, and all but 1 cup of the peas. Cover and simmer for 20 minutes.
5. In a food processor or by using an immersion blender purée the vegetables and liquid in batches. Return the processed soup to the pot.
6. Add the remaining cup of peas and season with salt and pepper. Simmer for several more minutes.

Serves 6
Preparation time about 35 minutes

ALL ABOUT LEEKS:
Leeks are from the onion family. In most cases they are very dirty. To clean a leek, cut in half lengthwise. Break apart the white leaves and soak the leek in a bowl of cold water. The dirt will fall to the bottom of the bowl. Remove the leek from the water, pat dry and continue with the recipe.

HELPFUL HINT:
The soup will be quite thick at this point. If you prefer a thinner soup add more chicken stock.

SETTING THE SCENE:
Present the soup in an oversized cup and saucer. Garnish the saucer with a sprinkling of chopped mint. Top the soup with a crouton made by brushing both sides of a slice of French bread with olive oil. Sprinkle one side with garlic powder and a dash grated Parmesan cheese. Bake for 5 minutes at 350°.

Curried Pumpkin Soup

The savory consistency of this silken soup is matched by its beautiful golden color. I usually make it during the fall season and wonder why I have waited so long in between to serve it.

1	medium yellow onion, diced (about ½ cup)
1	large leek, cleaned and sliced into thin rings (about 1 cup)
2	tablespoons olive oil
1	16-ounce can pumpkin
6	cups chicken stock
1	tablespoon brown sugar
1	teaspoon curry powder
½	teaspoon ground ginger
½	teaspoon ground cinnamon
2	cups half and half
	Salt and freshly ground pepper

Baked ham, finely diced (optional)
Green onions including tops, thinly sliced (optional)

1. In a large pot cook the onion and leek in the olive oil over medium high heat.
2. Stir in the canned pumpkin, chicken stock, brown sugar, curry powder, ginger, and cinnamon.
3. Cover the pot and simmer for 20 minutes.
4. In a food processor purée the soup in batches and return to the pot (or use an immersion blender).
5. Add the half and half and season with salt and freshly ground pepper.

Serves 6 to 8
Preparation time about 30 minutes

HELPFUL HINT:
Read about slicing and cleaning leeks on page 64.

SETTING THE SCENE:
Use a hollowed out pumpkin as your soup tureen. Cut the top from the pumpkin. Remove the seeds and some of the pulp to reveal a smooth inside cavity. Place the warm soup in the pumpkin. Garnish with diced baked ham and sliced green onion. Place the lid of the pumpkin tipped on its side.

Chilled Gazpacho Soup

There is a certain twang of flavors that bounce off each other in this soup. The hot pepper sauce runs right into the sweet plum tomatoes to produce a burst of yummmmm!

1	medium yellow onion, chopped (about ½ cup)
1	large leek, sliced (about 1 cup)
1	tablespoon olive oil
1	28-ounce can chopped tomatoes
2	cups chicken stock
1	tablespoon tomato paste
2	tablespoons fresh thyme
½	teaspoon sugar
1	tablespoon balsamic vinegar
¾	cup heavy cream
½	cup sour cream
⅓	cup fresh lime juice
2	to 4 drops hot pepper sauce
1	medium cucumber, peeled and chopped into ½-inch pieces (about 2 cups)
4	medium plum tomatoes, seeded and chopped (about 1 cup)
1	large green bell pepper, chopped into ½-inch pieces (about 1 cup)
½	medium red onion, diced into ¼-inch pieces (about ½ cup)
	Salt and freshly ground pepper

1. In a large pot cook the onion and leeks in the olive oil over medium high heat until softened. Do not brown.
2. Add the tomatoes and chicken stock and cook for several minutes.
3. Add the tomato paste, fresh thyme, sugar, and balsamic vinegar. Cover and simmer for 15 minutes.
4. Add the cream, sour cream, lime juice, and as much hot pepper sauce as you like.
5. In a food processor purée the soup in batches (or use an immersion blender.)
6. Transfer the soup to a large bowl or container.

PARTY FAVORS:
Serve frosty mugs of this soup at an outdoor get-together. It's a real "ice breaker."

SETTING THE SCENE:
Serve the soup in chilled beer mugs or frosted tall pilsner glasses. Garnish with a rib of celery and a slice of lime twisted on the rim of the glass.

7. Stir in the chopped cucumber, tomatoes, green pepper, and onion.
8. Season with salt and freshly ground pepper.
9. Cover the soup and place in the freezer for 2 hours.
   The soup should be served very cold.

Serves 8
Preparation time about 30 minutes

Potato, Carrot, and Leek Soup with Fresh Ginger

As a first course, serve this soup either hot or cold. The texture is rich and creamy. The aroma of the ginger and the sweetness of the carrot make the dish remarkably appealing.

2	**tablespoons olive oil**
1	**large leek, white part only, sliced (about ⅓ cup)**
1	**medium onion, diced (about ½ cup)**
4	**large carrots, peeled and diced (about 2 cups)**
6	**cups chicken stock**
3	**medium potatoes, peeled and diced (about 2 cups)**
1	**teaspoon freshly grated ginger**
½	**cup heavy cream**
1	**tablespoon chopped fresh chives**
	Salt and freshly ground black pepper

Sour cream, optional

1. In the bottom of a large pot heat the olive oil over medium high heat.
2. Add the sliced leek and diced onion. Cook until softened, about 5 minutes.
3. Add the carrots and cook 5 minutes more.
4. Pour in the chicken stock and add the potatoes. Cover and simmer about 15 minutes until the vegetables are softened.
5. With an immersion blender or food processor purée all of the ingredients. Return to the pot.
6. Add the fresh ginger and the cream and stir well.
7. Add the chopped chives and season with salt and pepper. Cover the pot and simmer for several minutes.
8. Serve the soup warm directly from the pot or transfer to a bowl and chill for at least 2 hours.

Serves 6 to 8
Preparation time about 30 minutes

This soup is a variation on the classic potato soup, vichyssoise. The addition of carrots and ginger give it just enough oomph to make it your own.

SETTING THE SCENE:
Garnish with a dollop of sour cream and an extra sprinkle of chopped chives.

Black Bean Soup with Toasted Corn and Rosemary

More than a traditional spicy black bean soup, this dish takes a veggie twist with chunks of diced carrots and kernels of crisp corn. Using canned corn makes this soup come together quickly for an excellent midweek meal.

1	12-ounce package dried black beans
1	14-ounce can corn
3	tablespoons olive oil
1	large yellow onion, diced (about 2 cups)
4	large carrots, peeled and diced (about 2 cups)
4	medium celery stalks, sliced (about 2 cups)
8	cups chicken stock
3	rosemary sprigs
	Salt and freshly ground pepper

1. Place the black beans in a pot. Cover with cold water. Bring to a boil. Remove from the heat and let the beans sit for 1 hour.
2. In a skillet cook the corn kernels in 1 tablespoon of olive oil over medium high heat about 5 minutes, until they just begin to brown. Set aside.
3. In a large soup pot heat the remaining olive oil over medium high heat.
4. Add the onions to the pot and cook for 5 minutes.
5. Add the carrots and celery to the pot. Reduce the heat to medium low and cook until the vegetables begin to soften, about 15 minutes.
6. Pour the chicken stock into the pot.
7. Drain the black beans and add to the pot.
8. Add the toasted corn kernels to the pot.
9. Place the whole rosemary sprigs into the soup. Season with salt and freshly ground pepper.
10. Cover and cook for 1 hour over medium low heat.

Serves 6 to 8

Preparation time about 30 minutes (plus 1 hour to soak beans)

SIMPLE SUBSTITUTION:
Experiment with white beans using this same recipe. Garnish with a teaspoon of olive oil that has been flavored with lemon juice and minced garlic. Yummm...

SETTING THE SCENE:
Serve the soup right out of the pot warming on the stove in big pottery bowls. Add a spoonful of sour cream and a grating of fresh pepper for garnish.

SIMPLE SUPPER

Black Bean Soup with Toasted Corn and Rosemary

Marinated Pork Tenderloins

Rum Soaked Sweet Potatoes

Traditional Black Bean Soup

The bowls full of extras add to this soup's universal appeal. There are a few must have accompaniments listed below. Can you think of some more?

1	**pound dried black beans**
1	**medium yellow onion, diced (about ½ cup)**
2	**medium celery ribs, diced fine (about 1 cup)**
2	**large carrots, peeled and diced (about I cup)**
1	**medium green bell pepper, diced (about ½ cup)**
2	**tablespoons olive oil**
2	**cloves garlic, minced (1 tablespoon)**
2	**quarts chicken stock**
1	**ham hock (or ham bone)**
1	**bay leaf**
½	**teaspoon ground cumin**
1	**tablespoon packed brown sugar**
	Salt and freshly ground pepper
1	**cup sherry, optional**

Cooked white rice, optional
Jalapeño pepper, seeded and diced (optional)
Tomato, seeded and chopped (optional)
Sharp cheddar cheese, shredded (optional)
Sour cream (optional)

1. Place the beans in a large pot. Fill the pot with enough cold water to cover by 3 inches. Bring the beans and water to a boil. Cook for 10 minutes. Cover the pot, turn off the heat, and let the beans sit for 1 hour. Drain the beans in a colander.
2. In a large pot cook the onion, celery, carrots, and bell pepper in the olive oil over medium high heat until the vegetables begin to brown.
3. Add the garlic and cook for several minutes.
4. Add the chicken stock, ham bone, bay leaf, ground cumin, brown sugar, and cooked black beans. Cover the pot and simmer for at least one hour.
5. Remove the ham hock and bay leaf from the soup.

SIMPLE SHORTCUT:
You can substitute canned black beans to save time. Do not cook the soup as long or it will be very mushy. You will not need to purée any of the beans because the canned beans produce a thicker result.

TECHNIQUE:
Dice the vegetables in a small dice for this soup recipe. You want small squares of similar size about the size of a pea.

SETTING THE SCENE:
Place a steaming bowl or tureen full of soup in the middle of the table. Surround it with small bowls filled with cooked white rice, diced jalapeño pepper, chopped tomatoes, grated cheese and sour cream.

KITCHEN SOUP PARTY MENU

Host an after-work gathering right off your kitchen stove! Serve huge bowls of Traditional Black Bean Soup with all of the accompaniments. Add a loaf of garlic bread and have your friends bring the dessert.

6. Place 3 cups of the beans into a food processor and purée. Return the puréed beans to the soup.
7. Season the soup with salt and freshly ground pepper. Add sherry to taste.

Serves 8
Preparation time about 30 minutes plus simmering

Velvety Split Pea Soup

Split peas cook in minutes, allowing you time to prepare the rest of this soup's ingredients. When you are ready, the peas take center stage to produce a savory soup that is a perfect starter.

1	20-ounce bag split peas
1	tablespoons olive oil
2	medium yellow onions, diced (about 1 cup)
½	large red bell pepper, diced (about ½ cup)
½	large green bell pepper, diced (about ½ cup)
2	clove garlic, minced (about 1 tablespoon)
8	cups chicken stock
1	teaspoon cumin
1	tablespoon chopped fresh rosemary
	Salt and freshly ground black pepper

1. Place the dried peas in the bottom of a heavy pot.
2. Cover the peas with water adding 1 inch on top.
3. Bring to a boil. Reduce the heat to a simmer and cook for 30 minutes.
4. In the bottom of a large pot heat the olive oil over medium high heat.
5. Add the diced onion and peppers. Cook until softened, about 5 minutes.
6. Add the garlic and cook several minutes more.
7. Pour in the chicken stock. Stir in the cumin and the softened peas.
8. Cover and simmer about 15 minutes.
9. Add the fresh rosemary and simmer for 5 minutes.
10. With an immersion blender or a food processor purée all of the ingredients. Season with salt and pepper.

Serves 6 to 8
Preparation time about 40 minutes

SIMPLE SUBSTITUTION:
Fresh out of fresh herbs? No problem. Substitute dried rosemary for fresh. Use less dried herb. A good rule is 1 teaspoon of dried herb to 1 tablespoon of fresh.

SETTING THE SCENE:
Garnish with a handful of homemade croutons.

Vegetable Soup with Lentils

The great news about lentils is that they are quick cooking. Unlike a dried bean, they do not require soaking or boiling before you include them in a soup. Try this quick soup with the added nourishment of lentils for a simple yet hearty meal.

3	tablespoons olive oil
1	large red onion, diced (about 2 cups)
2	large leeks, white part only, sliced (about 2 cups)
1	large fennel bulb, chopped (about 1 cup)
4	large carrots, peeled and diced (about 2 cups)
8	medium celery stalks, sliced (about 4 cups)
4	cloves garlic, minced (about 2 tablespoons)
1	teaspoon cumin
3	quarts chicken stock
1	28-ounce can chopped tomatoes
1	14-ounce package dried lentils
2	fresh rosemary sprigs
	Salt and freshly ground pepper

1. In a large soup pot heat the olive oil over medium high heat.
2. Add the onion to the pot and cook for 5 minutes.
3. Add the leeks, fennel, carrots, and celery to the pot. Reduce the heat to medium low and cook until the vegetables begin to soften, about 15 minutes.
4. Add the garlic and cumin, stir, and cook for 5 minutes.
5. Pour the chicken stock into the pot.
6. Stir in the tomatoes.
7. Add the dried lentils to the pot. Stir and simmer for at least 30 minutes.
8. Place the whole rosemary sprigs into the soup. Season with salt and freshly ground pepper.
9. Cover and cook for 15 minutes more until the lentils are tender. Remove the rosemary before serving.

Serves a crowd
Preparation time about 45 minutes

Lentils are easily made and full of good stuff. Cook them as a great side dish for grilled meat or fish. Season with fresh herbs and a drizzle of flavored olive oil.

SETTING THE SCENE:
Serve the soup with a garnish of fresh rosemary sprigs. Crostini topped with roasted garlic and melted mozzarella cheese makes the perfect accompaniment.

Swiss Cheese Soup

The consistency of this soup is smooth and velvety. The beer and the sherry add much to the aroma and flavor. Don't fret, the alcohol actually cooks out of the soup.

¼	pound bacon, cut into pieces (about 4 to 6 slices)
1	medium yellow onion, diced (about ½ cup)
¼	cup chicken soup base
7	cups milk divided into 6 cups and 1 cup
½	teaspoon hot pepper sauce
¾	teaspoon Worcestershire sauce
¼	cup cornstarch
1	pound Swiss cheese, shredded (about 2 cups)
1	12-ounce can beer
½	cup dry sherry
¼	teaspoon ground nutmeg
	Fresh chives, chopped
	Salt and freshly ground pepper

1. In a skillet cook the bacon pieces until crisp.
2. Add the onions and cook until they are soft but not brown. Drain off the fat.
3. Add the chicken soup base and stir for several minutes until thickened. Remove from heat and set aside.
4. Pour 6 cups of milk, the hot pepper sauce, and the Worcestershire sauce into a large pot. Stir over medium high heat.
5. Add the bacon and onion mixture to the milk and stir.
6. Mix the remaining 1 cup of milk with the cornstarch and add to the hot milk mixture.
7. Stir the soup until it begins to thicken.
8. Add the cheese and beer, stirring constantly.
9. Remove the onion and bacon pieces with a slotted spoon (or strain the soup through a colander), when the cheese is completely melted.
10. Add the sherry. Season with nutmeg, salt, and pepper. Cover and simmer over low heat for 5 to 10 minutes.

Serves 6 to 8
Preparation time about 1 hour

SIMPLE SUBSTITUTION:
Chicken soup base is a concentrated form of chicken bouillon, found in most supermarkets. One jar will last a long time. If it is not available, substitute chicken bouillon dissolved in a small amount of water.

SETTING THE SCENE:
Impress the guests at your next dinner party. In a large, shallow bowl ladle Swiss Cheese Soup on one side. Ladle Spinach and Avocado Soup with Tarragon (page 76) on the other side. Sprinkle with fresh chopped chives and a tarragon leaf.

Summer Corn Chowder

The inspiration for this light refreshing summer soup came from a beautiful display of gorgeous summer vegetables at dinner party. The hostess ordered an elaborate tray of specialty crudités as a delightful hors d'oeuvres. She served a terrific steamed seafood dish accompanied by ears and ears of boiled corn. There were tons of leftovers—and I grabbed them all offering to make a dish to share with everyone. This soup is the result.

1	tablespoon olive oil
1	medium onion, diced (about ½ cup)
2	large carrots, diced (about 1 cup)
2	large zucchini, diced (about 2 cups)
½	pound petite green beans
1	red bell pepper, diced (about 1 cup)
1	green bell pepper, diced
1½	cups corn kernels (scraped from 3 ears)
2	quarts chicken stock
2	tablespoons chopped fresh chives
1	teaspoon cumin
	Salt and freshly ground pepper
1	cup whipping cream
½	pound asparagus, blanched, some tips reserved
6	to 8 baby artichoke hearts, outer leaves removed, blanched, diced, 2 reserved for garnish

1. In a soup pot heat the olive oil over medium high heat.
2. Cook the onion in the oil until translucent.
3. Add the carrots, zucchini, green beans, peppers, and kernels of corn to the pot. Cook for 5 minutes.
4. Pour in the chicken stock and simmer for about 20 minutes until the vegetables are soft.
5. Season with fresh chives, cumin, salt, and pepper. Blend in the cream.
6. Garnish with blanched asparagus tips and baby artichoke hearts cut into quarters.

Serves a crowd
Preparation time 30 minutes

SIMPLE SUBSTITUTION:
This is the time to be creative. Substitute any veggies leftover from your cut up vegetable platter. Broccoli and cauliflower would be a great addition. If the baby artichoke garnish looks daunting—don't despair. You can substitute a homemade crouton or 2 cooked shrimp.

Leftovers are often the inspiration for a new and different meal. Take a look at the recipe for Sweet Potato Hash (page 199) to see what I mean!

Spinach and Avocado Soup with Tarragon

The color of this soup is a gorgeous green. It looks fabulous in a rimmed soup dish served as a first course. The great news is that the soup serves equally as well as a midweek supper because it is easy to make, low in calories, and richly satisfying.

2	tablespoons olive oil
2	medium yellow onions, diced (about 1 cup)
4	medium potatoes, diced (about 3 cups)
2	quarts chicken stock
2	tablespoons olive oil
3	cloves garlic, minced (about 3 teaspoons)
1	medium jalapeño pepper, seeded and diced (about 2 tablespoons)
1	10-ounce package fresh spinach leaves
1	medium ripe avocado, peeled and diced (about 2 cups)
2	tablespoons chopped fresh tarragon
	Salt and freshly ground black pepper

1. In a large pot heat the olive oil over medium high heat.
2. Add the diced onions and cook until soft.
3. Add the potatoes to the pot and stir.
4. Pour the chicken stock into the pot. Bring the soup to a boil. Reduce the heat and simmer for about 15 minutes or until the potatoes are softened.
5. In a skillet heat 2 more tablespoons of olive oil over medium high heat.
6. Add the garlic and jalapeño and cook for several minutes. (Be careful not to burn the garlic.)
7. Add the fresh spinach leaves. Cook until the spinach is wilted.
8. Add the diced avocado and the wilted spinach mixture to the soup. Cook for 5 minutes.
9. Add the chopped tarragon to the pot and simmer for 5 minutes more.

TECHNIQUE:
Prepare all of the diced vegetables before you begin the soup. To avoid browning, you may squeeze the juice of ½ fresh lemon over the diced avocado.

ALL ABOUT JALAPEÑOS:
The hot part of this pepper is found inside. Split the pepper in half. Use a spoon to remove the seeds and pulp. Dice the pepper to continue with the recipe. Wear rubber gloves or be sure to wash your hands after handling peppers.

SETTING THE SCENE:
To garnish the soup, use a plastic mustard or ketchup squeeze bottle. Place a small amount of sour cream in the bottle and thin it with a few drops of water. Swirl the sour cream mixture on top of the soup. Use additional chopped tarragon to line the rim of the soup dish.

10. Turn off the heat. In a food processor purée the soup
    in batches or use an immersion blender to emulsify
    the cooked vegetables into a creamy textured soup.
    Season with salt and pepper to taste.

Serves 6 to 8
Preparation time about 45 minutes

Tomato Soup with Melted Cheddar Cheese Sandwiches

This is a grown-up version of the canned tomato soup and grilled cheese sandwiches that served as a childhood staple. Fresh herbs and a dash of heat give the soup a whole new gusto. With just a few extra hours this soup transforms into a creamy chilled soup.

1	**medium red onion, chopped (about 1 cup)**
1	**tablespoon olive oil**
3	**green onions including tops, chopped (about ½ cup)**
1	**quart chicken stock**
1	**28-ounce can chopped tomatoes**
1	**tablespoon tomato paste**
½	**cup dry white wine**
1	**tablespoon fresh thyme**
1	**tablespoon fresh dill weed**
	Salt and freshly ground pepper
2	**to 4 drops hot pepper sauce**
½	**cup cream**
6	**slices thick bread**
2	**cups shredded Cheddar cheese**
2	**tablespoons butter**

FOR SOUP:

1. In a large pot cook the chopped red onion in the olive oil over medium high heat.
2. Add the green onion and cook for several minutes until soft.
3. Add the chicken broth, tomatoes, tomato paste, and white wine. Cook for about 15 minutes.
4. Add the chopped thyme and dill. Cover the pot, reduce the heat to low, and cook for 5 more minutes.
5. Season with the salt and pepper. Add a dash or more of the liquid hot pepper sauce.
6. Purée the soup in batches in a food processor (or use an immersion blender).
7. Return the soup to the pot, add the cream, and stir thoroughly.

SIMPLE SUBSTITUTION:

Chill the soup for several hours or overnight and serve cold on a hot afternoon. Accompany the soup with cold cucumber sandwiches cut into triangles.

This soup meal is an update on a family classic—what I call "new traditions." Start some new traditions with your family meals. Check out the recipe for Home Style Macaroni and Cheese (page 200) to see what I mean.

SETTING THE SCENE:

Ladle the soup into bowls and top with a sprinkle of fresh herbs. Place a cloth napkin over a dinner plate. Place the soup bowl on top of the napkin. Cut the sandwiches into triangles. Stand the triangles against each other around the soup bowl.

FOR SANDWICHES:

8. Sprinkle the cheese between 2 thick slices of bread and press down firmly.

9. Cook the sandwiches in the butter, turning once, until the cheese is melted and the bread is golden brown.

Serves 6

Preparation time about 30 minutes

Red Bean Soup with Chorizo Sausage and Brown Rice

Spicy sausage rings add an abundant amount of flavor to good-for-you red beans and brown rice. There are a couple of steps involved—but the results are worth the effort.

12	ounces dried red beans
10	cups chicken stock
1	bay leaf
2	sprigs fresh rosemary
2	tablespoons olive oil
1	large Vidalia onion, chopped (about 2 cups)
2	medium celery ribs, chopped (about 1 cup)
2	large carrots, peeled and sliced (about 1 cup)
1	medium green bell pepper, chopped (about ½ cup)
2	pounds Chorizo sausage links (about 6 links)
3	cloves garlic, minced (1 tablespoon)
½	cup plus 2 tablespoons red wine

Cooked brown rice

1. Place the beans in a large pot. Fill the pot with enough water to cover by 2 inches. Bring the water to a boil. Cook for 2 minutes. Cover the pot, turn off the heat, and let the beans sit for 1 hour. Drain.
2. Pour 8 cups of chicken stock into a large soup pot. Add the bay leaf and fresh rosemary. Add the drained beans. Cover and simmer until the beans begin to get tender, about 1 hour and 30 minutes to 2 hours.
3. Remove the bay leaf and thyme sprigs.
4. In a large pot heat the olive oil over medium heat and cook the onion, celery, carrots, and bell pepper until beginning to brown.
5. In a food processor purée the vegetables.
6. Add the puréed vegetables to the soup and simmer for 30 minutes more.
7. In a skillet cook the sausage links until browned.
8. Add the garlic and ½ cup of red wine to the sausage. Cover and cook for 15 minutes more.

SETTING THE SCENE:
Serve the soup in a large bowl. Place a heaping spoonful of rice in the center of the soup.

9. Remove the sausage to a platter. Add another 2 tablespoons of wine to the pan and stir up the brown bits. Add the mixture to the soup.
10. Cut the sausage into ½-inch slices. Add to the soup.

Serves 8
Preparation time about 30 minutes plus simmering

Super Sandwiches

When is a sandwich better than a sandwich? When you take the time to use fresh ingredients and pile them high between slices of fresh bread.

CALIFORNIA SANDWICH
2	slices whole wheat bread, toasted
3	slices cooked turkey breast
1	slice Swiss cheese
1	tablespoon alfalfa sprouts
4	slices avocado
1	tablespoon prepared Thousand Island dressing

QUICK RANCH SANDWICH
2	slices rye bread
3	slices pastrami
1	slice white Cheddar cheese
¼	cup coleslaw
1	tablespoon prepared Ranch salad dressing

TUNA AND VEGGIE SANDWICH
2	slices Italian bread
⅓	cup tuna fish salad
4	slices carrot
2	slices cucumber
1	sweet pickle, thinly sliced
1	tablespoon mayonnaise

For each sandwich, layer ingredients between bread slices.

Yield 1 sandwich per recipe
Preparation time about 15 minutes

TECHNIQUE:
Feel free to vary the combinations with anything that you have on hand and according to your individual taste. The basic idea is to build a better sandwich by combining fresh veggies (fruits and vegetables), cheese (dairy), meat and fish (protein) and vitamin rich breads (grain).

SETTING THE SCENE:
Share the sandwiches with a crowd. Line a picnic basket with a checkered napkin and place the sandwich halves inside. Serve the sandwiches with a chilled platter of Marinated Grilled Vegetables with Feta Cheese (see recipe page 127).

To share your favorite Super Sandwich recipe visit www.jorj.com.

More Super Sandwiches

Here are some more sandwich combinations for you to try. Remember to add your own touches and use these suggestions as a guideline.

CURRIED CHICKEN AND APPLE SANDWICH

2	slices whole grain bread, toasted
1	cup cubed cooked chicken breast
2	tablespoons mayonnaise
1	teaspoon prepared chutney
¼	teaspoon curry powder
½	medium apple, peeled, cored, and sliced
2	red lettuce leaves

PEPPERED STEAK SANDWICH

2	slices Ricotta Bread (see recipe page 236)
3	to 4 slices Island Spiced Flank Steak (see recipe page 125)
	Freshly ground pepper
1	slice Swiss cheese
2	slices beefsteak tomato
1	tablespoon prepared tangy mustard

BAKED HAM AND BRIE SANDWICH

2	slices Herb and Cheese Bread (see recipe page 237)
2	to 3 slices baked ham
2	ounces Brie cheese sliced
1	teaspoon prepared chili sauce
1	teaspoon mayonnaise

1. Prepare curried chicken by mixing together the cooked chicken, mayonnaise, and curry powder.
2. Continue to assemble the sandwiches by layering the ingredients between the bread slices.

Yield 1 sandwich per recipe
Preparation time about 10 minutes

SETTING THE SCENE:
Mini sandwiches, using the same ingredients and bite size muffins or biscuits work well as for appetizers.

Surprise your friends at work by bringing along extra super sandwiches to share.

Veggies on the Side

STEAMING, BOILING, AND ROASTING

Fresh vegetables are abundant and easily purchased either from the local grocer or from the corner produce market. My rule of thumb on fresh veggies is to cook them within three days of purchase to make sure that they maintain their maximum amount of nutrients and flavor. Canned and frozen vegetables are a perfectly acceptable substitution when time is short or when the veggie that you have your heart set on is temporarily out of season.

To cook the recipes in the Veggies on the Side chapter, read about steaming, boiling, and roasting in Chapter 1. Vegetables are prepared using many cooking processes. A few minutes of steaming a vegetable precooks it for further use in a recipe. A few minutes more and the veggie is ready to serve. The recipes in this chapter use one of two methods to steam. The stovetop method requires that you place the vegetable into a steamer basket insert that fits into a deep pan. The insert will have holes on the bottom to allow the steam to reach the vegetable. A wire mesh colander can be used in place of a steamer basket. Place one to two inches of water in the bottom of the pan. Bring the water to a boil over high heat. Cover the pan with a lid. Steam the vegetable for several minutes. Remove immediately and continue with the recipe. A microwave oven is another tool for steaming. Place the vegetable pieces into a microwave-safe dish. Place one to two inches of water in the bottom of the dish. Cover the dish with a lid or with plastic wrap. Microwave on high for a few minutes.

Roasting has become a popular method for cooking vegetables. The vegetable is cooked in the oven uncovered at medium high heat. The size of the vegetable piece directly affects the amount of cooking time required. Certain vegetables like bell peppers require that you char the skin of the pepper over direct heat. The heat of the broiling element of the oven, the flame of a gas stove top, or the heat of a barbecue grill all accomplish the task. After it is blackened the pepper is placed in a paper bag to steam, which continues the cooking process. Minutes later, the blackened skin can be peeled off and the pepper is seeded and sliced.

This chapter includes some basic sauces that are great accompaniments to freshly cooked vegetables. Read about cooking a roux in the first chapter, Getting Started. The terrific rich cheese sauce that is poured over steamed cauliflower begins with a roux. A tangy tuna and caper sauce or a salsa inspired mayonnaise can be made in a food processor rapidly. The sauces are easily interchanged with all types of veggies. Work with these recipes to prepare a tapestry of brightly flavored vegetables. Then use this inspiration to create your own special dish.

Find more information about the recipes in the Veggies on the Side chapter at www.jorj.com.

Broccoli with Garlic and Lemon

The preparation of this dish will work just as well with fresh green beans or asparagus. Add some color by tossing in a handful of crisp diced red or yellow bell pepper into the dish just before serving.

1   **medium bunch broccoli, stems and florets (about 2 cups)**
2   **tablespoons olive oil**
2   **cloves garlic, minced (about 1 tablespoon)**
     Juice of 1 medium lemon
     Salt and freshly ground pepper

1. Steam the broccoli until it is crisp tender. Drain.
2. In a large pan heat the oil over medium high heat.
3. Add the garlic and the broccoli to the pan and toss.
4. Squeeze the lemon juice over the broccoli.
5. Season with salt and freshly ground pepper.

Serves 4 to 6
Preparation time about 10 minutes

TECHNIQUE:
Steam the broccoli by placing the cut pieces into a steamer basket or colander and then into a pan that holds 1 to 2 inches of boiling water. Place a lid on top of the pan. Steam for several minutes until the broccoli turns a luscious green color yet remains somewhat crisp and not mushy. An alternative method is to place the broccoli pieces into a microwave safe dish in 1 to 2 inches of water. Cove the dish with a lid or plastic wrap. Microwave on high and test for doneness as described above.

Baked Cauliflower

Roasting the cauliflower in the oven gives it a rich, nutty flavor. Try this dish in place of potatoes for a satisfying accompaniment to your entrée.

1   large head cauliflower, leaves and stem removed (about 3 cups)
1   tablespoon olive oil
     Salt and freshly ground pepper
¼   cup seasoned bread crumbs

Preheat the oven to 350°.

1. Steam the cauliflower by placing the head in a casserole dish. Add 1 inch of water in the bottom of the dish. Cover with a lid or plastic wrap.
2. Microwave on high for 10 to 12 minutes or until the underneath stem begins to soften.
3. Remove the dish from the microwave and drain the water.
4. Drizzle the top of the cauliflower with the olive oil and season with salt and freshly ground pepper.
5. Sprinkle the breadcrumbs on top.
6. Bake uncovered for 10 to 15 minutes.

Serves 4 to 6
Preparation time about 10 minutes plus baking

SIMPLE SUBSTITUTION:
To add a dash of color to this dish, sprinkle with fresh, chopped parsley.

HECTIC TUESDAY SUPPER

Baked Cauliflower

Fresh Tilapia Filets with Sautéed Bananas

Vanilla Ice Cream with Warm Chocolate Sauce

Spinach with Caramelized Onions

Can you believe many people still wriggle their nose at the thought of eating spinach? This recipe is sure to change even the most faithful spinach-hater's mind. The sweetness of the caramelized onions blends with the balsamic vinegar to set off the tartness of the spinach.

2   tablespoons olive oil
1   medium red onion, sliced in thin rings (about 1 cup)
2   tablespoons balsamic vinegar
1   pound fresh spinach leaves, washed well and patted dry (about 4 cups)
     Salt and freshly ground pepper

1.   In a large skillet heat the olive oil over medium high heat.
2.   Add the onion rings and cook until the onions become brown.
3.   Pour the balsamic vinegar over the onion rings. Continue to cook for several minutes. The onions will begin to look syrupy.
4.   Add the spinach leaves to the pan and toss until just wilted.
5.   Season with salt and freshly ground pepper.

Serves 4
Preparation time about 15 minutes

HELPFUL HINT:
The spinach will begin to wilt immediately. Remove the pan from the heat to complete the gentle cooking of the spinach.

This recipe easily transforms into a great warm dip with just a few additions. Skip ahead to the recipe for Baked Spinach and Artichoke Dip (page 267) to see what I mean.

Fresh Lima Beans with Mint

The mint adds a fruity feel to these fiber filled beans.
There is a hidden spoonful of dark mustard that adds a lit-
tle twang.

ALL ABOUT LIMA BEANS:
Find fresh lima beans in the produce section of the grocery store. You may substitute dried, frozen, or canned beans. Follow the package directions to cook the beans and then continue with the recipe.

1   pound lima beans (about 3 cups)
2   tablespoons chopped fresh mint
1   tablespoon prepared mustard
1   tablespoon butter
     Salt and freshly ground pepper

1. Place the beans in a medium saucepan and cover with water.
2. Boil over medium high heat for 8 to 10 minutes, or until the beans are soft but not mushy.
3. Drain the beans in a colander and return to the saucepan.
4. Stir in the mint, mustard, and butter.
5. Season with salt and pepper.

Serves 4 to 6
Preparation time about 10 minutes

d Zucchini with Parmesan Cheese

This is a terrific way to prepare a sturdy vegetable. How thick you cut the zucchini determines the actual cooking time.

2   large zucchinis, sliced into 1½ inch pieces
     (about 4 cups)
2   tablespoons olive oil
3   tablespoons grated Parmesan cheese
3   tablespoons bread crumbs
1   teaspoon dried oregano
½   teaspoon garlic powder
     Salt and freshly ground pepper

Preheat the oven to 350°.

1. Place the zucchini pieces upright in a shallow baking dish that has been sprayed with a vegetable oil cooking spray.
2. Drizzle the olive oil over the top of each piece.
3. Sprinkle the Parmesan cheese generously over the top.
4. Combine the breadcrumbs, oregano and garlic powder. Sprinkle over the top of the zucchini.
4. Season with salt and freshly ground pepper.
6. Bake for 30 minutes or until the pieces become tender but not mushy.

Serves 4 to 6
Preparation time about 35 minutes

Serve Baked Zucchini with Parmesan Cheese with another family favorite, Chicken Pepperoni (page 186) for a quick and easy midweek meal.

Sherried Mushrooms

There is no better vegetable to accompany a sizzling steak that piping hot sautéed mushrooms. The secret is to make sure that the mushrooms are cleaned and dry and cooked quickly over high heat.

¼   **cup butter (½ stick)**
2   **cloves garlic, minced (about 1 tablespoon)**
1   **pound button mushrooms, sliced (about 3 cups)**
¼   **cup dry sherry**
     Salt and freshly ground pepper

1. In a skillet melt the butter over medium high heat.
2. Add the minced garlic. Be careful not to burn.
3. Add the mushrooms to the pan and stir until almost all of the liquid is absorbed.
4. Add the sherry to the pan and continue cooking for several minutes until the mushrooms are almost dry.
5. Season with salt and freshly ground pepper.

Serves 4
Preparation time about 20 minutes

HELPFUL HINT:
Mushrooms are spongy and like to soak up liquid. In order to make sure that they are clean, use a mushroom brush to brush off any residual dirt instead of soaking them in water.

SIMPLE SUBSTITUTION:
Turn this simple side dish into an elegant first course by adding chopped shallots, heavy cream, and a touch more sherry. Reduce until the sauce thickens. Serve over a cooked puff pastry shell. Garnish with fresh chopped parsley.

Candied Carrots

Serve the carrots crispy-crunchy for a satisfying taste. This is a super side dish that goes well with all types of meats and poultry.

4	**large carrots, peeled and sliced into rounds (2 cups)**
2	**tablespoons butter (¼ stick)**
1	**teaspoon brown sugar**
¼	**teaspoon cinnamon**
	Salt and freshly ground pepper
1	**tablespoon fresh mint leaves, chopped**

1. Drop the carrots into a pan of rapidly boiling water and boil for several minutes.
2. Remove them to a bowl of ice water to stop the cooking process.
3. In a small sauté pan heat the butter over medium high heat.
4. Add the brown sugar and cinnamon and stir.
5. Toss the carrots into the brown sugar mixture and cook for several minutes.
6. Season with salt and freshly ground pepper.
7. Sprinkle with fresh chopped mint.

Serves 4
Preparation time about 20 minutes

SETTING THE SCENE:
For an upscale version of this simple dish, purchase whole baby carrots with the green tops intact. Steam the carrots in the microwave. Place them side by side on a platter. Drizzle the brown sugar-butter sauce over the carrots. Sprinkle with fresh chopped mint.

Glazed Acorn Squash Rings

This is a terrific fall veggie that takes about a nanosecond to make. Kids and adults alike will love the fun taste.

1	**acorn squash, cut into ½ inch rings, center pulp removed**
2	**tablespoons butter**
½	**cup maple syrup**
2	**cups prepared apple sauce, room temperature**
¼	**teaspoon ground cinnamon**

Preheat the oven to 350°.

1. Spray a baking sheet with vegetable oil spray. Place the acorn rings onto the sheet.
2. In a small pan melt the butter over medium low heat. Stir in the maple syrup.
3. Drizzle the maple syrup mixture over the squash rings.
4. Bake for 15 to 20 minutes until the squash is tender.

Serves 4
Preparation time about 20 minutes

SIMPLE SUBSTITUTION:
For a heartier take on this fall veggie, split the acorn squash in half. Spray each half with vegetable oil cooking spray. Bake cut side down for 20 minutes at 350°. Turn the squash over. Fill each half with applesauce. Bake for 10 minutes more or until soft. Drizzle the maple-butter sauce over the top and add a dash of ground cinnamon.

SETTING THE SCENE:
To serve the dish, place the squash rings around the edge of a serving platter. Mount the apple sauce in the center of the dish and sprinkle with cinnamon.

Julienne of Zucchini, Yellow Squash, and Carrots in Rosemary Butter

Here is a simple and colorful presentation of quickly steamed vegetables that can be prepared well in advance.

1	large zucchini, cut into julienne (about 2 cups)
2	large carrots, peeled and cut into julienne (about 1 cup)
2	large yellow squash, cut into julienne (about 1 cup)
¼	cup butter (½ stick)
2	tablespoons chopped fresh rosemary
	Salt and freshly ground pepper

1. Steam the vegetables in a basket or colander over boiling water until just crisp tender.
2. In a small skillet melt the butter over low heat and add the chopped rosemary.
3. Remove the vegetables to a large bowl. Toss with the rosemary butter and season with salt and freshly ground pepper.

Serves 6 to 8
Preparation time about 20 minutes

TECHNIQUE:
Prepare all of the vegetables by peeling and cutting each one into small match stick size pieces known as julienne.

HELPFUL HINT:
Steam the carrots first because they require a longer cooking time than the zucchini and squash.

Herb Glazed Roasted Tomatoes

This dish is so pretty on the plate that it goes with everything. It is also a great way to utilize a tomato that is not quite ripe.

2	large tomatoes, sliced horizontally into 1 inch slices
2	tablespoons prepared mustard
2	tablespoons fresh parsley
2	tablespoons fresh dill
2	tablespoons grated Parmesan cheese
1	tablespoon mayonnaise
	Salt and freshly ground pepper

Preheat the oven to 400°.

1. Place the tomato slices on a cookie sheet that has been lightly coated with a vegetable oil cooking spray.
2. In a food processor combine the mustard, parsley, dill, Parmesan cheese and mayonnaise. Pulse briefly.
3. Generously coat each tomato slice with the mixture.
4. Season with salt and freshly ground pepper.
5. Bake for 15 minutes or until the topping begins to brown and bubble.

Serves 4
Preparation time about 20 minutes

TECHNIQUE:
A mini food processor is an excellent kitchen gadget for chopping herbs. Another great tool is the herb chopping blade and cutting board. The 6-inch square board has a well in the center so that the half-moon shaped chopping blade gently rocks back and forth to produce well chopped fresh herbs.

Cajun Potato Spears

This is a much lighter, more flavorful version of the steak fry. Feel free to vary the spices to create just the right amount of heat. It is the roasting that makes the potatoes so yummy.

4   large baking potatoes, cut in strips (about 6 cups)
2   teaspoon salt
1   teaspoon ground black pepper
½   teaspoon ground cayenne pepper
½   teaspoon paprika
⅓   cup olive oil

Preheat the oven to 400°.
1.   Peel the potatoes and cut into lengthwise strips.
2.   In a small bowl combine the salt, ground pepper, cayenne pepper and paprika.
3.   In a second bowl toss the potato spears in the olive oil.
4.   Place the potatoes on a baking sheet.
5.   Sprinkle the potatoes with the spice mixture, turning to coat evenly.
6.   Bake for 20 minutes, turning once, until the potatoes begin to brown.

Serves 6 to 8
Preparation time about 25 minutes

QUICK AND EASY MID-WEEK MEAL

Spiced Up Turkey Burgers

Cajun Potato Spears

Peanut Butter and White Chocolate Chip Cookies

Roasted Herb Potatoes

A variation on Cajun Potatoes, this dish offers the uniqueness of sweet potatoes and the addition of fresh herbs.

HELPFUL HINT:
Sweet potatoes cook a little faster than white potatoes. For even cooking time, make sure that you cut the sweet potatoes into slightly larger strips.

2   large white baking potatoes, cut into strips (about 3 cups)
1   large sweet potato, cut into strips (about 2 cups)
2   tablespoons olive oil
2   cloves garlic, minced (about 1 tablespoon)
2   tablespoons fresh chives
2   tablespoons fresh rosemary
2   tablespoons fresh thyme
      Salt and freshly ground pepper

Preheat the oven to 400°.

1. Wash the potatoes and slice them vertically into ½ inch wedges. (You do not need to peel them.)
2. Chop the garlic and herbs.
3. Place the olive oil in a shallow bowl. Toss in the potato wedges.
4. Sprinkle the herb mixture over the potatoes, making sure that each one is well coated.
5. Remove the potato wedges from the bowl and place them on a cookie sheet.
6. Season with salt and freshly ground pepper.
7. Roast the potatoes for 20 to 30 minutes, turning over at least once during the cooking time to make sure that they brown evenly.

Serves 6 to 8
Preparation time about 35 minutes

Cauliflower Gratin

To make this dish rich and creamy there is a cheesy sauce that accompanies the cauliflower. The result is a side dish that is packed with tang.

1	large cauliflower head, cut into florets (about 3 cups)
⅓	stick butter, less than 3 tablespoons
2	tablespoons all-purpose flour
2	cups milk
2	tablespoons prepared horseradish
1	tablespoon prepared mustard
¼	teaspoon nutmeg
	Salt and ground white pepper
2	tablespoons Fontina cheese, grated

Preheat the oven to 375°.

1. In a microwave safe dish place the cauliflower florets in 1 inch of water. Cover and microwave on high for 6 to 8 minutes.
2. In a small sauce pan melt the butter over medium high heat.
3. Stir the flour into the butter mixture until it becomes brown and bubbles.
4. Add the milk and continue stirring until the mixture thickens.
5. Stir in the horseradish, mustard, and nutmeg. Season with salt and ground white pepper.
6. Drain the cauliflower and place the florets into a baking dish.
7. Pour the sauce over top.
8. Grate the Fontina cheese over all.
9. Bake for 30 minutes or until the casserole bubbles and begins to brown.

Serves 6
Preparation time about 45 minutes

TECHNIQUE:
Combining butter and flour as in this recipe is known as preparing a roux. This is the basis for rich sauces. The secret is to cook the roux long enough so that the flour is thoroughly combined. The roux will darken as it is cooked. For this recipe the roux should be a golden brown color.

SIMPLE SUBSTITUTION:
The sauce works well on many different vegetables. Substitute steamed broccoli or a combination of boiled white and sweet potatoes.

Chilled Roasted Asparagus with Tomato Mayonnaise Salsa

Fresh asparagus signals the beginning of the summer season. This chilled dish is accented with a spicy mayonnaise that is full of gusto.

1	pound fresh asparagus spears (about 4 cups)
1	tablespoon olive oil
	Salt and freshly ground pepper

6	plum tomatoes, seeded and diced (about 2 cups)
½	medium red onion, finely diced (about ½ cup)
½	green bell pepper, finely diced (about ½ cup)
½	yellow bell pepper, finely diced (about ½ cup)
1	medium jalapeño pepper, seeded and finely diced (about 2 tablespoons)
1	tablespoon chopped cilantro
1	tablespoon balsamic vinegar
2	tablespoons mayonnaise

Preheat the oven to 350°.

1. Cut off the tough ends of the asparagus stalks. Peel the tough skin from the stalks with a vegetable peeler.
2. Place the asparagus on a rack in a shallow roasting pan.
3. Drizzle with olive oil and season with salt and freshly ground pepper.
4. Roast about 15 to 20 minutes until tender.
5. In a small bowl combine the tomatoes, red onion, bell peppers, jalapeño pepper, cilantro, vinegar, and mayonnaise. Season with salt and freshly ground pepper.

Serves 6 to 8
Preparation time about 45 minutes

SIMPLE SHORTCUT:
In place of chopping create a quick tomato mayonnaise salsa by stirring together 2 tablespoons of mayonnaise with 1 tablespoon of prepared salsa.

TECHNIQUE:
For small, thin asparagus spears reduce the roasting time to 5 to 10 minutes.

SETTING THE SCENE:
Lay the asparagus spears on a serving platter. Spoon the sauce over the center top. Garnish the platter with additional finely diced bell pepper.

Broccoli Cheese Casserole

A traditional dish, most of us have had some version of this casserole at family gatherings for years and years. This is one of the easiest and yummiest recipes that I have found. Feel free to add your "Aunt Harriett's" secret ingredient to make it your new tradition.

2	pounds fresh broccoli, leaves and tough stalks removed
1	medium yellow onion, diced (about ½ cup)
2	medium celery stalks, sliced (about 1 cup)
2	tablespoons butter
½	pound button mushrooms, sliced (about 1½ cups)
½	pound process cheese
1	10-ounce can cream of mushroom soup
	Salt and freshly ground pepper
½	cup prepared bread crumbs
1	cup shredded sharp Cheddar cheese

Preheat the oven to 350°.

1. Trim the broccoli, removing the leaves and tough end of the stalks. Cut into florets and slice the stalks into bite size pieces. Place the broccoli pieces into a microwave safe dish. Add 1 inch of water to the dish. Cover and microwave on high for 6 to 8 minutes or until the broccoli is just crisp tender. Drain.
2. In a large skillet cook the onion and celery in the butter over medium high heat until softened.
3. Add the mushrooms and cook for 5 minutes.
4. Add the broccoli to the pan and cook for 5 minutes more.
5. Soften the process cheese in the microwave using the low setting.
6. Combine the softened cheese with the soup and pour over the vegetables. Season the mixture with salt and freshly ground pepper.
7. Spoon the mixture into a 13 x 9 x 2-inch baking pan that has been sprayed with a vegetable oil spray.

HELPFUL HINT:
Make this dish into a weekday quick meal with the addition of cooked chicken of turkey chunks!

If casserole cooking is your thing, look ahead to the fun recipe for GLOP (page 201) for a tummy-filling midweek meal.

8. Sprinkle the top of the casserole with bread crumbs. Bake for 25 minutes.
9. Sprinkle the Cheddar cheese on top of the warm casserole. Bake for 5 minutes more until the cheese melts.

Serves 6 to 8
Preparation time about 45 minutes

Crispy Broccoli Corn Rice Cake

A great way to use left over rice, this crispy cake makes an excellent side dish. Substitute yellow rice for white, black beans in place of broccoli, and add a teaspoon of diced jalapeño peppers for a yummy spicy alternative.

2   **cups cooked white rice**
½   **cup corn flake crumbs**
½   **cup canned corn, drained**
1   **small stalk broccoli, cut into very small pieces (about ½ cup)**
1   **small yellow onion, diced (about ¼ cup)**
1   **whole egg, beaten**
2   **tablespoons chopped fresh cilantro**
     Salt and freshly ground pepper
½   **cup olive oil**

1. In a large bowl combine all of the ingredients except the olive oil.
2. Form the rice mixture into 6 cakes.
3. In a sauté heat the olive oil over high heat.
4. Place the cakes in the hot oil. Brown well turning once, about 5 minute per side.
5. Remove the cakes and drain on a paper towel.

Serves 6
Preparation time about 20 minutes

SIMPLE SUBSTITUTION:
For a fun twist on individual cakes, form the mixture into one large cake. Brown on both sides and continue cooking in a 350° oven for 10 to 15 minutes. Cut the cake into wedges like pizza!

TECHNIQUE:
Make sure that you drain the corn well. You don't want the cakes to be too wet.

Vegetable Party Platter

Arrange the green vegetables side by side on half of a large platter. Toss the cauliflower, potato pieces, olives, and cherry tomatoes together and place on the other half. Garnish with fresh thyme sprigs for an appealing vegetable presentation.

2	medium potatoes, peeled, cut into 2 inch pieces (about 3 cups)
1	pound fresh asparagus spears, stems trimmed (about 2 cups)
1	pound fresh green beans (about 3 cups)
1	large head cauliflower, broken into florets (about 3 cups)
1	head red leaf lettuce
1	pint cherry tomatoes (about 2 cups)
1	10¾-ounce can pitted black olives
4	to 5 fresh thyme sprigs
1	cup Tuna Sauce (see following recipe)

1. In a large pot boil the potatoes in water to cover until just tender. Rinse in cold water. Place in the refrigerator to cool.
2. Steam the asparagus for several minutes until just crisp tender. Remove to a bowl of ice water to stop the cooking process. Drain well and set aside.
3. Repeat for the green beans and cauliflower.
4. Arrange whole leaves of lettuce on a large platter.
5. Place the vegetables on the lettuce leaves. Garnish with the thyme sprigs.

Serves a crowd
Preparation time about 30 minutes

SETTING THE SCENE:
Serve the vegetable platter with the rich Tuna Sauce on the side. Tarragon Vinaigrette and Sun-Dried Tomato Thousand Island Dressing (recipes on page 34 and 50) are equally good substitutions.

HELPFUL HINT:
What to do with Vegetable Party Platter leftovers? Check out Summer Corn Chowder (page 75) for ideas!

Tuna Sauce

This is a very sturdy sauce that blends the interesting flavors of tuna, capers and lemon. It is the perfect accompaniment for a Vegetable Party Platter and can be equally exciting when drizzled on cooked chilled breast of chicken or turkey.

1   7¾-ounce can tuna packed in olive oil
1   7-ounce can anchovy fillets
3   to 4 tablespoons capers, drained
½   cup olive oil
    Juice of 1 medium lemon (about 2 to 3 tablespoons)
1½ cups mayonnaise
    Salt and freshly ground pepper

    Chopped parsley, optional
1   lemon, sliced, optional

1. In a food processor combine the tuna, anchovies, and capers. Pulse until smooth.
2. Add the olive oil through the feed tube with the motor running.
3. Add the lemon juice and pulse briefly.
3. Pour the mixture into a medium size bowl.
4. Fold in the mayonnaise.
5. Season with salt and freshly ground pepper.

Makes about 2 cups

SETTING THE SCENE:
Serve the sauce over cold veggies, chilled cooked chicken medallions, or turkey slices. Garnish the dish with fresh chopped parsley and lemon slices. Keep extra sauce in an airtight container for several days.

Ratatouille

This dish is rich enough to be a meatless main course especially when served with pasta or brown rice. As a side dish it adds all the veggies needed for a terrifically balanced meal.

This dish is super on a buffet table and special as a midweek side dish. Serve it with Poached Yellowtail snapper for your next everyday celebration.

¼   cup olive oil
2   large green bell peppers, chopped into 1-inch pieces (about 2 cups)
1   medium red onion, diced (about 1 cup)
1   medium eggplant, peeled and diced into ½-inch pieces (about 4 cups)
2   large zucchini, sliced into rounds (about 4 cups)
4   large yellow squash, sliced into rounds (4 cups)
1   28-ounce can tomatoes, crushed
1   tablespoon chopped fresh basil
1   tablespoon chopped fresh parsley
       Salt and freshly ground pepper
½   cup grated Parmesan cheese

Preheat the oven to 350°.
1. In a large pan heat the olive oil over medium high heat.
2. Cook the green peppers until soft.
3. Add the onion and cook until soft.
4. Add the eggplant, zucchini, and yellow squash and cook for several minutes.
5. Add the canned tomatoes and stir.
6. Season with the fresh basil, parsley, salt, and pepper.
7. Place the vegetable mixture in a baking dish that has been sprayed with vegetable cooking spray.
8. Sprinkle the cheese over top.
9. Bake for 20 to 30 minutes or until the casserole is bubbling and the cheese begins to brown.

Serves 6
Preparation time about 45 minutes

Rum Soaked Sweet Potatoes

Here is a Caribbean twist on the traditional baked potato. It is best served in its own dish so that the potato can swim in the terrific sauce.

4	**medium sweet potatoes**
1	**tablespoon olive oil**
4	**thyme sprigs**
½	**cup butter (1 stick)**
½	**cup packed dark brown sugar**
½	**cup dark rum**

Preheat the oven to 350°.
1. Wash each potato, dry, and rub with olive oil.
2. Wrap each potato in aluminum foil. Seal in a thyme sprig on top of the potato. Bake for 30 to 45 minutes until tender.
3. In a small pan melt the butter over medium heat.
4. Stir in the brown sugar and rum. Cook the sauce for several minutes until it becomes thick and bubbly.
5. Remove the foil from the potatoes. Make a slit in the top of the potato and gently squeeze with your finger to break up the flesh.
6. Pour the sauce over each potato slowly, allowing the potato to absorb as much as possible.

Serves 4
Preparation time about 45 minutes

This island inspired dish is a great accompaniment for fish. Team it with Vegetable Stuffed Whole Trout with Lemon Sauce (page 232) or Roasted Salmon in the Grass (page 224) for an upscale dinner.

Pommes Anna

The French inspired this spiral potato dish. It is easily made ahead and can be dressed with sour cream, caviar, or even salsa to blend in with any type of meal.

½   **cup butter (1 stick), melted**
1   **clove garlic, minced (1 teaspoon)**
3   **medium baking potatoes, peeled and thinly sliced (2 cups)**
    Salt and freshly ground pepper

    Sour cream
    Fresh chives, chopped

Preheat the oven to 375°.

1. In a medium skillet heat the melted butter over medium high heat.
2. Stir in the garlic and cook until soft.
3. Pour the butter garlic mixture into a bowl.
4. Place one-third of the butter and garlic mixture back into the bottom of the skillet.
5. Place one-third of the potatoes in an overlapping layer completely covering the bottom with potato slices.
6. Spoon the next one-third of the garlic butter over the first layer of potatoes. Season with salt and pepper.
7. Repeat with the next one-third of the potato slices and one-third of the garlic butter and seasonings. Create 3 layers.
8. Remove the pan from the heat, cover with a lid, and place in the oven.
9. Cook for 30 to 45 minutes or until the potatoes are well browned and fully cooked.

Serves 4 to 6
Preparation time about 20 minutes plus baking

HELPFUL HINT:
The bottom layer will eventually be the top of the potato cake. Use the best slices in the prettiest pattern for this layer.

SETTING THE SCENE:
Carefully invert the pan onto a serving plate. Allow the dish to rest for several minutes. Cut the potato cake into wedges. Serve each wedge with a dollop of sour cream and a sprinkling of chopped chives.

CANDLELIT DINNER

Sweet Pea Soup with Mint

Herb Crusted Rack of Lamb

Pommes Anna

Sticky Toffee Pudding
with Caramel Sauce

Stuffed Baked Potatoes

These potatoes are not only delicious, but also perfect for a dinner party or buffet. Prepare the potatoes up to a day in advance. Bake them just before you are ready to serve.

4	large baking potatoes
½	cup butter (1 stick), reserving 2 tablespoons
½	cup sour cream
½	cup plain yogurt
4	green onions, including tops (about 4 tablespoons)
4	tablespoons chopped garlic chives
	Salt and freshly ground pepper
1	cup grated sharp Cheddar cheese

Preheat the oven to 350°.

1. Bake the potatoes for approximately 1 hour or until they are tender. Cool for 20 minutes.
2. Slice each potato in half lengthwise.
3. Scoop out the inside leaving at least ¼ inch of the white potato with the skin. Set the shells aside.
4. In the bowl of an electric mixer combine the potatoes, 6 tablespoons of the butter, sour cream, yogurt, and onions and mix until blended.
5. Stir in the chives. Season with salt and pepper.
6. Place the potato shells on a cookie sheet and fill them with the potato mixture.
7. Place some of the grated cheese on each potato.
8. Cut the remaining 2 tablespoons of butter into small pieces and dot the tops of each filled potato.
9. Bake the potatoes for 30 minutes or until the tops brown.

Serves 8
Preparation time about 10 minutes plus baking twice

HELPFUL HINT:
Bake the perfect potato by first washing and patting dry. Pierce the outer skin with a fork in several places to allow the steam to escape. The potato is done when you can squeeze it with your fingers.

SIMPLE SUBSTITUTION:
Turn your stuffed baked potato into a weekday meal. Check out the recipe for Smothered Baked Potato with Broccoli, Garlic, and Cheese Sauce (page 146).

Hot off the Grill

MARINADES, MARINATING, AND GRILLING

Grilled food is most often thought of when the weather begins to warm. Spring is in the air along with feelings of new beginnings. In reality, grilling the food usually comes as the culmination of the meal-preparing process. The best grilled vegetables, poultry, and meat often begin in a marinade. A combination of spices, vinegar, oil, and other full-flavored ingredients combine to let the food absorb their zestiness. In this way grilled chicken can be served three nights in a row and each night offer a different taste and texture.

Grilling is a quick process because the food is cooked using a direct heat source and higher temperature than in other methods. While outdoor grilling is an activity within itself, the invention of the grill pan has opened the door to preparing grilled food all year round. A necessary tool, the grill pan enables you to very quickly prepare almost any meat or vegetable that can be broiled or baked. The food develops a delicious outdoor quality and for the most part cooks in its own juices. This technique produces rapid results and even faster cleanup.

To make your favorite Hot Off the Grill food read about marinades and marinating in the first chapter, Getting Started. When you are really pressed for time, there are several good quality marinades that you can substitute for the ones you prepare at home. For health reasons, after the food has been removed from its marinade, either discard the marinade or cook it to begin a sauce. A marinade that has been used for uncooked meat or poultry must be cooked before eating.

Several of the recipes in this chapter combine more than one cooking technique. In some cases you are asked to keep the food warm while you continue with another part of the recipe. A warming drawer produces the best results. However, you can place the food in an oven set on the lowest temperature. Loosely cover the food with aluminum foil. Continue with the recipe until the warm food is ready for presentation.

There is some debate on saucing the grilled food. In some portions of the country spicy barbecue sauce is brushed on the food during the grilling process. Other regional methods included basting the grilled food with one sauce and adding the barbecue sauce at the very end. For foolproof everyday outdoor grilling, I like a combination of methods to get great results. For long-cooking foods like chicken and ribs, precook by steaming with a basting liquid in the oven. Then finish the dish by grilling for a few minutes to complete the cooking process. Sauce is brushed on the meat while it is on the grill, which is at the absolute end of the process. More sauce is placed in warmed pitchers that sit nearby the main attraction.

In other recipes, the food is grilled and then baked or roasted in the oven. The fast searing of the food on a grill or in a grill pan seals in the juices while roasting completes the cooking process.

Grilling is a great answer to the "what's for dinner" question. This cooking method produces fast and healthy meals that taste great and clean up quickly. Why not incorporate grilling into your weekday routine? Use these Hot Off the Grill recipes to get you started.

Find more information about the recipes in the Hot Off The Grill chapter at www.jorj.com.

Big Juicy Hamburgers with Grilled Onions

Once you find out how easy and delicious a real, thick, juicy, grilled-to-perfection hamburger can be, you will never stop at a golden arch again. (Well, maybe not never....)

1½	**pounds lean ground beef, preferably sirloin**
1	**tablespoon olive oil**
1	**medium Vidalia onion, roughly chopped (1 cup)**
	Salt and freshly ground pepper
4	**hamburger buns**
1	**teaspoon butter, melted**
2	**ounces blue cheese, crumbled (optional)**
1	**ripe large tomato, sliced into 4 pieces (optional)**

1. Divide the beef into 4 portions and form into thick patties. Refrigerate for 20 minutes.
2. Heat a grill pan on the stove top over high heat.
3. Place the olive oil in the pan.
4. Toss the onion into the pan and grill for several minutes until the edges are browned. Transfer to a small bowl and keep warm.
5. Remove the hamburger patties from the refrigerator and season with salt and freshly ground pepper.
6. Grill the patties approximately 5 minutes per side for medium rare.
7. Brush the inside of the buns with butter at the same time that you are grilling the hamburgers. Toast the buns on a rack in the oven at 350° for several minutes.
8. Remove the hamburgers from the grill and place onto a bun. Top with grilled onions, blue cheese, and a tomato slice.

Serves 4
Preparation time about 20 minutes

TECHNIQUE:
If the weather permits, feel free to grill these fun burgers outdoors. Toast the buns on the grill in place of the oven.

SETTING THE SCENE:
The perfect accompaniment to Big Juicy Hamburgers with Grilled Onions is a platter of Roasted Herb Potatoes (see the recipe on page 95) and a Fresh Vegetable Salad with Tarragon Vinaigrette (see the recipe on page 34).

Spiced Up Turkey Burgers

Is there a difference between ground sirloin and ground turkey? Yep. The prevailing theory is that ground turkey has a lower fat content. That's the good news. The bad news is that as that fat departs it also takes with it some flavor. Here is a great recipe for spicing up that low fat burger choice by adding back lots of flavor.

1½	pounds lean ground turkey
1	medium jalapeño, seeded and finely diced (about 1 tablespoon)
1	small red bell pepper, finely diced (about ½ cup)
2	green onions, diced (about 2 tablespoons)
2	tablespoons finely chopped fresh cilantro
1	tablespoon Worcestershire sauce
1	egg, slightly beaten
	Salt and freshly ground pepper
1	teaspoon olive oil
4	whole grain hamburger buns
½	teaspoon garlic powder
2	ounces Monterey Jack cheese, shredded
1	medium red onion, sliced into thin rounds
1	ripe large tomato, sliced into 4 pieces
1	medium avocado, peeled and sliced

1. In a large bowl mix together the ground turkey, jalapeño pepper, red pepper, green onion, cilantro, Worcestershire sauce, egg, salt, and pepper.
2. Divide the turkey mixture into 4 portions and form into thick patties. Refrigerate for 20 minutes.
3. Heat a grill to medium high heat. Spray the surface with vegetable oil spray to prevent sticking.
4. Remove the hamburger patties from the refrigerator and season with salt and freshly ground pepper.
5. Grill the patties approximately 5 to 8 minutes per side for medium.

TUESDAY NIGHT SUPPER

Spiced Up Turkey Burgers

Cajun Potato Spears

Southern Style Slaw

6. Mix 1 tablespoon of olive oil with ½ teaspoon of garlic powder. Brush this mixture on the inside of the buns. Grill the buns garlic side down for several minutes.
7. Remove the turkey burgers from the grill and place each one onto a bun. Top with cheese, sliced red onion, a slice of tomato, and several slices of avocado.

Serves 4
Preparation time about 20 minutes

Best Barbecue Sauce

Leftover sauce is terrific on every kind of burger. Try this easy sauce the next time you are in the mood!

¼   cup cider vinegar
¼   cup Worcestershire sauce
¼   cup olive oil
1   medium white onion, diced (about 1 cup)
2   stalks celery, chopped (about 1 cup)
2   cloves garlic, minced (about 1 tablespoon)
1   tablespoon dark grain mustard
1   teaspoon granulated sugar
1   14-ounce bottle ketchup
½   can beer
     Salt and freshly ground pepper to taste

1. In a saucepan combine all of the ingredients and heat over medium high heat, stirring constantly.
2. Simmer for 15 to 20 minutes.

Makes 3 to 4 cups

Grilled Chicken Breasts with Vegetables

Here is an updated twist on the one pot supper. You only need one pan and a few minutes to make this dish. The chicken takes on an outdoor grill quality while the veggies remain crisp and lightly flavored.

¼	cup olive oil
¼	cup balsamic vinegar
2	cloves garlic, minced (about 1 tablespoon)
¼	medium red onion, chopped (about ¼ cup)
1	tablespoon chopped fresh basil
1	tablespoon chopped fresh oregano
	Salt and freshly ground pepper
1	tablespoon olive oil
¾	medium red onion, sliced into thin rings (about ½ cup)
½	medium head red cabbage, sliced into thin strips (about 2 cups)
2	large carrots, peeled and shredded (about 1 cup)
2	tablespoons chopped fresh thyme
	Salt and freshly ground pepper
4	6-ounce skinless, boneless chicken breasts halves, pounded to ½-inch thickness

1. In a small bowl combine the olive oil, vinegar, garlic, onion, basil and oregano to make a marinade for the chicken. Season with salt and pepper.
2. Marinate the chicken breasts in the mixture, covered in the refrigerator, for at least 30 minutes.
3. Heat the grill pan on the stovetop over high heat.
4. Drizzle 1 tablespoon of olive oil in the pan.
5. Remove the chicken from the marinade. Set aside the marinade for later use.
6. Grill the breasts, turning once, for 4 to 6 minutes per side until just cooked through. Remove the chicken to a platter and keep warm.
7. Heat the remaining marinade in the grill pan.

TECHNIQUE:
Heat the grill pan on high and then add the olive oil. The pan may smoke a bit—just like an outdoor grill. Add the food to the pan and then reduce the heat to control the smoking.

SIMPLE SHORTCUT:
Skip step 1 and substitute ½ cup of spicy bottled Italian salad dressing for the marinade.

SETTING THE SCENE:
Place a grilled chicken breast half in the center of a dinner plate. Top with a mound of grilled vegetables. Serve a spoonful of herbed rice on each side of the chicken. Sprinkle the plate with a splattering of fresh thyme.

8. Add the vegetables to the pan, tossing frequently. Continue cooking until all the vegetables are browned on the edges, about 5 to 10 minutes.
9. Sprinkle the vegetables with fresh thyme. Toss gently for another few minutes until no liquid is visible. Season with salt and freshly ground pepper.

Serves 4
Preparation time about 30 minutes

Spicy Tomato Barbecue Sauce

Spice up a plain grilled chicken breast by brushing on a great barbecue sauce. This one makes a bunch—save the extra for a busy day.

1	**28-ounce can tomato sauce**
½	**cup soy sauce**
½	**cup red wine vinegar**
1	**12-ounce can beer**
2	**medium jalapeño peppers, seeded, finely diced (about 2 tablespoons)**
4	**cloves garlic, minced**
	Salt and freshly ground pepper to taste

1. In a saucepan combine all of the ingredients and heat over medium high heat, stirring constantly.
2. Simmer for 15 to 20 minutes.

Makes 4 cups

Grilled Pork Chops with Mango Salsa

Fresh mango is the perfect accompaniment for the spicy seasoning of these pork chops.

½	teaspoon cumin
½	teaspoon garlic powder
¼	teaspoon cayenne pepper
¼	teaspoon salt
4	6-to 8-ounce pork rib chops, 1 inch thick

1	medium ripe mango, cut into ½-inch dice (about 1 cup)
1	medium red onion, diced (about ½ cup)
¼	cup chopped fresh cilantro
2	tablespoons balsamic vinegar
1	tablespoon olive oil

Heat the grill to medium high heat.
1. In a small bowl combine the cumin, garlic powder cayenne pepper and salt.
2. Sprinkle each side of each pork chop with the spice mixture.
3. Grill over medium high for about 4 to 6 minutes per side, turning once.
4. In a medium bowl toss together the mango, red onion, cilantro, balsamic vinegar, and olive oil.
5. Serve the pork chops with a spoonful of mango salsa on the side.

Serves 4
Preparation time about 20 minutes

TECHNIQUE;
Salsa is the blend of diced vegetables and fresh herbs. Mango adds a sweet taste to counter the sharp onion in this dish.

For more salsa fun check out the recipe for Black Bean and Toasted Corn Salsa (page 258).

Marinated Pork Tenderloin

Pork tenderloin is a flavorful, lean meat. It is readily found in the butcher section of the grocery store and usually comes two to a package.

2   **whole pork tenderloins, 1½ to 2 pounds total**
       Salt and freshly ground pepper

¼   **cup soy sauce**
½   **cup olive oil**
2   **tablespoons honey**
¼   **cup balsamic vinegar**
2   **cloves garlic, minced (about 1 tablespoon)**
2   **teaspoons grated fresh ginger**
3   **to 4 green onions including tops, chopped (about ½ cup)**
2   **to 4 rosemary sprigs**

1. Season the pork tenderloins with salt and pepper.
2. In a small bowl whisk together all of the remaining ingredients except for the rosemary sprigs.
3. Place the pork in a shallow dish. Pour the marinade over top. Place the rosemary sprigs around the pork.
4. Cover the dish with plastic wrap and refrigerate for at least 30 minutes (or as long as several hours).
5. Heat a grill pan on the stove top over high heat.
6. Remove the tenderloins from the marinade and place them into the pan. Reduce the heat to medium high.
7. Grill about 10 to 15 minutes per side for medium rare portions.

Serves 6
Preparation time about 20 minutes plus marinating

TECHNIQUE:
If the weather outside is smiling feel free to use a barbecue grill to cook the pork. Make sure that you light the fire and allow the grill to heat up before you begin to cook.

HELPFUL HINT:
Let the tenderloins rest for a few minutes after they are removed from the grill. When you are ready to serve cut the meat across the grain and into diagonally sliced medallions.

Spicy Caesar Salad with Sliced Grilled Chicken Breasts

Here is a contemporary twist on an old classic. This dish takes the place of a full dinner on those nights when quick preparation is a necessity.

½	cup fresh lime juice
⅓	cup peanut oil
3	to 4 green onions including tops, chopped (about ½ cup)
2	whole cloves garlic, minced (about 1 tablespoon)
1	tablespoons chopped basil
	Salt and freshly ground pepper
2	6-ounce skinless, boneless, chicken breast halves
1	2-ounce tin anchovy fillets (about 6 to 8)
1	medium jalapeño, seeded and diced (about 2 tablespoons)
2	tablespoons fresh cilantro
1	tablespoon Worcestershire sauce
1	tablespoon prepared mustard
1	tablespoon mayonnaise
1	clove garlic
1	teaspoon capers
	Juice from 1 medium lime (about 2 to 3 tablespoons)
¼	cup balsamic vinegar
½	cup olive oil
4	cups salad greens, torn into pieces
½	cup croutons
1	ounce Parmesan cheese, shaved (about ¼ cup)

SIMPLE SUBSTITUTION:
Use a prepared marinade or bottled salad dressing to save time. Bottled dressing makes a great marinade for those working late days. Feel free to take this shortcut.

SETTING THE SCENE:
To serve, slice each chicken breast into thin diagonal strips and place on top of the salad. Pass around the pepper mill.

1. In a small bowl combine the lime juice, peanut oil, onions, garlic, basil, salt, and pepper to make a marinade.
2. Pour the marinade over the chicken breasts in a shallow dish. Cover with plastic wrap and refrigerate for at least 30 minutes.

3. In the bowl of a food processor place the anchovies, jalapeño, cilantro, Worcestershire sauce, mustard, mayonnaise, garlic clove, capers, juice from 1 lime, and vinegar.
4. Add the olive oil through the feed tube with the motor running.
5. Remove the breasts from the marinade. Grill the chicken, turning once, about 5 to 6 minutes per side until cooked through. The breasts should be moist in the center and firm to the touch.
6. In a large salad bowl toss the salad greens with the croutons.
7. Drizzle the dressing over the salad and toss again.
8. Shave the Parmesan cheese on top of the dressed greens.

Serves 4
Preparation time about 20 minutes plus marinating

Garlic Infused Caesar Dressing

The next time you are in the mood for a spicy twist on the classic Caesar dressing, give this one a try. At first it may seem like a lot of garlic, but don't put in less. The garlic sweetens as the dressing sits. Trust me, the results are worth it.

SERVING SUGGESTION:
Break crisp Romaine lettuce leaves into bite size pieces. Dress the leaves with a squeeze of lemon juice. Toss with grated Parmesan cheese and home baked croutons. Drizzle the garlic dressing over the top until the leaves are just moist. Season with freshly ground pepper.

1 **tablespoon Dijon mustard**
Dash Worcestershire sauce
¾ **or more of 1.6-ounce tube anchovy paste**
¼ **cup plus 2 tablespoons balsamic vinegar**
10 **cloves garlic, pressed**
¾ **cup good quality olive oil**

1. In a small bowl combine the mustard, Worcestershire sauce, and anchovy paste.
2. Stir in the garlic.
3. Slowly whisk in the olive oil.
4. Allow the dressing to sit for several hours.

Grilled Chicken and Baby Back Ribs with Mustard "Cue"

"Cue" is a term used by Southerners when they talk about the rich sauce that coats grilled meat and chicken. There are several variations, each better than the one before. Plain yellow mustard gives this sauce its tangy taste.

2	8-ounce racks baby back ribs
4	8-ounce chicken breast halves with ribs
4	6-ounce chicken thighs
	Salt and freshly ground pepper
	Garlic powder
1	12-ounce can beer
	Rosemary sprigs

1	cup red wine vinegar
½	cup prepared mustard
¼	cup ketchup, or more
½	cup molasses
1	tablespoon honey
1	teaspoon chili powder
½	teaspoon Worcestershire sauce

Preheat the oven to 300°.

1. Lay the chicken and ribs on pieces of waxed paper. Season each piece with salt, freshly ground pepper, and garlic powder.
2. Place each piece on a rack in the bottom of a large baking (or roasting) pan.
3. Pour a full can of beer on the bottom of the pan surrounding the meat and poultry.
4. Place rosemary sprigs all around.
5. Cover the pan with aluminum foil and bake for 30 to 40 minutes.

To make the sauce:

6. In a saucepan combine the red wine vinegar, mustard, ketchup, molasses, honey, chili powder, and Worcestershire sauce.

HELPFUL HINT:
Precooking the food before it is grilled makes the cooking time shorter and guarantees a spectacular finish.

SIMPLE SHORTCUT:
There a great number of super tasting prepared barbecue sauces. Substitute your favorite when making your own is not on the agenda.

BACKYARD COOK-OUT MENU

Deviled Eggs

Dilled Potato and Egg Salad

Southern Style Slaw

Chilled Green Bean Salad with Mustard Shallot Vinaigrette

Apple Strawberry Cobbler

7. Stir over medium heat until the sauce reduces slightly and begins to thicken. Taste and adjust ingredients. Remove from the heat.
8. Complete the cooking of the ribs and chicken by grilling them over a medium high fire. Baste each piece generously with the sauce at the end of the grilling.

Serve 8
Preparation time about 1 hour

Red Wine Barbecue Sauce

Feel free to heat up the spice in this great sauce by adding a few extra drops of hot sauce.

1	cup butter (2 sticks)
2	medium white onions, diced (about 2 cups)
2	cloves garlic, minced
2	cups water
½	cup red wine
1	tablespoon brown sugar
1	teaspoon chili powder
⅓	cup ketchup
	Hot pepper sauce
	Salt and freshly ground pepper

1. In a saucepan melt the butter over medium high heat.
2. Cook the onions and garlic in the butter until soft.
3. Add the remaining ingredients. Stir.
4. Bring the sauce to a boil. Reduce the heat and simmer for 15 to 20 minutes.

Makes 2 to 3 cups

Moroccan Spiced Rotisserie Chicken

For outdoor entertaining there is nothing as easy as using the rotisserie attachment to your barbecue. The secret is to use the tongs that hold the meat onto the spit correctly. Try to scrunch the legs into the tongs instead of allowing the tongs to pierce the meat. This will insure that the juices remain inside the food.

1	whole chicken for roasting
1	tablespoon olive oil
¼	cup Hungarian paprika
2	tablespoons brown sugar
1	tablespoon cumin
1	tablespoon ground cinnamon
4	cloves garlic, minced
1	teaspoon salt
1	teaspoon ground pepper

1. Place the chicken on the spit of a rotisserie.
2. Rub the chicken with olive oil.
3. Mix the spices together and rub the mixture all over the chicken.
4. Roast the chicken over medium high heat for 40 minutes to one hour—using a meat thermometer to determine doneness.

Serves a crowd
Preparation time 50 to 70 minutes

SIMPLE SUBSTITUTION:
This cooking technique and combination of spices works well on all sorts of meat. A family favorite is a boneless leg of lamb and a super alternative is a whole beef tenderloin. Whichever you choose, make sure to use a meat thermometer to check for doneness as this cooking process works more rapidly than the traditional oven roasting method.

Grilled Chicken and White Bean Enchiladas

This filling meal covers all the food groups. What's more—
it's easy to make and fun to eat.

	Mexican flavored marinade
2	**8-ounce skinless, boneless, chicken breasts**
2	**tablespoons sour cream**
1	**16-ounce can cannelloni beans, rinsed and drained**
½	**cup grated sharp Cheddar cheese**
1	**large jalapeño pepper, seeded and chopped**
3	**large green onions, chopped (about 1 tablespoon)**
1	**tablespoon chopped fresh cilantro**
1	**teaspoon ground cumin**
2	**tablespoons olive oil**
6	**8-inch spinach-flavored flour tortillas**
1	**10-ounce can prepared enchilada sauce**
¼	**cup grated sharp Cheddar cheese**

Preheat the oven to 350°.

1. In a shallow dish pour the marinade over the chicken. Cover with plastic wrap and refrigerate for 30 minutes.
2. Remove the chicken from the marinade. In a grill pan cook the chicken, turning once, for about 5 minutes per side until cooked through. Cool. Slice into thin strips.
3. In a food processor combine the sour cream and cannelloni beans. Pulse to combine. Add the cheese, jalapeño, onions, cilantro, and cumin. Pulse briefly.
4. In a skillet heat the oil over medium high heat. Cook each tortilla in the oil until just beginning to brown, no longer than 1 minute. Place on paper towels.
5. Spray a baking dish with vegetable oil cooking spray. Place several strips of chicken in the center of each tortilla. Top with 2 tablespoons of the bean mixture. Roll the tortillas and place seam side down in the dish.
6. Spread with enchilada sauce and sprinkle with additional Cheddar cheese. Bake for 30 minutes.

Serves 6
Preparation time about 30 minutes plus baking

Grilled Artichokes and Baby Portabella Mushroom Salad

The dramatic presentation of this dish makes it look harder than it is. The warm artichokes and mushrooms sit atop chilled greens lightly tossed with oriental flavored vinaigrette.

2	whole artichokes, steamed
1	large lemon
1	pound whole baby portabella mushrooms
2	tablespoons olive oil
	Freshly ground pepper

⅓	cup rice wine vinegar
2	tablespoons soy sauce
1	teaspoon honey
1	tablespoon fresh garlic chives, snipped
½	teaspoon fresh ginger, grated
¼	cup olive oil

4	cups mixed fresh organic salad greens

1. Steam the artichokes. Slice into quarters, and remove the choke.
2. Clean the baby portabella mushrooms with a mushroom brush.
3. Heat a grill pan on the stovetop over high heat. Drizzle 1 tablespoon of olive oil in the pan.
4. Grill the artichokes in the pan, turning once. Season with salt and pepper as they grill. Drizzle with additional olive oil if needed.
5. Remove the artichokes from the pan and keep warm.
6. Place 1 tablespoon of olive oil into the pan. Grill the mushrooms in the pan, turning several times. Season with salt and pepper and drizzle with additional olive oil if needed.
7. Remove the mushrooms from the pan and keep warm.
8. In a mixing bowl combine the vinegar, soy sauce, honey, garlic chives, and ginger.

HELPFUL HINT:
The artichokes are steamed before they are grilled. To steam an artichoke, cut off the pointed edges of the outer leaves. Peel the tough skin from the stem leaving about 1 to 2 inches. Peel off the rough outer leaves. Cut off one-third of the top of the artichoke so that it opens. Squeeze lemon juice over the top. Place the artichokes in a casserole dish with 1 inch of water. Cover the dish and cook in a microwave oven on high for about 10 minutes or until a fork is easily inserted into the stem and bottom. Remove the artichokes from the dish. Cut each one in half. Use a spoon or sharp knife to remove the thorny choke portion from the middle of the artichoke.

SETTING THE SCENE:
Assemble the dish by placing the dressed greens on a large platter. Toss the warm artichokes, in the same bowl that held the greens, with a small amount of vinaigrette. Place the artichokes on top of the greens. Place the mushrooms in the bowl and toss with a small amount of vinaigrette. Scatter the mushrooms around the platter. The salad may be served warm or at room temperature.

9. Add the olive oil in a thin stream whisking constantly until well blended.
10. Place the salad greens in a large bowl. Drizzle a small amount of the vinaigrette over the top. Toss until the leaves are just moistened.

Serves 2 as an entrée or 4 as a salad
Preparation time about 30 minutes

Grilled Corn with Thyme-Infused Butter

What's a barbecue without corn on the cob? This preparation is not only delicious, but it offers a great way to present the veggie!

2   **tablespoons chopped fresh thyme**
¼   **cup butter, melted (½ stick butter)**
8   **ears corn on the cob**

1. In a saucepan stir the fresh thyme into the melted butter over medium heat.
2. Remove the pan from the heat, cover, and set aside for several minutes to allow the flavor of the herb to infuse the butter.
3. Peel down the husk from the corn, and remove the threads. Leave the husk attached at the stem.
4. Brush the corn with the savory butter.
5. Pull the husks back in place.
6. Grill the corn in the husks over a medium fire for 20 minutes. Make sure to turn frequently so you do not burn the husk.

Serves 8
Preparation time about 30 minutes

SETTING THE SCENE:
Serve the corn in a large festive pottery bowl or platter. Peel the husk from the corn leaving it attached at the bottom, like the leaves on a flower. Pour any remaining butter over the corn. Place bunches of thyme tied with thin strips of corn husks among the ears of corn. Place a butter dish filled with decorative corn holders nearby.

Share your favorite grilled food recipe at www.jorj.com.

Grilled Beef Tenderloin Steaks with Shiitake Mushroom Sauce

4	**6-ounce beef tenderloin steaks**
2	**teaspoons Worcestershire sauce**
1	**tablespoon butter**
1	**pound shiitake mushrooms**
¼	**cup balsamic vinegar**
½	**cup port wine**
3	**cups beef broth**
½	**teaspoon cornstarch, mixed with 2 tablespoons water**
2	**tablespoons butter, chilled**
	Salt and freshly ground pepper

1. Place the steaks in a shallow dish. Season with Worcestershire sauce and ground pepper. Marinate for at least 30 minutes.
2. In a medium skillet heat the butter over medium high heat.
3. Add the mushrooms and cook until just brown. Remove the mushrooms to a plate.
4. Pour the balsamic vinegar into the skillet. Add the port wine and cook until the liquid is reduced to about ⅓ cup.
5. Add the beef broth to the skillet and cook until the liquid is reduced by half.
6. Thicken the sauce with the cornstarch and water mixture.
7. Add the mushrooms and cook for 2 to 3 minutes.
8. Reduce the heat to low. Stir in the butter to produce a smooth and shiny sauce.
9. Grill the steaks over high heat turning once, about 4 minutes per side. Season with salt and pepper.
10. Serve each steak topped with mushroom sauce.

Serves 4
Preparation time about 20 minutes plus marinating

HELPFUL HINT:
The steaks will grill quickly. To have the sauce ready, but not overcooked; bring it to the stage where the mushrooms are added. Reduce the heat and stir in the butter just before you serve the steaks.

SETTING THE SCENE:
For an awesome presentation, quickly sauté fresh spinach leaves in a small amount of butter. Place the cooked spinach on the plate. Cut each steak diagonally. Set one half of the steak on top of the spinach. Stand the other half on its side resting on the first half. Spoon the mushroom sauce over top.

TECHNIQUE:
For a moist, delicious grilled steak, season with salt—just before grilling. Salting in advance tends to dry out the meat.

Island Spiced Flank Steak

For indoor grilling, make sure that your flank steak will fit into the grill pan. You may need to cut it into two pieces. When you are ready to serve cut the meat across the grain (from the narrow end of the steak) for the most tender slices.

1	1½-pound flank steak
	Salt and freshly ground pepper
2	tablespoons peanut oil
2	tablespoons olive oil
2	tablespoons fresh lime juice
2	tablespoons Worcestershire sauce
1	tablespoon chili powder
1	teaspoon ground ginger
1	teaspoon allspice
1	teaspoon ground celery seed
2	to 4 green onions including tops, chopped (about ½ cup)
	Rosemary sprigs

1. Season the flank steak with salt and freshly ground pepper.
2. In a small bowl whisk together all of the remaining ingredients except for the rosemary sprigs.
3. Place the steak in a shallow dish. Pour the marinade over top coating both sides. Place the rosemary sprigs around the steak.
4. Cover the dish with plastic wrap and refrigerate for at least 30 minutes or for several hours.
5. Heat a grill pan on the stove top over high heat.
6. Remove the steak from the marinade and place it into the hot pan.
7. Grill for 8 to 10 minutes for medium rare slices.

Serves 4 to 6
Preparation time about 15 minutes plus marinating

HELPFUL HINT:
Let the steak rest for a few minutes before you slice.

SIMPLE SUBSTITUTION:
This marinade and cooking technique also works well with skirt steak.

SETTING THE SCENE:
Leftover flank steak is terrific the next day served with a salad of fresh greens, peppers, and tomatoes, tossed with a favorite vinaigrette.

Try it with Greek Style Salad with Garlic Lemon Dressing (page 33).

Grilled Stuffed Veal Chops

Purchase a good quality, thick veal chop for this dish. The chops are seared in the grill pan and then finished in the oven.

4	**¾-pound veal rib chops, 2 inches thick**
1	**small eggplant, peeled and diced into ¼-inch cubes (about 3 cups)**
	Salt and freshly ground pepper
4	**ounces goat cheese, softened**
1	**teaspoon dried oregano**
1	**medium red bell pepper, roasted, sliced into quarters**
	Salt and freshly ground pepper
1	**tablespoon olive oil**

Preheat the oven to 350°.

1. Butterfly the veal chops by cutting the meat three quarters through to the bone. Pound each side of each chop with a meat mallet to about ½-inch thickness.
2. Season the eggplant with salt and pepper. Roast the eggplant cubes at 350° on a baking dish sprayed with a cooking spray for 10 minutes. Remove from the oven and allow to cool slightly.
3. Toss together the goat cheese and oregano with the eggplant in a small bowl.
4. Place one-fourth of the cheese mixture inside each veal chop. Top with a slice of roasted red pepper.
5. Close the two sides of the veal chop over the filling.
6. Heat the grill pan on the stove top over high heat.
7. Drizzle the olive oil in the pan.
8. Sear both sides of the chops in the pan for about 3 to 4 minutes per side.
9. Finish cooking the chops by placing the grill pan in the oven at 350° for 10 to 20 minutes.

Serves 4
Preparation time about 30 minutes plus baking

SIMPLE SHORTCUT:
Roasted peppers are available in a jar. If time does not permit roasting one yourself, this is a good substitution.

HELPFUL HINT:
1. The veal chops may be made ahead through step 5. Cover and refrigerate for several hours until you are ready to proceed. When you are ready to continue season both sides of the chops with salt and freshly ground pepper.

2. Remember to use a pot holder when you take the pan out of the oven!

Marinated Grilled Vegetables with Feta Cheese

These savory roasted vegetables take the place of a tossed salad on a buffet table. Make enough to serve as a treat for lunch the next day. Easily prepared in advance, the dish is served at room temperature.

1	large eggplant, peeled and sliced lengthwise into ¼-inch slices
2	large zucchini, peeled and sliced lengthwise into ¼-inch slices
4	yellow squash, peeled and sliced lengthwise into ¼-inch slices
2	large tomatoes, sliced into ½-inch slices
1	medium red onion, sliced into ¼-inch slices
½	cup olive oil, divided
	Salt and freshly ground pepper
¼	cup balsamic vinegar
1	tablespoon chopped fresh basil
	Juice of ½ medium lemon (about 1 tablespoon)
4	ounces Feta cheese, crumbled
	Fresh basil leaves

1. Brush each side of the vegetables lightly with ¼ cup of the olive oil. Season with salt and pepper.
2. Grill both sides over medium high heat using a grill pan or the outdoor grill. The vegetables will soften and begin to blacken very quickly. Be careful not to overcook or they will fall apart.
3. Remove the vegetables to a dish or shallow pan.
4. In a small bowl combine the remaining ¼ cup of olive oil, vinegar, chopped basil, and lemon juice.
5. Pour the marinade over the vegetables and chill for at least 30 minutes and up to 4 hours.
6. Remove the vegetables from the marinade and arrange each slice on a platter. Sprinkle the crumbled Feta cheese over all and season with pepper.

Serves 4

Preparation time about 30 minutes plus marinating

SETTING THE SCENE:

Choose a large white platter to serve this tapestry of grilled veggies. Arrange alternating slices of eggplant, zucchini, and yellow squash around the outside edge of the platter. Alternate slices of tomatoes and red onion in the center of the platter. Sprinkle the crumbled Feta cheese over top. Place a cluster of fresh basil leaves on top of the vegetable platter for the garnish.

COOK-IN–INSTEAD OF COOK-OUT– SUPPER MENU

Marinated Grilled Vegetables with Feta Cheese

Big Juicy Hamburgers with Grilled Onions

Rum Soaked Sweet Potatoes

Peach Pie Y'All

Grilled Swordfish Steaks with White Bean Relish

Swordfish steaks really hold up well to grilling. This dish blends a garlicky marinade with a Mediterranean inspired relish.

4	**6-ounce swordfish steaks, 1 inch thick**
	Juice of 1 medium lime (about 2 tablespoons)
2	**cloves garlic, minced (about 1 tablespoon)**
1	**tablespoon olive oil**
	Salt and freshly ground pepper
1	**15-ounce can cannelloni beans, drained**
4	**medium plum tomatoes, seeded and chopped (about 1 cup)**
1	**2¼-ounce can sliced black olives, drained (about ½ cup)**
1	**(or more) jalapeño pepper, seeded and diced (about 1 tablespoon)**
2	**tablespoons chopped fresh rosemary**
1	**tablespoons balsamic vinegar**
1	**tablespoon olive oil**

Heat the grill to medium high heat.

1. Place the swordfish steaks in a shallow dish.
2. Sprinkle each side with lime juice, minced garlic, olive oil, salt, and pepper. Refrigerate for at least 30 minutes.
3. In a small bowl combine the drained beans, chopped tomatoes, black olives, jalapeño, and rosemary. Toss to combine.
4. Sprinkle the mixture with balsamic vinegar and olive oil. Toss and let sit for at least 30 minutes.
5. Grill the swordfish over medium high heat for about 4 to 6 minutes per side, turning once.
6. Serve the swordfish with the white bean relish on the side.

Serves 4
Preparation time about 30 minutes

ENTERTAINING THE BOSS DINNER MENU

Mixed Greens with Goat Cheese, Walnuts, and Chili Vinaigrette

❧

Chilled Roasted Asparagus with Tomato Mayonnaise Salsa

❧

Grilled Swordfish Steaks with White Bean Relish

❧

Warm Apple Tart with Almond Creme and Caramel Sauce

Grilled Herb Shrimp

Serve this dish as an appetizer when friends come to visit. The shrimp are grilled in advance and chilled before serving. You are free to enjoy your guests.

2	dozen large shrimp

1	cup olive oil
	Juice from 2 medium lemons (about ½ cup)
	Salt and freshly ground pepper

2	tablespoons chopped fresh oregano
2	tablespoons chopped fresh thyme
2	tablespoons chopped fresh basil
2	tablespoons chopped fresh rosemary

1. Remove the shells from the shrimp keeping the tails in place. Pull out the dark vein.
2. In a small bowl mix together the olive oil and lemon juice. Season with salt and freshly ground pepper.
3. In a separate bowl combine the chopped herbs.
4. Dip each shrimp first into the olive oil mixture and then roll it into the herbs. Place onto a baking sheet. Continue until all of the shrimp have been dipped.
5. Grill the shrimp, turning once, about 3 minutes per side until they turn opaque.
6. Remove the shrimp and chill.

Serves 6
Preparation time about 15 minutes

HELPFUL HINT:
A mini food processor is an excellent tool to use when chopping fresh herbs. It makes fast work of a busy process. Try to remove as many stems from the herbs as you can before you place them into the bowl of the processor.

SETTING THE SCENE:
Serve the shrimp in a chilled bowl or a glass bowl sitting in a larger bowl filled with ice. Sauce Remoulade (page 129), Dilled Mustard Sauce (page 213), and Black Bean and Toasted Corn Salsa (page 258) are each terrific accompaniments for this dish.

Grilled Florida Lobster Tail with Garlicky Tomato Sauce

Florida lobster tail comes into season for a short time at the end of the summer. It is well worth the wait. The sweet meat is easily prepared in a variety of ways. Try this grilled version using my favorite kitchen gadget—the grill pan!

4	1- to 1½-pound fresh Florida lobster tails
	Juice of 1 medium lemon, about 2 to 3 tablespoons
	Salt and freshly ground pepper
2	tablespoons olive oil, divided

1	tablespoon olive oil
2	medium shallots, diced (about 2 tablespoons)
4	to 6 cloves garlic, minced (about 2 to 3 tablespoons)
½	cup white wine
1	10½-ounce can chopped tomatoes
	Juice of 1 medium lemon (about 2 to 3 tablespoons)

Preheat the oven to 375°.

1. Butterfly the lobster tails by cutting through the bottom shell and meat leaving the end section attached. Pull the meat from the tail to loosen. Set it back into the shell.
2. Season the lobster with lemon juice and pepper.
3. In a grill pan heat 1 tablespoon of olive oil on high heat.
4. Place the lobster into the pan with the meat side down. Reduce the heat to medium high. Cook until the meat begins to color, about 4 minutes.
5. Use tongs to turn the lobster and cook for 2 minutes more. Place the grill pan into the oven and cook for 5 to 8 minutes.
6. In a skillet heat the remaining olive oil over medium high heat.
7. Cook the shallots in the oil until just beginning to brown. Add the garlic and cook for 1 to 2 minutes, being careful not to burn.

HELPFUL HINT:
Remember to use a pot holder when you take out the pan!

SIMPLE SUBSTITUTION:
Florida lobster is only available for a few months at the end of the summer. Not to worry, frozen lobster tails will work quite well, as will fresh dolphin or sea bass.

SETTING THE SCENE:
Place a lobster tail on each dinner plate. The meat will easily pull free from the shell. Ladle a generous spoonful of sauce over top. Accompany the dish with oven roasted vegetables like carrots, onions, or sweet and white potatoes tossed with a touch of thyme.

8. Add the white wine to the pan and reduce for several minutes.
9. Add the chopped tomatoes and lemon juice. Season the sauce with salt and pepper.
10. Remove the grill pan from the oven.

Serves 4
Preparation time about 30 minutes

Grilled Calamari

This dish is a fast and festive party starter or a quick, light midweek meal. Either way, the secret is to find fresh squid that is cleaned well.

1   **tablespoon olive oil**
1   **pound squid, cleaned and cut into rings and tentacles**
     Juice of 1 medium lemon
     Salt and freshly ground pepper
     Chopped fresh parsley

1. Heat a grill pan on the stove top over high heat.
2. Drizzle the olive oil into the pan.
3. Place the squid pieces in the pan.
4. Drizzle the lemon juice over top of the squid. Turn frequently.
5. Remove the calamari from the pan as it begins to turn opaque in color, about 2 minutes.

Serves 4 to 8
Preparation time about 15 minutes

HELPFUL HINT:
The trick to preparing great calamari is to cook it either under 2 minutes or over 1 hour. Otherwise it can be tough.

TECHNIQUE:
Make bruschetta by slicing thick pieces of Italian bread. Melt butter together with a sprinkling of garlic powder. Brush the butter mixture onto both sides of the bread. Grill the bread in the grill pan, turning once, until it just begins to brown.

SETTING THE SCENE:
Place the calamari in a pasta serving bowl. Season with salt and freshly ground pepper. Sprinkle fresh chopped parsley over the top. Serve with a basket of warm bruschetta.

Totally Take-Out

COOKING FAST FOOD FAVORITES

Think about a late-night craving for a quick, good meal and several tastes come to mind. A shared slice of pizza, the fun of take-out Chinese, or the spicy flavors of Mexican food are just a few of the ethnic foods that satisfy our appetite needs. You can create these dishes at home with little fuss and gain the benefits of guaranteed "on-time," piping hot, great quality food made from the freshest ingredients.

The pizza recipes in this chapter are a simple guideline for discovering your own array of deluxe toppings. Follow my one rule of thumb to insure a great result: use a fast melting cheese as the "glue" that holds on all of the other ingredients. Puff pastry adds delicateness to the dish that pushes pizza beyond take out and onto an appetizer plate for any party. After that, your individual taste buds take over the recipe.

Asian flavorings blend sweet and tangy tastes to many types of food such as vegetables, chicken, and beef. You can easily alternate the sauces with the different kinds of food. Ginger is a common spice used in these dishes. It is purchased in a ground or dried form in the spice section of the grocery. Fresh ginger is more pungent. It is peeled and finely chopped with a small hand-held grater. Pickled ginger can be found in the refrigerated section of the produce department. Inspired cooks choose fresh ginger for the fabulous aroma.

The Mexican origins of quesadillas have given way to the infused direction of today's cooking. Because it is rapidly prepared, a quesadilla is filled with ingredients that span ethnic cuisine. *Fusion cuisine* is the phrase coined to describe various ethnic foods infused into other ethnic cooking techniques. For example, smoked trout and Brie cheese are more often found on a bagel than in a quesadilla. The next time your schedule calls for a quick meal, use the ingredients that you keep on hand and the recipes in this chapter to gratify your appetite.

The beauty of cooking the Totally Take-Out foods that you love at home is also in the ease of presentation. A pizza served on a china platter and garnished with fresh chopped cilantro has much more eye appeal that the one that you eat from a box. Likewise, baked plump chicken wings that surround a bowl of fragrant peanut sauce attract a crowd much more quickly than those served from a folded carton. Colorful earthen bowls brimming with fresh salsas hold much more charm than pre-packaged condiments tossed onto a table next to an insulated cardboard container of chili.

Experiment with the presentation of food and you will soon discover that eye appeal is as important as taste and aroma. Create your own Totally Take-Out favorites and invite your friends to share the results.

Find more information about the recipes in the Totally Take Out chapter at www.jorj.com.

Pizza with Sun-Dried Tomatoes, Basil, and Goat Cheese

Much better than take-out, this pizza comes from your oven, bubbly hot and fragrant. The extra bonus is that you don't have to tip the delivery dude!

1	8-ounce frozen puff pastry sheet
	Dash flour
1½	cups shredded mozzarella cheese
1	7-ounce jar sun-dried tomato halves in oil, drained, sliced, oil reserved
1	bunch fresh basil leaves, 12 or more whole leaves
4	ounces goat cheese
½	medium red onion, thinly sliced (about ½ cup)
⅓	cup grated Parmesan cheese
2	tablespoons chopped fresh oregano
	Freshly ground pepper

Preheat the oven to 450°.

1. Remove 1 sheet of frozen puff pastry and thaw according to package directions.
2. Spray a baking sheet (or jelly roll pan) with vegetable oil spray.
3. Roll out the dough to approximately ⅛-inch thickness and place it on the cookie sheet. (You may lightly flour the rolling pin and surface.) Crimp the edges to form a ridge on all sides. Pierce the bottom of the dough with a fork.
4. Sprinkle the mozzarella cheese evenly over the dough.
5. Scatter the sun-dried tomatoes over the cheese. Place the basil leaves around the tomatoes.
6. Crumble (or spread) the goat cheese on top of the basil leaves.
7. Place the red onion rings over the basil and tomatoes.
8. Drizzle the pizza with the 1 tablespoon of the reserved oil from the sun-dried tomatoes. Season with pepper.
9. Top with the grated Parmesan cheese.

HELPFUL HINT:
To create your own individual pizza, try the following combinations. Always start by layering the pizza dough with mozzarella (or other easily melted cheese) to secure the other toppings.

- Pizza sauce, pepperoni, and green peppers
- Sliced tomatoes, black olives, and feta cheese

SETTING THE SCENE:
Sprinkle chopped fresh oregano over a large platter. Place the pizza slices on top of the herbs. Garnish with a bouquet of fresh basil leaves.

10. Bake the pizza for 14 to 18 minutes. The crust ridge will be puffed and golden brown and the cheese melted and bubbling. Let the pizza rest for a minute or two before cutting.

Serves 6
Preparation time about 30 minutes

SPORTS BAR BUFFET PARTY MENU

Black Bean and Toasted Corn Salsa

Super Nachos Two Ways

Buffalo Style Chicken Wings

Chicken Chili with Veggies

Vegetable Party Platter

Chocolate Cookie Cheesecake Bars

Inspired Greek Pizza

Here is another quick pizza recipe. This one uses frozen pizza dough and a few Mediterranean inspired ingredients. Feel free to create your own specialty pizza by substituting your favorite stuff.

1	**10-ounce frozen pizza dough, thawed**
	Dash flour
¾	**pound ground lamb**
½	**small eggplant, peeled and diced, about**
4	**cloves garlic, minced**
½	**teaspoon ground cinnamon**
½	**teaspoon ground cumin**
1	**teaspoon ground oregano**
½	**medium red onion, chopped (about ½ cup)**
½	**cup chopped pitted Kalamata olives**
3	**to 4 plum tomatoes, sliced (about 1 cup)**
½	**cup crumbled feta cheese**
	Salt and freshly ground pepper

Preheat the oven to 475°.

1. Spray a baking sheet with vegetable oil spray.
2. Roll out the dough to approximately ⅛-inch thickness and place it on the cookie sheet. (You may lightly flour the rolling pin and surface.) Crimp the edges to form a ridge on all sides. Pierce the bottom of the dough with a fork.
3. Cook the lamb in a skillet over medium high heat until just beginning to brown.
4. Add the diced eggplant, stir, and cook for several minutes.
5. Add the minced garlic, cinnamon, cumin, and oregano to the lamb. Stir. Remove from the heat.
6. Spread the lamb mixture over the pizza dough.
7. Scatter the chopped red onion, chopped olives, and plum tomatoes over the top.
8. Sprinkle the crumbled feta cheese evenly over the pizza. Season with salt and pepper.

HELPFUL HINT:
Follow the direction on the package to thaw the pizza dough. If you plan ahead, you can thaw it in the refrigerator the night before. Or allow up to three hours for it to sit on your counter. You may want to try to defrost the dough in a hurry using the microwave oven. Lightly oil the dough. Place it in a plastic bag. Seal the bag and pierce it with the tines of a fork. Microwave on the defrost setting for about 4 minutes. Check the dough every 30 seconds, turning the dough each time. Remove the dough from the bag and allow it to rest for several minutes before you begin to roll it out.

9. Bake the pizza for 14 to 18 minutes. The crust ridge should be lightly brown. The cheese is melted and bubbling. Let the pizza rest for a minute or two before cutting.

Serves 4 to 6
Preparation time about 30 minutes

Mexican Spiced Pizza

Don't stop now! Pizza toppings go on and on and on. Here is a combination that is simply irresistible. Remember to use this and other recipes as a guideline to create your own favorite home made pizza.

1	**10-ounce frozen pizza dough, thawed**
	Dash flour
½	**pound bacon, diced**
½	**pound mild sausage, sliced**
1	**7-ounce jar roasted red pepper strips**
1	**jalapeño pepper, sliced**
1	**medium zucchini, thinly sliced**
1	**cup grated Monterey Jack cheese**

Preheat the oven to 475°.

1. Spray a baking sheet with vegetable oil spray.
2. Roll out the dough to approximately ⅛-inch thickness and place it on the cookie sheet. (You may lightly flour the rolling pin and surface.) Crimp the edges to form a ridge on all sides. Pierce the bottom of the dough with a fork.
3. In a skillet cook the bacon over medium high heat for several minutes.
4. Add the sliced sausage and cook until brown. Remove from the heat. Drain well.
5. Spread the bacon and sausage mixture over the pizza dough.
6. Scatter the roasted red pepper strips, jalapeño, and zucchini slices over top.
7. Sprinkle the grated cheese evenly over the pizza.
8. Bake the pizza for 14 to 18 minutes. The crust ridge should be lightly brown. The cheese is melted and bubbling. Let the pizza rest for a minute or two before cutting.

Serves 4

Preparation time about 30 minutes

HELPFUL HINT:

Do you have a taste for Mexican tonight? Here are a few more Mexican-inspired suggestions:

- Mushroom, Bacon, and Jack Cheese Quesadillas (page 157)
- Dolphin Fajitas (page 154)
- Super Nachos Two Ways (page 260)
- Iced Orange Treats (page 284)

Spicy Fried Chicken

Make this chicken as spicy as you like by increasing the amount of seasonings. Serve warm with roasted potatoes and sautéed green beans or at room temperature with picnic style potato salad and deviled eggs.

4	8-ounce chicken breast halves with rib
6	chicken thighs
6	chicken legs
	Canola oil
2	eggs, slightly beaten
½	cup beer
1	cup corn flake crumbs
1	cup all-purpose flour
1	teaspoon paprika
1	teaspoon chili powder
¼	teaspoon red pepper flakes
	Salt and freshly ground pepper

Preheat the oven to 350°.

1. Rinse the chicken pieces and pat dry with paper towels.
2. In a large skillet heat about 1 inch of canola oil over high heat.
3. In a shallow bowl combine the beaten egg and beer.
4. In a second bowl combine the corn flake crumbs, flour, paprika, chili powder, red pepper flakes and salt and freshly ground pepper.
5. Dip the chicken pieces into the egg and then into the flour mixture, coating each piece thoroughly.
6. Cook the chicken pieces in the skillet, turning once, until golden brown.
7. Remove the chicken to a rack placed in the bottom of a broiler pan.
8. Bake the chicken until cooked through, about 20 minutes.

Serves 8
Preparation time about 30 minutes

HELPFUL HINT:
Do not crowd the chicken in the skillet. Allow plenty of room between each piece so that the oil has room to move. If you cook the chicken in batches, make sure that you allow the oil to come up to heat in between each group.

FOURTH OF JULY PICNIC BASKET MENU

Chilled Gazpacho Soup
(packed in a thermos)

Spicy Fried Chicken

Marinated Grilled Vegetables
with Feta Cheese
*(packed in individual
disposable containers)*

Apple Streusel Muffins

Buffalo Style Chicken Wings

Not only are these wings great tasting but, they also are easily be made in advance and reheated for a half time snack for your favorite couch potato's big game.

1	to 2 pounds chicken wings, cut into 2 pieces, tips discarded (24 pieces)
	Salt and freshly ground pepper
½	cup butter (1 stick)
4	large cloves garlic (about 2 tablespoons minced)
¼	cup red wine vinegar
1	to 2 tablespoons hot pepper sauce
½	cup canola oil

1. Pat the chicken pieces with a paper towel to make sure that they are very dry. Season with salt and pepper.
2. In a shallow skillet melt the butter over medium high heat.
3. Cook the garlic in the butter until soft.
4. Add the red wine vinegar and as much of the hot sauce as you desire. (You can add more later.) Keep the sauce warm.
5. In a large skillet heat the canola oil over high heat.
6. Cook the wings in the hot oil turning once.
7. Remove the cooked wings from the oil and place them directly into the warm sauce. Repeat until all wings have been cooked. Simmer the wings in the sauce for 20 to 30 minutes, or bake in the oven for 20 to 30 minutes at 350°.
8. Adjust the seasonings by adding more vinegar or hot sauce.

Serves a crowd
Preparation time about 45 minutes

HELPFUL HINT:
The oil needs to be very hot to produce a crispy wing. Be careful of splatters as you place the wings into the oil. Do not crowd the pan. The temperature of the oil will come down as you add the wings. Maintain the heat by cooking the wings in batches. Things wings are messy. To save on clean up time, cover the pan with a splatter reducing shield.

TECHNIQUE:
To cut the wings into pieces, snip off the pointed tip with poultry scissors. Use your hands to separate the drummette from the mid section. Snap at the joint. Cut through the flesh at the joint to get two pieces.

SETTING THE SCENE:
Serve the wings in a large shallow dish with stacks of celery and carrot sticks. Add a glass full of prepared blue cheese salad dressing for dipping.

Chicken Wings with Peanut Sauce

Bite size drumettes make a great finger food. Make a bunch and save some for a snack the next day.

½   cup teriyaki sauce
2   cloves garlic, minced (1 tablespoon)
2   tablespoons fresh lemon juice
1   tablespoon grated fresh ginger
1   tablespoon brown sugar

1½   pound chicken wings, cut into 2 sections, tips discarded (24 pieces)

½   cup peanut butter
¾   cup chicken stock
2   tablespoons fresh lemon juice
1½   tablespoon brown sugar
1   tablespoon soy sauce
1   tablespoon grated fresh ginger

Canned Chinese noodles

1. In a small bowl stir together the teriyaki sauce, garlic, lemon juice, ginger, and sugar until the sugar dissolves.
2. Place the chicken wings in a shallow baking pan. Pour the marinade over the top. Cover and refrigerate for at least 30 minutes or as long as several hours.
3. In a saucepan warm the peanut butter over medium heat.
4. Stir in the chicken stock, lemon juice, sugar, soy sauce, and fresh ginger until the mixture is smooth.
Preheat the oven to 375°.
5. Remove the wings from the marinade and place on a baking sheet or in a shallow pan.
6. Roast the wings turning once until they are cooked, about 30 to 40 minutes.

Serves a crowd
Preparation time about 30 minutes plus marinating and baking

SIMPLE SHORTCUT:
You can find chicken wings that have been cut into pieces in the frozen food section of the meat department in your grocery store. You may also choose to use only the drumette portion of the wing.

HELPFUL HINT:
This sauce is great on barbecued shrimp and flank steak as well as sliced chicken breast. Give it a try the next time you are in a peanutty mood.

SETTING THE SCENE:
Serve the wings on a large platter. Place a bowl full of peanut sauce in the center. Garnish with canned Chinese noodles crushed over the top.

Chicken Chili with Veggies

This chili is milder than it's traditional meat counterpart, yet just as flavorful. Place a bottle of hot pepper sauce close by to please the avid spice fans.

4   6- to 8-ounce) boneless, skinless chicken breasts, cut into 1-inch pieces
1   tablespoon olive oil
    Salt and freshly ground pepper
1   medium red onion, chopped into ¼-inch pieces (about 1 cup)
1   green bell pepper, chopped into ½-inch piece (about 1 cup)
3   large carrots, peeled and diced into ½-inch pieces (about 1½ cups)
¾   pound yellow squash, diced into ½-inch pieces (about 1½ cups)
2   cloves garlic, minced (about 1 tablespoon)
1   jalapeño pepper, seeded and finely diced (about 2 tablespoon)
2   28-ounce cans chopped tomatoes
2   tablespoons tomato paste
1   cup beer
1   16-ounce can pinto beans, drained
2   tablespoons chili powder, more or less
½   teaspoon ground cinnamon
1   tablespoon chopped fresh cilantro

Green onion, chopped (optional)
Avocado, chopped (optional)
Sharp Cheddar cheese, shredded (optional)
Baked tortilla chips (optional)

1. In a large pot cook the chicken pieces in 1 tablespoon of olive oil over high heat. Season with salt and freshly ground pepper as they brown.
2. Remove the chicken from the pot and set aside.
3. Sauté the onion in the same pot until it begins to brown.

HELPFUL HINT:
Cut the chicken and chop all of the vegetables before you start the dish. As you add a bowl of diced squash or a splash of fresh herbs, you will feel like a chef in a gourmet restaurant.

SETTING THE SCENE:
Serve the chili in a tureen surrounded by bowls of diced green onions, chopped avocado, grated Cheddar cheese and baked tortilla chips.

4. Add the green pepper, carrots, and squash. Reduce the heat to medium. Cover the pot and cook, stirring occasionally, about 5 to 10 minutes until the vegetables are softened. Season with salt and freshly ground pepper.
5. Add the garlic and jalapeño pepper, cover the pot, and cook for several more minutes.
6. Pour the tomatoes into the pot and stir. Reduce the heat to medium low.
7. Add the tomato paste and the beer and stir.
8. Place the browned chicken pieces into the pot with the vegetables.
9. Stir in the pinto beans.
10. Add the chili powder, cinnamon, cilantro, salt, and freshly ground pepper and stir to combine. Simmer for at least 15 minutes.

Serves 8
Preparation time about 45 minutes

Chili Con Carne with Gusto

2	medium yellow onions, chopped (about 2 cups)
2	large green bell pepper, chopped (about 2 cups)
3	tablespoons olive oil
4	cloves garlic, minced (about 2 tablespoons)
1	pound lean ground beef
¾	pound mild Italian sausage
2	28-ounce cans chopped tomatoes
½	cup burgundy wine
1	6-ounce can tomato paste
1	bay leaf
1	teaspoon sugar
1	teaspoon dried oregano
2	tablespoons chili powder, more or less
2	tablespoons chopped fresh parsley
1	16-ounce can kidney beans (optional)
	Salt and pepper

Jalapeño pepper, finely diced (optional)
Sharp Cheddar cheese, grated (optional)
Sour cream (optional)

1. In a large pot cook the onion and green pepper in olive oil over medium high heat.
2. Add the garlic and cook until soft.
3. Add the beef and the sausage and cook until browned.
4. Pour in the chopped tomatoes and burgundy wine.
5. Stir in the tomato paste.
6. Add the bay leaf, sugar, dried oregano, and as much of the chili powder as you desire.
7. Add the fresh parsley, canned beans with the liquid, and season with salt and freshly ground pepper.
8. Cover the pot with a lid and simmer over medium-low heat for 30 minutes. Adjust the seasonings.

Serves 6 to 8
Preparation time about 40 minutes

HELPFUL HINT:
Chili is sometimes better the second day than the first! It freezes well for future use. Make a double batch, as insurance, for a day when cooking is not high on the priority list.

SETTING THE SCENE:
Serve the chili in a large bowl or on top of rice or pasta. For garnish offer fresh chopped jalapeño, grated cheese, and sour cream.

Ultimate Potato Skins

A staple on every fast food take out menu is the crispy potato skin. Easily made at home, you can have inspired skins filled with your favorite cheese and spice.

4	medium baking potatoes
2	tablespoons canola oil
	Salt and freshly grated pepper

½	pound bacon, diced
1½	cups grated Monterey Jack cheese
1½	cup grated sharp Cheddar cheese
1	tablespoon finely chopped fresh parsley

6	green onions, sliced (about 1 cup)
	Sour cream

Preheat the oven to 425°.
1. Wash the potatoes. Dry well. Rub each one with canola oil.
2. Bake the potatoes on the center rack of the oven for 1 hour or until just tender. Cool.
3. Cut each potato. Scoop out the center leaving a ¼-inch layer of potato with the shells.
4. Spray a baking sheet with vegetable oil cooking spray. Place each potato half on the baking sheet. Season with salt and pepper.
5. In a medium skillet cook the diced bacon over medium high heat until crisp. Drain.
7. In a small bowl mix together the Monterey Jack cheese, the sharp cheese, the fresh parsley and the cook bacon. Fill each skin with the mixture.
8. Bake until the skins are crisp and the cheese is melted, about 20 to 30 minutes.

Serves 4
Preparation time about 15 minutes plus baking

SETTING THE SCENE:
Place the potato skins on a large platter. Sprinkle sliced green onion over the top and serve with a generous dollop of sour cream.

Smothered Baked Potato with Broccoli, Garlic, and Cheese Sauce

This dish has everything needed for a yummy fast midweek supper or on-the-run lunch.

4	medium baking potatoes
2	tablespoons canola oil
1	stalk broccoli, cut into florets (about 1 cup)
	Salt and freshly grated pepper
4	cloves garlic
½	cup olive oil
½	teaspoon red pepper flakes
4	tablespoons butter
4	tablespoons all-purpose flour
2	cup milk
2	cups grated sharp Cheddar cheese

Preheat the oven to 425°.

1. Wash the potatoes. Dry well. Rub each one with canola oil.
2. Bake the potatoes on the center rack of the oven for 1 hour or until just tender.
3. Place the broccoli in a microwave safe dish. Add about 1 inch of water. Microwave on high for 5 to 6 minutes. Drain and finely chop. Season with salt and pepper.
4. Place the cloves garlic in a small pan. Cover with olive oil. Cook until the garlic browns, about 6 minutes. Add the red pepper flakes.
5. Remove the cloves garlic and slice.
6. In a small pan cook the butter and flour until golden brown over medium high heat. Pour the milk slowly into the pan and stir until thick, about 5 minutes. Add the cheese and blend thoroughly.
7. In a small bowl mix together the chopped broccoli and sliced garlic with a small amount of the olive oil.

SIMPLE SUBSTITUTIONS:
Try filling your baked potato with one of these great "tato-fillers:"

- Chili Con Carne (page 144)
- Ratatouille (page 102)
- Sherried Mushrooms (page 89)

The next time you have an urge for a great baked potato, check out these recipes:

- The Overachiever's Twice Baked Potatoes (page 336)
- Stuffed Baked Potatoes (page 105)
- Rum Soaked Sweet Potatoes (page 103)

8. Cut a slit into each baked potato. Press the sides together to open. Fill each potato with the broccoli garlic mixture and smother with the cheese sauce.

Serves 4
Preparation time about 25 minutes plus baking

Slow Roasted Country Style Ribs

Take out ribs are always a treat. But home cooked ribs are the real McCoy. The slow roasting process tenderizes these thick ribs to produce a great tasting dish. Pull the ingredients together in the pan, set in the oven, and don't come back for at least an hour. That's plenty of time to go rent a great video.

6	**4- to 6-ounce country style pork ribs**
¼	**cup apple cider vinegar**
	Salt and freshly ground pepper
	Garlic powder
1	**apple, sliced into wedges**
	Rosemary sprigs

Barbecue sauce

HELPFUL HINT:
Check out these recipes for home-made barbecue sauce:

- Best Barbecue Sauce (page 111)
- Spicy Tomato Barbecue Sauce (page 113)
- Red Wine Barbecue Sauce (page 119)

Preheat the oven to 300°.
1. Place the ribs in a large baking (or roasting) pan.
2. Pour the apple cider vinegar over the top.
3. Season with salt, pepper, and garlic powder.
4. Place the apple slices and rosemary sprigs all around.
5. Roast for 1 hour.
6. Remove the pan from the oven. Transfer the ribs to a plate. Remove the apple and juices from the pan. Place the ribs back in the pan and pour barbecue sauce on the ribs. Place the pan back in the oven.
7. Roast the ribs for another 20 minutes or until the sauce begins to caramelize and form a glaze.

Serves 4 to 6
Preparation time about 10 minutes plus roasting

Sesame Beef Stir Fry

The interesting crunch of flavors in this dish is achieved by not overcooking the vegetables. The red pepper flakes add some spunk to the oriental style sauce. Feel free to add water chestnuts or cashews for an extra bite full of crunch!

1	1- to 1½-pound flank steak
2	tablespoons sesame seeds
2	broccoli stalks, including stems (about 4 cups)
1	large yellow bell pepper, sliced lengthwise in strips (about 1 cup)
1	large red bell pepper, sliced lengthwise in strips (about 1 cup)
1	large green bell pepper, sliced lengthwise in strips (about 1 cup)
1½	cups beef stock
¼	cup soy sauce
1	tablespoon finely grated fresh ginger
4	cloves garlic, minced (about 2 tablespoons)
2	teaspoons cornstarch dissolved in 2 tablespoons water
2	tablespoons olive oil
½	teaspoon red pepper flakes

1. Chill the flank steak before cutting. With a sharp knife cut against the grain on a diagonal to get thin strips. Place the sliced steak in a bowl and sprinkle with the sesame seeds. Toss well and set aside.
2. Prepare the broccoli by peeling the stems with a vegetable peeler. Slice the stems into ¼-inch rounds. Cut the florets into bite-size pieces.
3. Place the broccoli and the sliced peppers in a bowl and set aside.
4. In a third bowl combine the beef stock, soy sauce, grated ginger, and garlic. Add the dissolved cornstarch.
5. In a large sauté pan or wok warm the olive oil over medium high heat.

SIMPLE SHORTCUT:
Substitute ½ teaspoon of ground ginger if fresh ginger is not available.

SETTING THE SCENE:
Serve the beef stir fry from a decorative tureen. Small bowls of white rice can be placed at each place. Individual pitchers of soy sauce are a must on the table.

Share your favorite stir fry recipe at www.jorj.com.

6. Cook the steak slices in the pan until just brown. Remove them with a slotted spoon to a bowl, leaving the juices in the pan.
7. Add the broccoli and peppers to the pan and cook until they are crisp-tender.
8. Add the sauce to the vegetables and stir. The dissolved cornstarch will thicken the sauce.
9. Add the beef and any juices left in the bowl to the pan and stir together.
10. Mix in the red pepper flakes, taste, and adjust seasonings.

Serves 6
Preparation time about 30 minutes

Lemon Chicken with Baby Artichokes, Sun-Dried Tomatoes, and Shiitake Mushrooms

Gourmet take-out shops are springing up all over town. But who says take-out is the only way to eat gourmet? Give this upscale dish a try the next time you get a craving for take-out gourmet!

4	**6-ounce skinless, boneless chicken breast halves, pounded to ½-inch thickness**
	Salt and freshly ground pepper
1	**tablespoon olive oil**
½	**cup flour, for dredging**
1	**medium lemon**
2	**pounds baby artichokes, outer leaves removed, stems trimmed**
1	**7½-ounce jar sun-dried tomatoes in oil**
1	**3½-ounce container shiitake mushrooms, cleaned and chopped**
½	**cup chicken stock**
1	**tablespoon butter**

1. Season the chicken with salt and pepper.
2. In a skillet warm the olive oil over medium high heat.
3. Dip the chicken breasts in flour. Shake off the excess.
4. Cook the chicken in the oil until browned on both sides, about 4 minutes. Drizzle the chicken with the juice of ½ lemon while cooking. Remove the chicken to a baking dish. Bake at 325° for 10 to 15 minutes.
5. Place the artichokes in a pot of boiling water and cook for 10 minutes until soft. Drain in a colander.
6. Drizzle 1 tablespoon of oil from the sun-dried tomatoes into the skillet used for the chicken. Heat over medium high heat.
7. Add the mushrooms and cook for several minutes.
8. Drain the remaining oil from the sun-dried tomatoes. Add the tomatoes to the pan.
9. Add the artichokes. Pour in the chicken stock and simmer for 5 minutes.

HELPFUL HINT:
To prepare the artichokes, remove the dark green outer leaves until the pale yellow leaves remain. Trim the stem and cut off the tops of the remaining leaves. Place the trimmed artichokes in a bowl of cold water with a slice of lemon. The lemon will prevent browning. Repeat with all of the artichokes.

SETTING THE SCENE:
Place a breast half in the center of a dinner plate. Top with a mound of baby artichoke sauce. Serve with a spoonful of herbed cous cous.

10. Reduce the heat to low. Squeeze the juice from ½ lemon into the sauce. Stir in the butter. Season with salt and pepper.

Serves 4
Preparation time about 30 minutes

Quick Veggie Stir Fry

An easy method for cooking vegetables, this dish is also a yummy companion to Fried Spiced Rice (page 155). Alternate the veggies to create new partners.

HELPFUL HINT:
Blanch the vegetables in a pot of boiling water until they are just beginning to soften but remain crisp. Refresh in a bowl of ice water. Pat dry and set aside until ready to proceed with the recipe.

2   tablespoons peanut oil
1   pound green beans, blanched (about 3 cups)
4   large carrots, peeled and sliced into thin strips, blanched (about 2 cups)
½   large head cauliflower, cut into florets, blanched (about 1½ cups)
1   tablespoons grated fresh ginger
¼   cup chicken stock
2   tablespoons fresh lime juice
2   tablespoons sesame oil
       Salt and freshly ground pepper

1. Heat a large skillet or wok over high heat.
2. Pour the peanut oil in the skillet.
3. Add the green beans, carrots, and cauliflower to the wok, stirring frequently.
4. Add the ginger and pour the chicken stock into the wok.
5. Remove the vegetables to a large bowl.
6. Season with lime juice, sesame oil, salt, and freshly ground pepper.

Serves 6 to 8
Preparation time about 30 minutes

Chicken Enchiladas with Black Bean Mole Sauce

If you are a spice lover, you will enjoy the unique sauce drizzled over these creamy enchiladas. This is a terrific way to use leftover chicken and turkey.

1	tablespoon olive oil
1	medium yellow onion, diced (about ¾ cup)
1	jalapeño pepper, seeded and diced (about 1 tablespoon)
3	to 4 cups cooked chicken or turkey, diced into ¼-inch cubes
1½	cups grated sharp Cheddar cheese Salt and freshly ground pepper

½	cup canola oil
10	6- or 8-inch round flour tortillas

2	cups chicken stock
1	clove garlic, minced (about 1 teaspoon)
1	ounce bittersweet chocolate
1	tablespoon chili sauce
1	tablespoon chili powder
¼	teaspoon nutmeg
½	cup canned black beans, drained
½	cup sour cream

Preheat the oven to 350°.

1. In a skillet heat 1 tablespoon of olive oil over medium high heat.
2. Cook the onion and the jalapeño pepper until just brown.
3. Place the chicken and 1 cup of cheese in a bowl. Add the cooked onion mixture and stir. Season with salt and pepper.
4. In a skillet heat the canola oil over medium high heat. When the oil is hot, place one tortilla shell into the oil.

HELPFUL HINT:
The tortilla shell will cook very quickly. It will begin to bubble almost immediately. Remove it from the oil after several seconds and drain it on paper towels.

SETTING THE SCENE:
Garnish the enchiladas with a dollop of sour cream, a spoonful of salsa, and a drizzle of fresh chopped cilantro.

5. Place a spoonful of the filling onto the shell while it is still warm. Roll the shell into a tube. Place the enchilada seam side down into a baking dish. Repeat using all of the shells and all of the filling.

FOR SAUCE:

6. Heat the chicken broth in a pan over medium high heat.
7. Add the garlic, chocolate, chili sauce, chili powder, and nutmeg. Cook for about 20 minutes or until the liquid is reduced by half.
8. Add the black beans to the sauce. Mash the beans into the sauce with a potato masher while the sauce is simmering.
9. Remove the sauce from the heat. Stir in the sour cream.
10. Drizzle the sauce over the enchiladas. Sprinkle with ½ cup of the cheese. Bake for 20 to 30 minutes.

Serves 4 to 6
Preparation time about 30 minutes plus baking

COZY SUNDAY SUPPER

Tortilla Soup

Chicken Enchiladas
with Black Bean Mole Sauce

Key Lime Buttery Cake

Dolphin Fajitas

A tropical twist on a Mexican favorite, this dish comes together quickly by using either a grill pan in the kitchen or an outdoor barbecue.

4	ounces Mexican or dark beer
1	medium yellow onion, chopped (about ½ cup)
4	cloves garlic, minced (about 2 tablespoons)
	Juice of 1 medium lime (about 2 tablespoons)
1	tablespoon chopped fresh cilantro
½	teaspoons dried red pepper flakes
	Salt
1½	pounds dolphin fillets

1	large red pepper, sliced into strips (about 1 cup)
1	large red onion, sliced (about 1 cup)
8	6- to 8-inch flour tortillas
½	medium head iceberg lettuce, shredded (about 3 cups)
6	to 8 plum tomatoes, seeded and diced (about 2 cups)

Salsa
Chopped avocado
Hot pepper sauce
Fresh cilantro, chopped

1. In a small bowl combine the beer, onions, garlic, lime juice, cilantro, red pepper flakes, and salt.
2. Pour all but ¼ cup of the marinade over the fish fillets. Cover and refrigerate for 30 minutes.
3. Remove the fish from the marinade. Discard this marinade.
4. In a grill pan cook the dolphin fillets over medium high heat for 5 minutes per side, turning once. Keep warm.
5. Cook the onion and red pepper in the same pan until just beginning to brown.
6. Brush the fish with the reserved ¼ cup of marinade. Drizzle 1 to 2 tablespoons over the cooked vegetables.

HELPFUL HINT:
Warm tortillas by spraying each one lightly with vegetable oil cooking spray. Layer on top of each other and wrap in aluminum foil. Place in the oven on 300° for 10 to 15 minutes.

SIMPLE SHORTCUT:
Use roasted red pepper in a jar when time does not allow roasting one yourself. Slice the pepper and cook the strips in olive oil. You may cook the sliced onion in the same pan.

7. Assemble the fajita by slicing the fillets into thin strips. Arrange fish strips, red pepper strips, red onion slices, shredded lettuce, and diced tomato on each warm tortilla. Garnish with prepared salsa, chopped avocado, hot pepper sauce, and fresh chopped cilantro.

Fried Spiced Rice

What's take out without a version of fried rice? This rice dish covers all of the flavors. Feel free to add stir fried vegetables, cooked chicken or cashews for your favorite fried rice compliment to complete the experience.

HELPFUL HINT:
Cook white rice according to the directions on the package. For added flavor substitute chicken stock for the water and add ½ teaspoon of ground cinnamon while it is cooking.

1	to 2 tablespoons peanut oil
2	eggs, beaten
1	medium onion, chopped (about ½ cup)
1	medium jalapeño pepper, seeded and diced (about 2 tablespoons)
½	teaspoon turmeric
1	pound cooked white rice
1	bunch green onions including tops, chopped (1 cup)

1. Heat a large skillet or wok over high heat.
2. Pour 1 tablespoon of peanut oil in the skillet.
3. Cook the eggs in the oil and remove when done.
4. Pour 1 more tablespoon of peanut oil into the skillet.
5. Cook the onion and jalapeño in the peanut oil until just beginning to brown.
6. Stir in the turmeric.
7. Add the cooked white rice and stir to combine.
8. Add the cooked egg to the rice.
9. Stir in the chopped green onion.

Serves 6 to 8
Preparation time about 20 minutes

Smoked Trout and Brie Quesadilla with Dill Cream Guacamole

This quesadilla combination makes a great addition to a brunch table or can be a sophisticated midnight supper.

4	10-inch flour tortillas
1	cup Brie cheese, sliced
½	pound smoked trout
½	medium red onion, sliced into thin rings (about ½ cup)
2	tablespoons capers
4	plum tomatoes, seeded and diced (2 cups)
1	medium avocado chopped (1 cup)
2	tablespoons chopped fresh dill
2	tablespoons sour cream
	Salt and freshly ground pepper

1. Spray one side of each tortilla with vegetable oil cooking spray.
2. Heat the skillet over medium high heat.
3. Place the sprayed side of the tortilla face down into the pan.
4. Top with half of the Brie cheese slices, half of the smoked trout slices, half of the sliced red onion, and 1 tablespoon of capers.
5. Top with the nonsprayed side of another tortilla.
6. Cover the pan briefly, allowing the cheese to melt. Be careful not to burn the tortilla.
7. Use 2 spatulas to carefully turn over the quesadilla. Brown the other side and continue melting the cheese.
8. Remove the quesadilla to a platter. Repeat with the remaining tortillas and filling.
9. In a medium bowl mix together the tomatoes, avocado, dill, and sour cream to make a chunky sauce. Season with salt and pepper. Top the quesadillas with sauce.

Serves 2 to 4

Preparation time about 15 minutes

HELPFUL HINT:
The tortillas can be assembled for cooking and grilled on an outside grill in place of sautéing for an interesting quesadilla twist.

HELPFUL HINT:
There is no end to the great combinations of fresh ingredients that you can sandwich between tortillas. For instance, substitute smoked salmon for trout or cream cheese for Brie, just like a breakfast bagel. Try some of these combinations:

- Spinach, plum tomatoes, feta cheese and kalamata olives
- Bean sprouts, sliced flank steak, fontina cheese, and slivered sun-dried tomatoes
- Grilled chicken breast strips, roasted red peppers, Monterey Jack cheese, cilantro pesto
- Turkey sausage, sweet corn, black beans, and Muenster cheese

SETTING THE SCENE:
Serve the quesadilla in wedges with the dill cream guacamole sauce on the side.

Mushroom, Bacon, and Jack Cheese Quesadilla

Quesadilla is anything melted between two tortillas and served with tangy condiments. Traditionally a Mexican inspired dish, the concept of quesadilla lends itself to great innovation and easy cooking. This favorite can be cut into triangles for a quick appetizer or served whole as a super supper.

4	10-inch flour tortillas
1	cup grated sharp Cheddar cheese
1	cup grated Monterey Jack cheese
½	pound bacon, cooked and crumbled (8 to 10 slices)
½	pound mushrooms, sliced (2 cups)
3	to 4 green onions including tops, sliced (about ½ cup)

Salsa (optional)
Sour cream (optional)
Guacamole (optional)
Black olives, sliced (optional)
Jalapeño pepper, seeded and thinly sliced (optional)

1. In a skillet cook the bacon and mushrooms.
2. Spray one side of each tortilla with vegetable oil cooking spray.
3. Heat the skillet over medium high heat.
4. Place the sprayed side of the tortilla face down into the pan.
5. Top with ½ cup of the Cheddar cheese, ½ cup of the Monterey Jack cheese, half of the bacon, mushrooms, and green onions.
6. Top with the nonsprayed side of another tortilla.
7. Cover the pan briefly, allowing the cheese to melt. Be careful not to burn the tortilla.
8. Use 2 spatulas to carefully turn over the quesadilla. Brown the other side, continuing to melt the cheese.
9. Remove the quesadilla to a platter. Repeat with the remaining tortillas and filling.

Serves 2 to 4
Preparation time about 15 minutes

HELPFUL HINT:
Cook the bacon in a 12-inch skillet. Remove the bacon from the pan, drain on a paper towel, and crumble into small pieces. Cook the mushrooms in the same pan. Remove with a slotted spoon. Use the same skillet to continue.

SETTING THE SCENE:
Cut into wedges. Serve with salsa, sour cream, and guacamole. Garnish with sliced black olives and thinly sliced jalapeño peppers.

To share your favorite quesadilla recipe visit www.jorj.com.

Shrimp, Roasted Corn, and Jalapeño Cheese Quesadilla

Try this combo for an inspired seafood quesadilla. Invite your friends and guests to help you assemble the condiments while you cook.

2   medium ears corn, roasted (about 1 cup kernels)
½   pound cooked medium shrimp (about 1 cup)
½   teaspoon cumin
       Salt and freshly ground pepper
8   6-inch spinach tortillas
1   cup grated jalapeño sharp Cheddar cheese
3   to 4 green onion including tops, sliced (½ cup)

       Black bean salsa (optional)
       Sour cream (optional)
       Chopped cilantro (optional)
       Lime wedges (optional)

SIMPLE SHORTCUT:
Use leftover corn that has been roasted on the grill for this recipe. If this is not available, use fresh or frozen corn.

HELPFUL HINT:
Buy pre-cooked shrimp to cut down on preparation time. Chop the shrimp into bite size pieces.

SETTING THE SCENE:
Serve a whole quesadilla on a medium size plate. Just before serving, top with a spoonful of salsa with black beans and a dollop of sour cream. Sprinkle the plate with chopped cilantro and garnish with lime wedges.

1. In a small skillet sauté the corn in olive oil over high heat until the kernels just begin to toast.
2. Add the shrimp, and season with cumin, salt, and pepper. Heat just until the shrimp is warmed through.
3. Spray one side of each tortilla with cooking spray.
4. Heat the skillet over medium high heat. Place the tortilla sprayed side down into the pan.
6. Top with one-fourth cup of the jalapeño Cheddar cheese, one-fourth of the corn kernel-shrimp mixture, and one-fourth of the green onions.
5. Top with the nonsprayed side of another tortilla.
6. Cover the pan briefly, allowing the cheese to melt. Be careful not to burn the tortilla.
7. Use 2 spatulas to carefully turn over the quesadilla. Brown the other side, continuing to melt the cheese.
8. Remove the quesadilla to a platter and keep warm while you continue the recipe.

Serves 4
Preparation time about 30 minutes

The Corner Italian Restaurant

PASTA AND SAUCES

Italian cuisine is as much about rich heritage and tradition as it is about remarkable food. The diversity of Italian cooking is as expansive as the ingenuity of its cooks, where the simplest ingredients create some of the most flavorful meals. Italian inspired food has become a standard in the American meal plan.

Imagine the spice-filled smells of your neighborhood corner Italian restaurant. What comes to mind? Stewing tomato sauces, crusty baked breads, and roasted vegetables that are enhanced with basil, parsley, and, of course, garlic. Garlic is the fragrant, sometimes pungent bulb that is basic to Italian cuisine. Purchase a bulb that is smooth and heavy, with no signs of gray or brown spots, to insure freshness. Grocery store produce departments offer pre-chopped or minced garlic in a jar that must be kept refrigerated. Read about the garlic press in the Getting Started chapter to familiarize yourself with mincing garlic.

This chapter introduces the pasta machine for rolling out pasta dough at home. This machine replaces a heavy rolling pin for thinning the pasta dough before it is cut or forged into the many different shapes of pasta. Some heavy-duty electric mixers come with pasta dough attachments and now electronic pasta machines can blend ingredients and propel the pasta shapes all in one step. Cooking pasta is an easy process. I recommend that pasta be cooked al dente, meaning that pasta is cooked firmly and not overcooked and mushy.

A note about substituting ingredients is essential when talking about Italian cuisine. The entire nature of this food is to create a dish that uses the freshest seasonal ingredients in a simple cooking style. A pasta recipe in this chapter that includes broccoli raab offers a perfect guideline for your favorite pasta combination. In some areas and in certain seasons, broccoli raab may be unavailable. Substitute any similar ingredient that is readily obtainable such as spinach, Swiss chard, Romaine lettuce, or another robust leafy vegetable.

Olive oil, the staple of Italian cuisine, is as variable in quality, flavor, and aroma as the wide variety of wines. Italian olive oil comes from different regions of the country such as Tuscany or Sardinia. Categories of olive oil, as in virgin or extra virgin, denote the manner of pressing the olives. As in all essential cooking ingredients, choose a good quality olive oil and use it frequently so that it stays fresh in your pantry.

This sampler of basic Italian favorite recipes is only a great beginning to cooking pasta and sauces at home. After you have worked with these recipes, enjoy creating your own pasta dish. Remember to use the freshest ingredients to add depth and flavor to the specialty meals offered at your Corner Italian Restaurant.

Find more information about the recipes in The Corner Italian Restaurant chapter at www.jorj.com.

Basic Marinara Sauce

You say tomatto, I say tomatow. You say tomato sauce, the Italians call it marinara. No matter what it is called, this simple red sauce is the basics of many great Italian dishes. Double the recipe to make a large pot, and save some for quick use on a busy day.

1	medium onion, diced (about ½ cup)
1	tablespoon olive oil
1	to 2 cloves garlic, minced (about 1 teaspoon)
1	15-ounce can chopped tomatoes
2	tablespoons chopped fresh basil
1	teaspoon granulated sugar
1	tablespoon grated Parmesan cheese

1. In a pot cook the onion in the olive oil over medium high heat until soft.
2. Add the garlic and cook for 1 to 2 minutes.
3. Add the tomatoes, basil, sugar, and cheese to the pot. Stir well.
4. Emulsify the sauce in batches using a food processor or an immersion blender.

Makes about 2 cups
Preparation time about 15 minutes

HELPFUL HINT:
It is not necessary to process the marinara sauce as stated in step 4. However, this method produces a smooth, blended sauce that works well in other recipes.

Basic Pasta

Just in case you have some extra time on your hands and feel the knead to work with them, here is a simple recipe for making homemade pasta.

1½   cups all-purpose flour

3   eggs

1. Make a well with the flour.
2. Break the eggs into the middle of the well.
3. Use a fork to beat the eggs together.
4. Blend small amounts of flour into the beaten eggs from the inside of the well.
5. Continue until all of the flour is absorbed and comes together to form a dough.
6. Knead the dough for 10 minutes. Let the dough rest for 20 minutes.
7. Divide the dough into 3 equal sections.
8. Process each section of dough through a pasta machine beginning with the thickest setting and working down to the thinnest.
9. Cut into noodles and let dry until ready to use.
10. Cook the pasta in salted boiling water for several minutes.

Serves 4 to 6
Preparation time about 45 minutes plus boiling

TECHNIQUE:
Make the dough on a clean floured surface.

HELPFUL HINT:
The humidity of the day may affect the quantity of flour that you need to form a dough. You can add a little more if needed. The end result is a dough that is not too wet and not too dry.

SIMPLE SUBSTITUTION:
If you are feeling creative, now is the time to incorporate ingredients into the dough to create a flavored, colorful pasta. Try a tablespoon of fresh basil, chopped spinach, beet juice, or finely diced sun-dried tomatoes.

ABOUT THE PASTA MACHINE:
A pasta machine is a non electric tool that thins out the pasta dough. An alternative to this machine is to roll out the dough using a rolling pin. Most pasta machines come with several settings. Start with the thickest (usually setting 7) and continue to the thinnest (setting 1). You may want to cut the dough in half as you progress. The machine also comes with a cutting attachment to cut the dough into your desired pasta shape (spaghetti, fettuccini, ravioli etc.) The noodles can dry for an hour or up to 24 hours. They can also be frozen for later use. Do not store them in the refrigerator as they will not dry properly.

Roasted Garlic Tomatoes

Slow roasting is the secret to the rich taste of garlic fused into tomatoes. Simply savory as a side dish, the finished tomatoes also make a great warm salad when chopped and added to a handful of fresh croutons and tossed with vinaigrette.

4	**tomatoes, cored and halved**
1	**clove garlic, minced (1 teaspoon)**
1	**teaspoon dried cilantro**
	Salt and freshly ground pepper
1	**teaspoon olive oil**

1. Squeeze the seeds from the tomato halves.
2. Place the tomatoes on a baking sheet.
3. Place a small amount of the minced garlic on each tomato.
4. Sprinkle the dried cilantro over each.
5. Season with salt and freshly ground pepper.
6. Drizzle a small amount of olive oil over the tomatoes.
7. Bake the tomatoes on low heat for several hours depending on available time.

Serves 6 to 8
Preparation time about 10 minutes plus roasting

TECHNIQUE:
Cook the tomatoes for as much as 6 hours at 250° or as little as 2 hours at 300°.

SIMPLE SUBSTITUTION:
Chop the tomatoes into chunks and serve over pasta dressed with olive oil for a light, flavorful side dish.

Vermicelli with Olive Oil and Fresh Parsley

A very simple pasta presentation is just what is needed as a side dish for many classic Italian dinners. To serve the pasta, mound the noodles in a circle that is larger at the base than at the top.

8	ounces dried vermicelli
⅓	cup olive oil
1	clove garlic, minced (about 1 teaspoon)
1	tablespoon chopped fresh parsley
	Salt and freshly ground pepper
2	tablespoons grated Parmesan cheese

1. Prepare the pasta according to the package directions.
2. In a small saucepan warm the olive oil over medium heat.
3. Sauté the garlic in the olive oil until just cooked, being careful not to burn.
4. Remove the pan from the heat.
5. Drain the pasta.
6. In a bowl (or in the pan used to cook the pasta) combine the pasta with the oil. Add the parsley and toss.
7. Season with salt and freshly ground pepper. Sprinkle grated Parmesan cheese over the top.

Serves 4
Preparation time about 20 minutes

VALENTINE'S DAY SUPPER

Sweet Cucumbers and Mandarin Orange Salad

Herb Crusted Rack of Lamb

Vermicelli with Olive Oil and Fresh Parsley

Fresh Lima Beans with Mint

Hazelnut Heart Cookies

Creamy Fettuccine

Here is a recipe for a flavorful pasta that works well as a side dish or stands on its own as a light meal. If you are low on fresh herbs (shame on you), you can substitute smaller amounts of dried herbs.

8	to 10 ounces fettuccine
¼	cup butter (½ stick)
2	tablespoons all-purpose flour
½	cup dry white wine
	Juice of 1 medium lemon
1	clove garlic, minced (about 1 teaspoon)
1	tablespoon chopped fresh basil
1	tablespoon chopped fresh dill weed
	Salt and freshly ground pepper
1	cup sour cream
1	cup grated Parmesan cheese

1. Cook the pasta according to the package directions.
2. In a medium saucepan melt the butter.
3. Whisk in the flour and continue to cook.
4. Whisk in the white wine and lemon juice.
5. Stir in the basil, dill weed, and garlic.
6. Season with salt and freshly ground pepper.
7. Stir in the sour cream and Parmesan cheese.
8. Drain the pasta and add it to the sauce. Toss and serve.

Serves 6
Preparation time about 20 minutes

HELPFUL HINT:
Use a mini food processor to chop the herbs and garlic before you begin the rest of the preparation.

SIMPLE SUBSTITUTION:
You can use this sauce over penne or ziti pasta and bake for several minutes in the oven to make a rich casserole side dish.

SETTING THE SCENE:
This easy dish transforms into an upscale showstopper with the addition of Garlic Spiced Shrimp. Sauté garlic in olive oil over medium high heat. Toss in ¾ pound of medium shrimp that have been peeled and deveined. Cook for several minutes until the shrimp turn opaque. Toss the shrimp with the pasta. Serve in large, shallow pasta bowls.

Rigatoni with Sausage, Sun-Dried Tomatoes and Broccoli Raab

For a quick meal on a busy evening try this pasta recipe. Once you get the hang of it, you will be able to substitute with various ingredients.

8	ounces rigatoni
1	bunch broccoli raab
½	pound mild Italian pork sausage, sliced into rings
1	7-ounce jar sun-dried tomato halves in oil, sliced lengthwise into strips
	Salt and freshly ground pepper
4	ounces Parmesan cheese, shaved
	Fresh basil, chopped

1. Prepare the rigatoni according to the package directions.
2. Blanch the broccoli raab. Drain well and chop into pieces.
3. In a skillet brown the sausage slices over medium high heat.
4. Add the broccoli raab to the pan and stir.
5. Drain the sun-dried tomatoes, reserving the oil that they are packed in. Cut the tomatoes into strips.
6. Add both the tomato strips and the reserved oil to the pan.
7. Add enough pasta water to the pan to make a sauce.
8. Drain the rigatoni and add it to the pan. Toss well.

Serves 4 to 6
Preparation time about 45 minutes

HELPFUL HINT:
Broccoli raab is a green leafy vegetable that looks like a bunch of stringy broccoli! You may easily substitute with broccoli florets, spinach, or kale!

SETTING THE SCENE:
Transfer the pasta to a serving bowl. Season with salt and freshly ground pepper. Shave pieces of Parmesan cheese over top and sprinkle with chopped basil for garnish.

Share your best new pasta recipe at www.jorj.com.

Spaghetti with Shrimp and Artichoke Hearts

Here is a great throw together pasta meal that is another fine example of how easy fresh ingredients blend with what you have on hand in the pantry to make a super quick midweek supper.

8   ounces spaghetti

2   tablespoons olive oil
1   pound medium shrimp, peeled and deveined
4   green onions, sliced (about ½ cup)
       Juice of 1 lime (about 2 tablespoons)
2   cloves garlic, minced (about 1 tablespoon)
4   plum tomatoes, diced (about 1 cup)
½   cup white wine
1   15-ounce can artichoke hearts, drained and
       chopped, reserve the liquid
2   tablespoons chilled butter
2   tablespoons chopped fresh dill
       Salt and freshly ground pepper
4   ounces Parmesan cheese, shaved

1. Cook the spaghetti according to the package directions.
2. In a skillet heat the olive oil over medium high heat. Cook the shrimp for several minutes until they turn pink in color. Remove the shrimp from the pan.
3. Reduce the heat to medium. Add the chopped green onions, lime juice, minced garlic, tomatoes, and white wine to the pan. Cook until the liquid reduces slightly, about 5 minutes.
4. Add the canned artichoke hearts and the juices to the pan. Cook for 5 minutes more.
5. Reduce the heat to low. Stir in the butter.
6. Add the fresh dill to the sauce. Return the shrimp to the pan. Season with salt and pepper.
7. Drain the rigatoni and add it to the pan. Toss well.

Serves 4 to 6
Preparation time about 30 minutes

SIMPLE SUBSTITUTION:
Don't hesitate to play with this recipe. Substitute mussels, scallops, or grilled chicken for the shrimp. Add cauliflower or broccoli to sneak in some veggies. Or toss in a handful of black olives for an extra flavor boost.

SETTING THE SCENE:
Transfer the pasta to a serving bowl. Use a vegetable peeler to shave curls of Parmesan cheese over the top. Sprinkle with freshly ground pepper.

Penne Pasta with Ham, Sweet Peas, and Vodka Cream Sauce

The wonderful simplicity of pasta allows for substitutions on a classic dish that appear to be innovations. The addition of a hint of vodka and sweet peas makes this basic pasta dish an upscale dining experience with very little effort!

1	**pound penne**
1	**7-ounce jar sun-dried tomato halves in oil**
1	**medium onion, finely diced (about ½ cup)**
¼	**pound extra lean ham, julienned into 1-inch strips**
⅓	**cup vodka**
¾	**cup milk**
¾	**cup cream**
2	**tablespoons tomato paste**
	Salt and freshly ground pepper
¾	**cup canned peas**
2	**tablespoons chopped fresh basil**
	Parmesan cheese

1. Cook the penne pasta according to the directions on the package. The pasta should be cooked *al dente.*
2. Remove the sun-dried tomatoes from the oil and cut them into thins strips. Reserve the oil.
3. In a large pan sauté the onions in the reserved oil over medium heat.
4. Add the strips of ham and stir.
5. Add the sun-dried tomatoes to the pan and stir again.
6. Drain off any fat from the pan.
7. Add the vodka to the pan and reduce until no liquid remains.
8. Add the milk and the cream and reduce until the sauce just begins to thicken.
9. Stir in the tomato paste and season with salt and freshly ground pepper.
10. Gently stir the peas into the sauce.

Serves 6 to 8

Preparation time about 20 minutes

HELPFUL HINT:
Al dente means firm and not mushy.

SIMPLE SUBSTITUTION:
Try chopped bacon or prosciutto instead of ham. In place of the peas you can use asparagus tips or sliced green beans

SETTING THE SCENE:
In a pasta bowl toss together the penne and the sauce. Sprinkle the dish with Parmesan cheese and fresh chopped basil. Add crusty bread and a tossed salad with a light vinaigrette for a true comfort meal.

Tortellini with Bolognese Sauce

After spaghetti (ground meat and jar sauce) has been mastered, you may want to prepare this rich sauce served over cheese-filled pasta. Make enough for a crowd, because if you cook it, they will come.

⅓   cup olive oil
2   medium ribs celery, chopped (about 1 cup)
2   carrots, chopped (about 2 cups)
6   cloves garlic, chopped (about 3 tablespoons)
½   pound bacon, chopped into pieces (about 8 to 10 slices)
1½   pounds ground veal
1½   pounds ground pork
¼   cup chopped fresh parsley
2   cups chicken stock
½   cup white wine
1   6-ounce can tomato paste

2   pounds tortellini

¼   cup butter (½ stick)
¼   cup whipping cream
2   tablespoons chopped fresh sage
⅔   cup grated Parmesan cheese
     Salt and freshly ground pepper

1. In a large pan heat the olive oil over medium high heat.
2. Add the celery and carrots and cook until softened.
3. Add the garlic and cook, being careful not to burn.
4. Add the bacon and cook until just crisp.
5. Add the ground veal and pork. Cook the mixture for at least 15 minutes until it reduces slightly.
6. Reduce to medium heat and add the parsley, chicken stock, white wine, and tomato paste.
7. Cover and simmer for at least 30 minutes or up to 2 hours. Stir occasionally.
8. Cook the tortellini according to the package directions.

HELPFUL HINT:
This sauce works well over any pasta that you have on hand. Save the leftover sauce in a container with a tight fitting lid in the freezer.

ITALIAN PARTY MENU

Chopped Salad with Gorgonzola
and Sun-Dried Tomato
Thousand Island Dressing
❧
Tortellini with Bolognese Sauce
❧
Easy Garlic Bread
❧
Gingerbread with Poached Pears

9. Complete the sauce by adding the butter, whipping cream, fresh sage, and Parmesan cheese. Season with salt and freshly ground pepper.
10. Add the sauce to the cooked tortellini in a large bowl and sprinkle with grated Parmesan cheese.

Serves a crowd
Preparation time about 45 minutes

Easy Garlic Bread

Warm, fragrant garlic bread is as easy as slicing and baking!

1	loaf crusty bread
½	cup olive oil
1	teaspoon garlic powder
2	tablespoons Parmesan cheese

Preheat the oven to 350°.
1. Cut the bread into 1-inch slices, only cutting three-fourths of the way through the loaf.
2. In a small bowl stir together the olive oil and garlic.
3. With a pastry brush spread olive oil mixture over the top of the bread and between the slices.
4. Sprinkle with Parmesan cheese.
5. Bake for 15 to 20 minutes, until warmed through.

Makes 1 loaf

Linguini Carbonara

This sauce is a classic one that highlights cooked bacon, cream and eggs. Feel free to add veggies or Prosciutto ham to take this country pasta dish to updated new tradition fare.

1	**pound linguini**

¾	**pound bacon, diced**
2	**tablespoon butter**
1	**cup half and half**
¾	**cup grated Parmesan cheese**
4	**egg yolks**

Salt and freshly ground pepper

1. Cook the linguini according to the package directions.
2. In a skillet cook the bacon and butter over medium high heat until crisp.
3. Remove the bacon from the pan and drain on paper towels.
4. In a small bowl whisk together the half and half, Parmesan cheese, and egg yolks.
5. Stir 1 tablespoon of the bacon drippings into the cream mixture.
6. Drain the pasta and return it to its pan.
7. Stir in the cream mixture and toss. Cook the pasta and the sauce over medium heat for several minutes until the sauce cooks through. Do not boil.
8. Add the bacon to the pasta. Stir.

Serves 4 to 6
Preparation time about 20 minutes

SETTING THE SCENE:
Garnish the pasta with additional Parmesan cheese and a grating of fresh pepper.

Baked Ziti

This traditional Italian casserole fits the bill on a cold winter's evening. Serve with a toss salad and warm garlic rolls for an yummy meal.

1	**pound ziti**
4	**tablespoons butter**
4	**tablespoons all-purpose flour**
2½	**cups milk**
¼	**teaspoon ground nutmeg**
½	**cup Parmesan cheese**
2	**cups Basic Marinara sauce (page 160)**
1	**pound fresh mozzarella cheese, shredded**
1	**cup grated Parmesan cheese**
½	**cup bread crumbs**
	Salt and freshly ground pepper

Preheat the oven to 375°

1. Prepare the ziti according to the package directions.
2. In a saucepan heat the butter over medium high heat. Stir in the flour. Cook until golden brown.
3. Add the milk to the flour mixture and stir constantly until thickened, about 10 to 15 minutes. Stir in the nutmeg and Parmesan cheese.
4. Drain the pasta and pour into a large 13 x 9 x 2-inch baking dish.
5. Add the Basic Marinara sauce, the white sauce, mozzarella, and Parmesan cheese to the pasta. Stir well.
6. Sprinkle the bread crumbs over the top.
7. Bake for 20 to 30 minutes until bubbly. Turn on the broiler for 2 to 4 minutes to make a crispy top crust.

Serves 4 to 6
Preparation time about 50 minutes

SIMPLE SUBSTITUTION:
Feel free to substitute 2 cups of prepared spaghetti sauce when time does not permit you to make Basic Marinara Sauce.

SETTING THE SCENE:
Make this casserole an upscale supper by using individual baking dishes. Divide the pasta and sauces into 4 ovenproof dishes. Sprinkle each with cheeses and breadcrumbs. Cook as directed, reducing the time by 5 to 10 minutes. Serve the individual dishes on napkin-lined dinner plates.

Baked Eggplant Parmesan

This meatless entree is a favorite. The eggplant is cooked in oil, drained and then layered in a casserole to bake. The result is a rich blend of tomato sauce and spicy that easily becomes a light supper.

2	**medium eggplants, sliced into ¼-inch rounds**
	Salt
½	**cup olive oil, or more**
1	**cup bread crumbs**
4	**cups Basic Marinara Sauce (page 160)**
2	**cups shredded mozzarella cheese**
1	**cup grated Parmesan Cheese**

Preheat the oven to 350°

1. Sprinkle the sliced eggplant with salt and allow to drain in a colander while you make the sauce.
2. Place the bread crumbs in a shallow dish.
3. Dip the eggplant slices into the bread crumbs, coating both sides lightly.
4. In a large pan heat 2 tablespoons of olive oil over high heat.
5. Cook the eggplant in batches until they begin to soften. Turn once. Remove from the pan and drain well on paper towels.
6. Place a small amount of Basic Marinara in the bottom of an oven proof baking dish.
7. Layer the dish with eggplant followed by tomato sauce, mozzarella cheese, and Parmesan cheese. Continue layering until all ingredients are used, ending with Parmesan cheese.
8. Bake for 30 to 35 minutes or until brown and bubbly.

Serves 6
Preparation time about 1 hour

HELPFUL HINT:
As you cook you will need to add olive oil to the skillet. The eggplant absorbs a lot. Remember to heat the oil after each addition. The hotter the oil and the quicker the cooking, the less oil is absorbed. Drain each eggplant slice well on paper towels.

Meatballs with Eggplant Topped with Muenster Cheese

If you are trying to sneak some extra veggies into your every day meal, here is an excellent combination. The roasted eggplant takes the place of breadcrumbs as a binding for the meatballs. The interesting taste of Muenster cheese blends the old world with the new!

SIMPLE SUBSTITUTION:
Vary the "sneaky veggie" in this dish. Shredded zucchini and carrots work well.

Share your favorite "sneaky veggie" dish at www.jorj.com.

1	tablespoon olive oil
2	medium shallots, minced (about 2 tablespoons)
1	medium eggplant, peeled and finely diced into ⅛-inch cubes (about 4 cups)
4	cloves garlic, minced (about 2 tablespoons)
	Salt and freshly ground pepper
1½	pounds ground sirloin
2	cups Basic Marinara Sauce (page 160)
8	ounces Muenster cheese, sliced

Preheat the oven to 350°.

1. In a hot pan heat the olive oil over medium high heat.
2. Cook the shallots until soft.
3. Add the eggplant and garlic and cook for several minutes. Season with salt and freshly ground pepper.
4. Remove the pan from the heat and allow to cool.
5. In a large bowl combine the ground sirloin and the eggplant mixture.
6. Form into 1-inch meatballs and place on a baking sheet.
7. Bake for 10 to 20 minutes or until cooked through.
8. Pour ½ cup of the marinara sauce into a large baking dish. Place the meatballs in the dish.
9. Pour the remaining sauce on top and place a piece of cheese on each one.
10. Bake for 20 to 30 minutes until the cheese begins to melt.

Serves 6 to 8
Preparation time about 1 hour

Bow Tie Pasta with Zucchini, Yellow Squash, Prosciutto, and Pesto

Make sure that you cut the zucchini and squash into similar size pieces to blend with the pretty bow ties and vibrant green sauce.

1	**pound bow tie pasta**
1	**bunch fresh basil (about 1 cup)**
2	**cloves garlic**
2	**tablespoons pine nuts, lightly toasted**
½	**teaspoon salt**
½	**cup olive oil**
⅓	**cup Parmesan cheese**
1	**large zucchini, cut into 1-inch pieces (about 2 cups)**
2	**large yellow squash, cut into 1-inch pieces (about 2 cups)**
8	**ounces prosciutto, cut into strips**

1. Prepare the pasta according to the package directions.
2. In the bowl of a food processor place the basil, garlic, pine nuts, and salt. Pulse to combine.
3. Pour in the olive oil with the blade running. Pulse until smooth.
4. Pour the sauce into a bowl. Stir in the cheese.
5. Cook the zucchini and squash in boiling water for several minutes until just crisp tender.
6. Drain the vegetables.
7. Drain the pasta and return it to its pan.
8. Add the vegetables, prosciutto, and pesto sauce to the pasta. Toss well.

Serves 4 to 6
Preparation time about 30 minutes

TECHNIQUE:
Toast the pine nuts on a baking sheet for 5 to 10 minutes at 350°. Cool before continuing with the sauce.

SETTING THE SCENE:
Garnish the pasta with additional Parmesan cheese and a sprinkling of fresh basil.

Risotto with Wild Mushrooms

The secret to a really silky risotto is to slowly add the warm liquid a ladleful at a time so that the Arborio rice emits a creamy starchiness.

8	cups chicken stock
2	tablespoons olive oil
1	medium yellow onion, finely diced
2	cloves garlic, minced
1	pound arborio rice
1	cup white wine
½	pound portabella mushrooms, sliced
½	pound shiitake mushrooms, sliced
⅓	cup grated Parmesan cheese
2	tablespoons fresh cream
1	tablespoon chopped fresh thyme
	Salt and freshly ground pepper

1. In a saucepan heat the chicken stock over medium heat.
2. In a skillet heat the olive oil over medium high heat.
3. Cook the diced onion and garlic in the olive oil until soft.
4. Add the arborio rice to the skillet and stir.
5. Pour the wine into the pan and cook until most of the liquid disappears.
6. Cover the rice with a ladle full of hot chicken broth. Simmer until the liquid disappears.
7. Stir the sliced mushrooms into the rice. Pour another ladle of stock into the pot.
8. Repeat this procedure until all of the chicken stock is incorporated into the rice.
7. Stir in the Parmesan cheese, cream, and fresh thyme. Season with salt and ground pepper.

Serves 4 to 6 for supper
Preparation time about 40 minutes

SIMPLE SUBSTITUTION:
This is a great dish to experiment with. For a really wild mushroom risotto, add equal amounts of button, portabella, shiitake, and chanterelle mushrooms. Or you can add any fresh vegetable or combination of veggies in place of mushrooms. Asparagus, green peas, beans, and roasted peppers will all work well. For seafood risotto, add cooked shrimp or scallops.

Veal and Spinach Filled Manicotti

This great dish is worth the extra effort. Make enough to freeze an extra pan full of manicotti for use on a day when time is limited.

1	tablespoon olive oil
1	small onion, diced (about ½ cup)
1	pound ground veal
	Salt and freshly ground black pepper
1	10-ounce package frozen chopped spinach, cooked and squeezed dry
¼	cup heavy cream
½	cup grated Parmesan cheese
4	tablespoons butter
4	tablespoons all-purpose flour
2½	cups milk
¼	teaspoon ground nutmeg
½	cup Parmesan cheese
1	16-ounce package manicotti
2	cups Basic Marinara Sauce
½	cup Parmesan cheese
2	tablespoons butter

Preheat the oven to 350°.

1. In a skillet heat the olive oil over medium high heat and cook the onions until soft.
2. Add the ground veal and cook until browned. Season with salt and pepper.
3. Place the veal mixture into the bowl of a food processor. Add the drained spinach, heavy cream, and Parmesan cheese. Pulse to combine. Set aside.
4. In a saucepan whisk together the butter and flour over medium high heat until brown and bubbling.
5. Add the milk and continue to whisk until the sauce begins to thicken. Season with nutmeg and Parmesan cheese. Reduce the heat and set the béchamel sauce aside.

TECHNIQUE:

If you are a cannelloni lover, this recipe will work just as well. Use homemade pasta sheets cut into 4 x 6-inch rectangles. Place 2 to 3 tablespoons of filling onto each sheet. Roll into a tube. Place seam side down in the baking dish over the marinara sauce. Continue with the recipe.

6. Cook the manicotti according to package directions. Rinse and remove to a cookie sheet sprayed with vegetable oil spray.
7. Place ¼ cup of the marinara sauce in the bottom of each of a shallow baking dish. Fill each noodle with some of the veal mixture and place in the pan.
8. Pour the béchamel sauce over the pasta. Pour the remaining tomato sauce over the béchamel. Sprinkle the dish with Parmesan cheese and dot the top small pieces of butter.
9. Bake at 350° for 20 to 30 minutes until cooked though and beginning to bubble.

Serves 6 to 8
Preparation time about 40 minutes plus baking

Antipasti

The perfect accompaniment to every Italian meal.

½   **pound salami, cut into ½-inch cubes**
½   **pound Provolone cheese, cut into ½-inch cubes**
1   **15-ounce can marinated artichoke hearts**
½   **pound roasted asparagus**
½   **pound grilled shrimp**
    Breadsticks
    Olive oil
    Basil

1. Arrange all of the ingredients on a large platter.
2. Drizzle with olive oil and fresh chopped basil.

HELPFUL HINT:
Although there are no real "dos and don'ts" in creating your own combinations, there are some common characteristics. A great antipasti combines finger foods that are fresh, easy to eat, and even easier to prepare.

Lasagna

This is a g— dish to serve for a party. Most of the preparation is done in advance. About 15 minutes before you are ready to serve the dish, take it out of the oven and let the great aroma invite your guests to the table.

Tomato and Sautéed Vegetable Sauce (page 180)

1	32-ounce container ricotta cheese
1	10-ounce package frozen chopped spinach, cooked and squeezed dry
½	cup grated Parmesan cheese
2	eggs

12	ounces shiitake mushrooms, sliced in half
1	tablespoon butter
1	tablespoon fresh rosemary

1	16-ounce package lasagna noodles
1	pound Fontina cheese, grated
¾	cup grated Parmesan cheese

1. Prepare the Tomato and Sautéed Vegetable Sauce.
2. In a bowl mix together the ricotta cheese, drained spinach, Parmesan cheese, and eggs and set aside.
3. Sauté the mushrooms in the butter until cooked. Sprinkle with rosemary and set aside.
4. Cook the lasagna noodles according to package directions. Drain well and place them on a baking sheet that has been sprayed with vegetable oil spray.
5. Place ½ cup of the Tomato and Sautéed Vegetable Sauce in the bottom of a lasagna pan or deep baking pan.
6. Place a layer of lasagna noodles in the bottom of the pan.
7. Top the noodles with sauce, one-third of the ricotta cheese mixture, and one-fourth of the Fontina cheese. Sprinkle with grated Parmesan cheese.

HELPFUL HINT:
The lasagna can be covered with plastic wrap and refrigerated at this point. When you are ready to continue, preheat the oven to 350°. Cook the lasagna for 30 minutes covered with aluminum foil. Uncover and continue cooking until it begins to bubble and the cheese is melted on the top, about 20 minutes more. Let the lasagna stand at least 15 minutes before serving. Serve with a bowl of grated Parmesan cheese and extra Tomato and Sautéed Vegetable Sauce on the side.

8. Repeat with a layer of noodles, sauce, ricotta cheese, and Fontina cheese. Add the sautéed mushrooms and sprinkle with Parmesan cheese.
9. Layer again with noodles, sauce, the remaining ricotta cheese, and Fontina cheese.
10. The final layer is noodles, tomato sauce, and the remaining Fontina and Parmesan cheese.

Serves a crowd
Preparation time about 1 hour plus baking

Grilled Mozzarella and Sun-Dried Tomato Skewers

This is a terrifically simple appetizer to serve with your favorite Italian supper.

½ **pound mozzarella cheese, cut into 1-inch cubes**
1 **7-ounce jar sun-dried tomatoes, drained, oil reserved, cut into 1-inch pieces**

1. Skewer the cheese and tomato pieces on bamboo skewers that have been soaked overnight. Start and end with cheese.
2. Heat a grill pan over medium high heat. Brush the pan with a dash of the reserved oil.
3. Grill the skewers until the cheese just starts to melt, turning once, about 2 to 3 minutes.

Tomato and Sautéed Vegetable Sauce

This pasta sauce is full of healthy vegetables. Be sure that you chop each vegetable the so the pieces are uniform in size. This makes for a presentation that is attractive as it is delicious.

SETTING THE SCENE:
Serve this sauce over the top of a bowl of cooked pasta. Shave Parmesan cheese over the top and sprinkle with fresh basil.

2	tablespoons olive oil
1	large onion, chopped (about 2 cups)
1	large zucchini, chopped (about 2 cups)
2	large squash, chopped (about 2 cups)
1	small eggplant, chopped (about 3 cups)
4	cloves garlic, minced (about 2 tablespoons)
1	pound button mushrooms, sliced (about 3 cups)
2	28-ounce cans chopped tomatoes
2	tablespoons tomato paste
2	tablespoons chopped basil
1	tablespoon chopped oregano
1	tablespoon sugar
	Salt and freshly ground pepper

1. In the bottom of a large pot heat the olive oil over medium high heat.
2. Cook the onions in the pot for several minutes.
3. Add the zucchini and squash and cook until the vegetables begin to soften.
4. Add the eggplant and cook just until it begins to soften.
5. Add the garlic and mushrooms and cook for 5 minutes more.
6. Add the chopped tomatoes, tomato paste, basil, oregano, and sugar. Simmer for 15 minutes. Season with salt and pepper.

Serves a crowd
Preparation time about 30 minutes

The Cozy Comfort Diner

ROASTING, BRAISING AND STEWING

What is comfort food? Visualize your favorite Sunday supper. The table is laid with bowls of steamy vegetables. In the center is a platter of roasted chicken or a tureen brimming with beef stroganoff. The serving vessels are passed from place to place and generous spoonfuls of each dish find their way to your plate. Think about mashed potatoes, buttered noodles, rich sauces, and red meat. Out of fashion for a while, these old-time culinary favorites have reappeared, spiked with exotic ingredients, to become unforgettable dishes now prepared in many of the most upscale restaurants. Do you remember a time when Monday night was synonymous with a dinner of meat loaf and mashed potatoes? Fast forward to today, add some roasted garlic to the mashed potatoes and fresh herbs to the meat loaf, and the dish is now served at many fashionable cafés in town.

To visit the Comfy Cozy Diner in your house read about sauces in the first chapter, Getting Started. The recipes in this chapter include several sauces, some of which are called gravy. The terms are mostly interchangeable. You can probably find a small distinction between the two, but when sauce is sopped up with a crusty heel of bread—it's just as good as any gravy. Here is a little fine point to consider: some sauces are finished with a tablespoon or two of butter at the very end of the cooking process. When butter is added to a sauce to produce a velvety shine, in most cases it should not be boiled to thicken. A gravy begins with the juices left in the pan from cooking meat or poultry. When a mixture of flour and water is added to the pan juices, the gravy must be boiled in order to thicken. In this way a gravy may be thought of as a sturdier, less delicate sauce and a perfect accompaniment to mashed potatoes and roasted poultry.

In order to roast the perfect chicken, I recommend the purchase of an upright roasting rack. The metal rack is inserted into the cavity of the chicken. It sits upright in a baking pan allowing the juices to flow to the meatiest part of the chicken, while the extra fat drips to the bottom of the pan.

Refresh your memory on the cooking terms *braising, roasting,* and *stewing* that are discussed in Chapter I. These are the cooking methods that are most often used with the recipes in this section. Meat is braised by browning the pieces in oil or butter. The meat is not actually cooked during the browning process. It is then submerged in fragrant liquids and allowed to slow cook to absorb the flavors while it tenderizes. For purposes of these dishes, stewing is essentially the same process. Roasting occurs in the oven. The roasted food is usually cooked uncovered to prevent steaming.

Today's Cozy Comfort Diner, while reminiscent of years past, offers meals with fresher, more savory ingredients. In many cases the dish comes together with a healthier balance of great gusto and sensible choice. Don't be afraid to hanker back to the good old days of iceberg lettuce and blue cheese dressing. Spend the time to make these traditional dishes for delicious, lip-smacking results. The benefit of cooking at home for your family and friends is that seconds are on the house!

Find more information about the recipes in The Cozy Comfort Diner chapter at www.jorj.com.

Stuffed Chicken Breasts with Ham and Swiss Cheese

When I first started in the catering business, my partner and dear friend, Mary, introduced me to this recipe. We served it for every occasion. It works well for large crowds, and is quite good served at room temperature sliced into pinwheels. This dish is one of my favorite week night meals and is easily adapted to chicken fingers!

HELPFUL HINT:
To make simple chicken fingers using this recipe, cut the breasts into strips. Dip them into the butter, then into the bread crumb mixture. Lay them in a baking dish. You will need to adjust the cooking time. About 20 minutes will produce fun fingers!

6	**6- to 8-ounce skinless boneless chicken breast halves**
¾	**cup bread crumbs**
1	**teaspoon dried basil**
1	**teaspoon paprika**
	Salt and freshly ground pepper
½	**cup butter (1 stick)**
⅓	**cup Parmesan cheese**
3	**ounces sliced Swiss cheese (6 slices)**
3	**ounces sliced baked ham (6 slices)**

Preheat the oven to 350°.

1. Pound each chicken breast half to about ¼-inch thickness between 2 pieces of plastic wrap, using a mallet.
2. In a shallow bowl combine the bread crumbs, basil, paprika, salt, and pepper.
3. In a shallow bowl melt the butter in a microwave oven on low heat. Stir the Parmesan cheese into the butter.
4. Dip 1 chicken breast half first into the butter mixture, and then into the bread crumb mixture, and place on the work surface. Repeat with the remaining breasts.
5. Lay one slice of the cheese on top of each chicken breast.
6. Top the cheese with one slice of ham.
7. Roll the chicken breast around the ham and cheese. Place it seam side down in a baking dish. Drizzle any remaining butter over the top.
8. Bake for 30 minute or until the chicken is browned and cooked through.

Serves 6
Preparation time about 15 minutes plus baking

Roasted Chicken and Vegetables

The best part of this dish is the aroma the drifts through every room in the house as the meal cooks. Be prepared to pass around seconds to everyone at the table.

2	tablespoons olive oil
1	4½- to 5-pound whole chicken
	Salt and freshly ground pepper
2	tablespoons chopped fresh thyme
2	tablespoons chopped fresh rosemary
	Juice of ½ medium lemon (about 1 tablespoon)
4	medium potatoes, peeled and cut into pieces (about 3 cups)
4	large carrots, peeled and cut into pieces (about 2 cups)
4	medium onions, peeled and cut into pieces (about 2 cups)

Preheat the oven to 375°
1. Place 1 teaspoon of the olive oil in the palm of your hand and rub it onto the chicken.
2. Sprinkle the chicken with salt and freshly ground pepper and 1 tablespoon of each of the herbs.
3. Place the chicken on an upright roasting rack placed into a baking pan. Drizzle the juice of ½ lemon over the chicken.
4. Cut the vegetables into pieces that are similar in size.
5. In a small bowl toss the vegetable pieces in the remaining olive oil.
6. Remove the vegetables from the oil and place them in the bottom of the roasting pan.
7. Sprinkle the vegetables with the remaining herbs and season with salt and freshly ground pepper.
8. Roast the chicken and vegetables for 45 to 55 minutes.

Serves 6
Preparation time about 15 minutes plus roasting

TECHNIQUE:
Place the baking pan on the lowest rack of the preheated 375° oven. An upright roasting rack is inserted into the cavity of the chicken and stands tall in the pan. It cooks the chicken in the same manner as a rotisserie.

HELPFUL HINT:
1. The chicken is done when a fork pierces the meat behind the thigh and the juices that run out are clear, not red or pink.

2. Always let the chicken rest before carving (at least 10 to 15 minutes depending on size).

White Raisin Dressing for Poultry

Like many of my comfort food dishes, this one is passed down from earlier generations. The raisins add a moist fruity taste to the rich turkey dressing. This recipe makes enough dressing to accompany a large bird and plenty of people. If you are having a more intimate setting, feel free to cut everything in half!

HELPFUL HINT:
You can refrigerate the dish after step 6, When you are ready to bake, remove the dish from the refrigerator and continue with the recipe.

2	large yellow onions, chopped (about 2 cups)
8	stalks celery, chopped (about 4 cups)
1	cup butter (2 sticks)
2	16-ounce packages stuffing cubes (the herb variety)
2	10¾-ounce cans cream of celery soup
2	10¾-ounce cans cream of mushroom soup
3	to 4 cups chicken broth
2	cups white raisins
2	tablespoons butter, additional, cut into small pieces

Preheat the oven to 350°

1. In a large sauté pan cook the onion and celery in the butter over medium high heat. Cover the pan and simmer until the vegetables are soft, about 20 minutes.
2. In a large bowl combine the stuffing cubes, soups, and cooked vegetable mixture. Stir until all the cubes are moistened.
3. Add as much chicken broth as need to reach to reach the desired stuffing consistency.
4. Toss in the white raisins and blend together.
5. Prepare a baking dish by spraying it first with a vegetable oil cooking spray. Spoon the stuffing into the dish.
6. Dot the top of the stuffing with butter pieces.
7. Bake for 30 to 45 minutes until cooked through and golden brown on top.

Serves 10 to 12 people with plenty left over
Preparation time about 30 minutes plus baking

Chicken Pepperoni

Here is fast, easy chicken dish that can be made with very little preparation. If you are in a rush, substitute a jar of prepared pizza sauce instead of making your own tomato sauce.

4	**6-ounce skinless boneless chicken breasts**
3	**tablespoons olive oil**
½	**cup bread crumbs**
1	**teaspoon dried oregano**
½	**teaspoon garlic powder**
	Salt and freshly ground pepper

1	**16-ounce can chopped tomatoes**
1	**teaspoon sugar**
½	**teaspoon dried oregano**
½	**teaspoon dried basil**
½	**teaspoon garlic powder**

2	**ounces pepperoni, sliced in thin rounds (8 slices)**
½	**cup shredded mozzarella cheese**

Preheat the oven to 350°.

1. Pound the chicken breast halves between 2 sheets of plastic wrap to about ½-inch thickness.
2. In a shallow skillet heat the olive oil over medium high heat.
3. In a bowl combine the bread crumbs with the oregano and garlic powder. Season the mixture with salt and freshly ground pepper.
4. Coat the chicken breasts with the bread crumbs.
5. Sauté in the olive oil until browned, about 4 minutes each side.
6. Remove the chicken cutlets to a baking dish. Set aside.
7. In a saucepan combine the tomato, sugar, oregano, basil, and garlic powder. Cook over medium heat for 10 minutes. Season with salt and freshly ground pepper.

TECHNIQUE:
A meat mallet is the kitchen tool used to pound meat. Good alternatives are a rolling pin, spatula, or the flat handle on a knife.

SIMPLE SUBSTITUTION:
Instead of the whole chicken breast, you can substitute chicken cutlets to skip step 1.

8. Pour the sauce over the chicken in the baking pan. Place the slices of pepperoni on top of each cutlet. Sprinkle the tops with cheese.
9. Bake for 20 to 30 minutes at 350° or until the cheese melts and just begins to brown.

Serves 8
Preparation time about 20 minutes plus baking

Ooey Gooey Rolls

You can make these rolls in a flash. They puff up out of the oven and go great with every comfort meal.

1	**package prebaked dinner rolls**
⅓	**cup butter, softened**
⅓	**cup sour cream**
⅓	**cup mayonnaise**
⅓	**cup Parmesan cheese**

Preheat the oven to 350°.
1. Mix together the butter, sour cream, mayonnaise, and Parmesan cheese.
2. Spread the mixture over the top and sides of each roll.
3. Bake the rolls on a baking sheet for 20 to 25 minutes, until they begin to brown and bubble.

Makes about 6 servings
Preparation time about 5 minutes plus baking

Pan Chicken with White Wine "Gravy"

Chicken any way you prepare it is an excellent mid week meal. This dish holds well when you are trying to balance several different schedules. Serve it with lightly buttered egg noodles or yellow rice and a tossed veggie salad.

4	6-ounce boneless skinless chicken breast halves
1	cup all-purpose flour, divided ½ cup and ½ cup
	Salt and freshly ground pepper
2	large eggs
½	cup corn flake crumbs
1	teaspoon Old Bay seasoning
1	teaspoon paprika
½	teaspoon red pepper flakes
3	tablespoons olive oil
1	tablespoon butter
1	bunch green onions including tops, chopped (about 1 cup)
¾	cup white wine
1½	cups chicken stock
1	teaspoon prepared mustard
1	teaspoon all-purpose flour, mixed with cold water (optional)
3	tablespoons garlic chives

SIMPLE SUBSTITUTION:
For a variation of this recipe substitute red wine for white, tomato paste for mustard, and basil for chives. Continue to experiment with what you have on hand!

1. Rinse the chicken breasts and pat dry. Place the chicken between 2 pieces of plastic wrap and pound to ¼-inch thickness, using a meat mallet.
2. In a shallow bowl place ½ cup of the flour. Season with salt and freshly ground pepper.
3. Whisk the eggs with 2 tablespoons of water in a second bowl.
4. In a third bowl combine the remaining ½ cup of flour with the corn flake crumbs and the seasonings.
5. In a shallow skillet heat the olive oil and butter on medium high heat.
6. Dip the chicken breasts into the flour followed by the egg and then into the seasoned flour and corn flake crumb mixture.

7. Place each one in the skillet and brown on both sides, about 3 to 5 minutes per side. Remove the breasts to a platter and keep warm in an oven set on low heat or in a warming drawer.
8. Add the chopped green onions to the pan and cook until softened.
9. Pour the white wine into the pan and deglaze by scraping and stirring the browned bits from the bottom. Add the chicken stock to the pan and reduce for 5 minutes over medium high heat. Add the mustard and stir thoroughly.
10. Add the chopped chives and season with salt and freshly ground pepper.

Serves 4
Preparation time about 30 minutes

HELPFUL HINT:
You may thicken the sauce at step 9 with a thin flour paste (flour mixed with cold water) to give it a gravy consistency.

Sautéed Cabbage

This easy to make veggie is a perfect side dish for chicken entrées.

2	**tablespoons olive oil**
1	**head savoy cabbage, sliced**
1	**Granny Smith apple, peeled, thinly sliced**
2	**tablespoons balsamic vinegar**
	Salt and freshly ground pepper

1. In a skillet heat the olive oil over medium high heat and sauté the cabbage for 10 minutes.
2. Add the apple and vinegar, and cook for 10 minutes more, until the cabbage is soft.
3. Season with salt and pepper.

Makes 4 to 6 servings
Preparation time about 25 minutes

Rustic Cinnamon Roasted Chicken

This dish blends the aroma of cinnamon with the taste of spicy roasted vegetables. Serve the chicken pieces with yellow rice, a ladle full of sauce, and a generous sprinkling of grated cheese.

4	chicken thighs
4	chicken legs
1	teaspoon ground cinnamon
1	teaspoon chili powder
	Salt and freshly ground pepper
1	teaspoon olive oil
3	portabella mushrooms, sliced into ¼-inch strips (about 3 cups)
1	medium onion, sliced (about ½ cup)
6	to 8 medium plum tomatoes, quartered (about 2 cups)
3	jalapeño chilies, seeded and sliced (about 6 tablespoons)
2	cups tortilla chips
1	tablespoon olive oil
1	cup beef stock
½	cup red wine
½	cup shredded Monterey Jack cheese (optional)

Preheat the oven to 350°.

1. Season the chicken pieces with cinnamon, chili powder and salt and pepper.
2. Place all of the vegetables and the tortilla chips in the bottom of a large 13 x 9 x 2-inch baking dish. Drizzle 1 tablespoon of olive oil over the top.
3. Brush each chicken piece with the remaining olive oil.
4. Place the chicken pieces on top of the vegetables.
5. Bake for approximately 45 minutes or until the chicken is done.
6. Remove the chicken to a platter and keep warm in an oven set on low heat or in a warming drawer.

SETTING THE SCENE:
To serve the dish family style, ladle the sauce onto a large serving platter. Place the chicken pieces on top and sprinkle everything with shredded Monterey Jack cheese.

7. Heat the baking dish with the vegetables over medium high heat on the top of a stove. Add the beef stock to the vegetables and cook for several minutes.
8. Add the red wine to the dish, and continue to cook for 5 more minutes.
9. Place the vegetables and liquid in a food processor and pulse to emulsify the mixture. Season with salt and freshly ground pepper. The sauce will be chunky and spicy.

Serves 4
Preparation time about 1 hour

Family Style Rice

You can easily turn packaged rice into your new family favorite with just a few additions.

2   tablespoons olive oil
2   cloves garlic, minced
3   to 4 green onions, chopped
1   package yellow rice
1   16-ounce can chicken broth

1. In a skillet heat the olive oil and cook the garlic and onions until soft.
2. Add the rice and cook for 5 minutes.
3. Add the chicken broth and additional water if required on the rice package directions. Bring to a boil.
4. Reduce the heat and cover. Cook according to the rice package directions.

Rock Cornish Game Hens with Wild Rice Stuffing and Orange Cranberry Glaze

Rock Cornish game hens were a staple on the dinner party menu of the late 60s. Today they're making a comeback, just like bell-bottom jeans. Try this updated twist on roasting the hens the next time your in the mood for nostalgia.

2	**Rock Cornish game hens**
1	**tablespoon olive oil**
1	**medium shallot, finely diced (about 2 tablespoons)**
½	**yellow bell pepper, finely diced**
1	**8-ounce can sliced water chestnuts, drained**
1	**cup uncooked wild rice**
3	**cups chicken broth**
1	**teaspoon fresh sage, chopped**
	Salt and freshly ground pepper
1	**cup orange juice**
½	**can jellied cranberry sauce (1 cup)**

1. Rinse the inside of the game hens thoroughly. Cut each one in half.
2. In a saucepan heat the olive oil over medium high heat and cook the shallot and bell pepper until tender.
3. Add the water chestnuts and rice to the pan. Stir.
4. Pour in the chicken broth. Bring to a boil. Reduce the heat to low, cover the pan and cook until all of the liquid is absorbed about 20 minutes.
5. Add the sage to the rice and season with salt and pepper. Place the rice mixture in a shallow baking dish.
6. Place the game hen on the rice layer, skin side up. Season with salt and pepper.
7. In a saucepan whisk together the orange juice and cranberry sauce over medium heat until well mixed.

TECHNIQUE:
Check the directions on the package of rice. Certain brands will require more or less stock.

8. Pour the orange glaze over the game hens, allowing the extra to spill over onto the rice stuffing.
9. Roast the hens for 40 to 50 minutes.

Serves 4
Preparation time about 30 minutes plus roasting

Baked Apples

A simply baked apple, quartered, and served alongside a great comfort food dish is a super sweet garnish.

2	**Granny Smith apples, cored**
½	**cup hot water**
2	**tablespoons brown sugar**
1	**tablespoon butter**

Preheat the oven to 375°.
1. Place the apples in a baking dish.
2. Pour the hot water into the bottom of the dish.
3. Sprinkle brown sugar in the center of the apples, where the core was removed.
4. Dot the top of the apples with butter.
5. Bake for 30 minutes. Baste with pan juices.

Serves 2
Preparation time about 5 minutes plus baking

Herb and Sherry Roasted Turkey with Savory Gravy

The big debate when choosing a turkey revolves around fresh versus frozen. I have used both successfully. My favorite is the fresh turkey, because no additional fat has been incorporated into the meat. But in a pinch, a frozen turkey will do quite nicely.

1	large fresh turkey, 10 to 12 pounds or more
1	to 2 apples or oranges, cut in quarters
¼	cup butter, melted
¼	cup finely chopped fresh rosemary
¼	cup finely chopped fresh thyme
¼	cup finely chopped basil
¼	cup finely chopped oregano
½	cup sherry, or dry white wine
	Salt and freshly ground pepper
	Turkey giblet, liver, heart, and neck parts
1	bunch parsley
½	onion, sliced
1	stalk celery
1	bay leaf
¼	cup all-purpose flour, mixed with ½ to 1 cup cold water

1. Rinse the inside of the turkey thoroughly. Place pieces of apple or orange in the cavity of the bird.
2. Brush the skin of the turkey with the melted butter.
3. In a small bowl combine the herbs. Rub the mixture over the top and under the skin of the turkey.
4. Place the turkey on a rack in a heavy roasting pan. Drizzle the sherry over the turkey and let it run off into the bottom of the pan. Season with salt and freshly ground pepper.
5. Cover the turkey loosely with a foil tent to prevent over browning. (You may place some water in the bottom of the pan.) Roast according to the directions on the package for an unstuffed turkey.

TECHNIQUE:
Preheat the oven to 450°. Place the turkey in the oven and immediately reduce the heat to 325°. Cooking time is 15 to 20 minutes per pound. For a bird over 16 pounds, reduce the time to 13 to 15 minutes per pound. Add 5 minutes per pound if the bird is stuffed.

HELPFUL HINT:
For a richer colored gravy you may add a dash of any gravy browning liquid.

6. Remove the foil with about 1 hour left to cook, and baste with the pan juices every 15 minutes. Let the bird stand for 30 minutes before carving.

FOR GRAVY:

7. Remove the turkey parts from inside the uncooked turkey and place them in a large stock pot covered with water. Add the parsley, onion, celery stalk, and bay leaf to the pan.
8. Simmer over low heat for at least 1 hour adding water if the stock cooks down too quickly.
9. Add the left over pan juices to the stock pot after the turkey has been removed.
10. Strain the mixture through a colander and return the gravy to the pan.
11. Thicken the gravy with the flour and water mixture. Add a little at a time and whisk briskly to avoid lumps.

Serves 15 to 20 people with plenty left over
Preparation time about 20 minutes plus roasting

NEW TRADITIONS THANKSGIVING MENU

Herb and Sherry Roasted Turkey with
Savory Gravy

White Raisin Dressing for Poultry

Roasted Garlic Mashed Potatoes

Corn Soufflé Casserole

Yam Pudding

Sautéed Green Beans
with Caramelized Pearl Onions

Perfect Pumpkin Pie

Meat Loaf with Mushroom Gravy

The key to a moist meat loaf is to incorporate fresh, lean ground beef with equally fresh bread crumbs. You may easily substitute ground turkey or veal, but don't cut back on the fresh herbs.

1	medium onion, diced about ½ cup
1	teaspoon olive oil
1	pound lean ground beef
1	pound ground veal
1	to 1½ cups bread crumbs
2	cloves garlic, minced (about 1 tablespoon)
1	teaspoon chili powder
1	teaspoon chopped fresh thyme
1	teaspoon chopped fresh rosemary
1	egg, lightly beaten
1	tablespoon tomato paste
¼	to ½ cup cream
	Salt and freshly ground pepper

1	tablespoon olive oil
½	pound button mushrooms, sliced (about 1½ cups)
½	cup red wine
1½	cups beef stock
1	tablespoon all-purpose flour mixed with ½ to 1 cup cold water

Preheat the oven to 350°.

1. In a skillet cook the diced onion in the olive oil until the pieces just begin to brown.
2. In a large bowl combine the ground beef, ground veal, sautéed onion, fresh bread crumbs, minced garlic, chili powder, fresh herbs, beaten egg, and tomato paste.
3. Add just enough cream to the mixture so that it comes together. Season the ingredients with salt and freshly ground pepper.
4. Form the mixture into a loaf and place into a 9 x 5 x 3-inch loaf pan that has been sprayed with vegetable cooking spray.

SETTING THE SCENE:

To serve the dish, place a spoonful of Roasted Garlic Mashed Potatoes (recipe on page 198) on a dinner plate. Tilt two slices of meat loaf on either side of the potatoes. Drizzle the mushroom gravy over top. Sprinkle the entire plate with chopped garlic chives and freshly ground pepper.

5. Bake the meat loaf for 45 minutes to 1 hour. Let it sit for 15 minutes before slicing.
6. In a small skillet heat the olive oil over medium high heat. Add the mushrooms and cook for several minutes.
7. Pour the red wine into the pan and reduce until most of the liquid is evaporated.
8. Pour the beef stock into the pan and reduce until half of the liquid is evaporated.
9. Whisk together the flour and water to form a smooth liquid.
10. Stir the flour mixture into the gravy. It will thicken as it cooks. You may add more water until you reach the desired consistency for gravy. Season with salt and freshly ground pepper.

Serves 6 to 8
Preparation time about 30 minutes plus baking

IT'S NOT YOUR GRANDMA'S SUNDAY SUPPER MENU

Meat Loaf with Mushroom Gravy

Roasted Garlic Mashed Potatoes

Sweet Pea Purée

Glazed Acorn Squash Rings

Cinnamon Bread Pudding with Bourbon Sauce

Sweet Pea Purée

Here is an update on a Sunday supper staple. Only you won't try to hide these peas in your mashed potatoes!

1   **10-ounce package frozen peas**
3   **tablespoons cream**
    Salt and freshly ground white pepper

1. Cook the peas in the microwave oven according to the package directions. Drain.
2. Place the peas in the bowl of a food processor. Add the cream and pulse until puréed.
3. Season with salt and white pepper.

Serves 4
Preparation time about 15 minutes

Roasted Garlic Mashed Potatoes

Once a staple at Grandma's Sunday night table, potatoes have been elevated to new heights with innovative presentations and ingredients like roasted garlic and fresh snipped chives.

4	**large baking potatoes, peeled and cut into pieces (about 6 cups)**
4	**to 6 cloves garlic, roasted (see Helpful Hint at right)**
6	**tablespoons butter (¾ stick)**
½	**to 1 cup milk**
2	**tablespoons snipped garlic chives**

1. Boil the potatoes in water until they are cooked, about 20 minutes.
2. In an electric mixer bowl combine the potatoes, roasted garlic, and butter. Mix on the medium high speed to blend.
3. Add enough milk to reach the desired consistency. For thicker potatoes use less milk. For thinner potatoes use more milk.
4. Mix in the garlic chives and season with salt and freshly ground pepper.

Serves 8
Preparation time about 30 minutes

HELPFUL HINT:
Use a toaster oven as a quick method to roast cloves garlic. Place the cloves on a baking sheet. Drizzle with a small amount of olive oil. Sprinkle with dried oregano, salt, and freshly ground pepper. Bake at 375° for 15 to 20 minutes.

SETTING THE SCENE:
Want to have some fun at your next party? Treat your guests to a Mashed Potato Martini. Stack layers of martini glasses on a table. Use a warming tray to keep large pans of Roasted Garlic Mashed Potatoes hot. Fill bowls with any of the following: grated Cheddar cheese, snipped chives, green onion rings, sour cream, yogurt, caramelized onions, cooked bacon and toasted pine nuts. Each guests receives a martini glass filled two-thirds full with mashed potatoes. Add the toppings of their choice. Top each serving with a green olive on a toothpick. Don't stop there: add a pan of mashed sweet potatoes for an extra layer of fun!

Sweet Potato Hash

I like to make this dish when I have left over cooked beef or poultry. However, it makes a beautifully blended vegetable side dish without these additions. As always, use the freshest ingredients to prepared the best hash.

1   large sweet potato, peeled and diced (about 2 cups)
2   large baking potatoes, peeled and diced (about 3 cups)
½   pound bacon, diced (about 8 to 10 slices)
1   medium onion, diced (about 1 cup)
1   green bell pepper, diced (about 1 cup)
1   tablespoon chopped fresh rosemary
      Salt and freshly ground pepper

1   cup cooked turkey, diced (optional)

1. Blanch the sweet potatoes for 5 minutes. Drain and set aside.
2. Blanch the white potatoes for 7 minutes. Drain and set aside.
3. In a skillet cook the diced bacon until crisp. Transfer the pieces to a bowl with a slotted spoon and set aside.
4. Cook the onion and green pepper in the bacon fat until browned.
5. Add the potatoes to the pan and brown well.
6. Add the bacon back to the pan and stir.
7. Season with the fresh rosemary, salt, and freshly ground pepper.

Serves 4
Preparation time about 25 minutes plus baking

HELPFUL HINT:
The secret to this dish is preparing all of the ingredients into a similar sized dice.

HELPFUL HINT:
To make the hash a simple main dish, add cooked meat or poultry such as diced cooked turkey, ham, beef or chicken to the pan. Warm the hash by placing the contents of the into a baking dish that has been sprayed with a vegetable cooking spray. Bake at 325 for 20 minutes or until ready to serve.

Home Style Macaroni and Cheese

Here is a creamy casserole that becomes a meal by itself with the addition of chunked baked ham or pieces of smoked turkey. Have fun substituting different types of cheese to create your own family favorite.

SIMPLE SUBSTITUTION:
Feel free to try different cheese. Yellow American and extra sharp Cheddar are great, but don't forget blue cheese or Fontina for a fun dish!

4	tablespoons butter (½ stick)
1	medium yellow onion (dice about ½ cup)
¼	cup all-purpose flour
4	cups milk
2	cups cubed sharp white Cheddar cheese
1	cup sour cream
	Salt and freshly ground pepper
1	pound pasta such as macaroni or rigatoni
⅓	cup seasoned bread crumbs

Preheat the oven to 350°.

1. In a saucepan melt the butter over medium high heat.
2. Add the diced onion and cook until just beginning to brown.
3. Add the flour and stir to make a paste.
4. Add the milk and stir until the sauce is thick, about 15 to 20 minutes.
5. Stir in the cheese.
6. Add the sour cream and stir.
7. Season with salt and freshly ground pepper.
8. Cook the pasta according to the directions on the package. Drain and place into a casserole dish.
9. Stir the sauce into the pasta. Sprinkle with bread crumbs.
10. Bake for 20 to 25 minutes until the top begins to brown and the casserole bubbles.

Serves 4 to 6
Preparation time about 30 minutes plus baking

GLOP

This recipe has roots in the American kitchen of the 60s— everything casserole. I have updated it using fresh ingredients in the tomato sauce. But in a pinch a jar of prepared sauce will work quite well.

2   tablespoons olive oil
1   large yellow onion, diced (about 1 cup)
1   medium green bell pepper, diced (about 1 cup)
1   medium red bell pepper, diced (about 1 cup)
1½   pounds lean ground sirloin beef
2   cloves garlic, minced (about 1 tablespoon)
1   teaspoon ground oregano
1   teaspoon dried basil
1   28-ounce can chopped tomatoes
2   tablespoons tomato paste
     Salt and freshly ground pepper

1   pound bow tie pasta, cooked
2   cups shredded sharp American cheese

Preheat the oven to 350°.

1.   In a large pot heat the olive oil over medium high heat.
2.   Add the onion and peppers to the pot and cook until softened, about 5 to 10 minutes.
3.   Add the ground sirloin and brown well.
4.   Stir in the garlic, oregano, and basil.
5.   Pour the chopped tomatoes into the pot.
6.   Stir in the tomato paste and season with salt and freshly ground pepper.
7.   Stir and simmer for at least 10 minutes.
8.   Place the cooked pasta into a large baking dish. Add the sauce to the pasta and stir to combine.
9.   Generously sprinkle cheese over the casserole.
10. Bake for 20 to 30 minutes, until the cheese begins to brown and the casserole bubbles.

Serves 6
Preparation time about 15 minutes plus baking

SIMPLE SUBSTITUTIONS:
Make this dish even easier by substituting with a prepared pasta sauce. Brown the ground meat in a skillet and stir in the prepared sauce. Continue with the recipe. Another fast and favorite tip is to substitute thick slices of processed cheese that will quickly melt into the pasta for the shredded sharp cheese.

Peppered Pork Chops with Tomato Caper Cream Sauce

Use a medium thick pork chop for this dish. Serve with broccoli and cauliflower for a satisfying week night special meal.

SETTING THE SCENE:
Serve the dish by placing a pork chop on each plate and drizzle the sauce around the sides.

4	6-ounce pork chops, ½ inch thick
	Salt
2	tablespoons olive oil
2	tablespoons butter, divided
1	tablespoon crushed black peppercorns
3	to 4 green onions including tops, sliced (½ cup)
1	cup chicken stock
4	medium plum tomatoes, diced (about 1 cup)
1	tablespoon capers
1	tablespoon prepared mustard
⅓	cup half and half
1	tablespoon chopped fresh thyme

1. Season the pork chops on both sides with salt.
2. In a sauté pan heat the olive oil and 1 tablespoon of the butter over medium high heat. Stir in the crushed peppercorns.
3. Cook the pork chops in the mixture turning once, approximately 8 minutes per side until browned.
4. Remove the chops to a dish and keep warm in an oven on low heat.
5. Drain most of the fat from the pan.
6. Cook the onions until they are soft.
6. Deglaze the pan with chicken stock and reduce to about ½ cup.
7. Add the chopped tomatoes, capers, and mustard to the pan.
8. Stir in the half and half and cook for 5 minutes.
9. Reduce the heat to low. Whisk the remaining 1 tablespoon of butter into the sauce.
10. Sprinkle the fresh thyme into the sauce.

Serves 4
Preparation time about 25 minutes

Dilled Beef Stroganoff

Some versions of this dish call for a hint of tomato in the sauce. I prefer an abundance of mushrooms and fresh dill. Serve the dish over wild rice or wide, flat, buttered noodles.

2	pounds sirloin tip steaks, cut into 1 inch pieces
	Salt and freshly ground pepper
2	tablespoons butter
1	medium onion, diced (about ½ cup)
1	pound button mushrooms, sliced (about 3 cups)
1	10¾-ounce can beef broth
1	cup sour cream
2	tablespoons chopped fresh dill weed

1. Season the steak pieces with salt and freshly ground pepper.
2. In a large skillet melt the butter and brown the steak in batches over medium high heat. Transfer the pieces to a bowl and set aside.
3. Brown the onions in the same pan.
4. Add the mushrooms and cook for several minutes.
5. Pour the beef broth into the pan and reduce by half.
6. Reduce the heat to low. Stir a tablespoon of the hot sauce from the pan into the sour cream to temper. Pour the mixture back into the skillet. Stir the sauce.
7. Add the beef and beef juices to the pan.
8. Stir in the fresh dill and season with salt and freshly ground pepper.

Serves 4
Preparation time about 20 to 30 minutes

TECHNIQUE:
Each steak cube should be well browned on the outside and pink on the inside.

HELPFUL HINT:
When making a warm sauce that incorporates a cold ingredient it requires that you temper the cold ingredient to prevent curdling the sauce. Pour a small amount of the warm sauce into the cold ingredient and stir quickly. Now you may pour the tempered cold ingredient into the warm sauce and continue with the recipe.

Baked Veal Chop with Red Wine Mushroom Cream Sauce

Here is a yummy way to prepare veal chops. Pounding the chop produces a very tender piece of veal. It's also a great way to reduce the stress of a busy workday. Pound away!

4	**8-ounce veal chops, 1-inch thick**
½	**cup bread crumbs**
½	**cup cornmeal**
1	**teaspoon garlic powder**
1	**teaspoon dried oregano**
	Salt and freshly ground pepper
1	**tablespoon olive oil**
2	**tablespoons butter**
1	**pound sliced button mushrooms**
1	**cup red wine**
1½	**cups beef stock**
1	**tablespoon Dijon mustard**
⅓	**cup half and half**
2	**to 3 fresh thyme sprigs**

Preheat the oven to 375°.

1. Pound the veal chops with a meat mallet to ½-inch thickness.
2. Mix together the bread crumbs, cornmeal, ½ teaspoon of garlic powder, ½ teaspoon of dried oregano, salt, and pepper in a shallow bowl.
3. In a skillet heat the olive oil and 1 tablespoon butter over medium high heat.
4. Dredge the veal chops on both sides in the bread crumb mixture.
5. Cook the veal chops in the hot oil turning once, until golden brown. Remove to a baking dish. Cook in the oven for 5 minutes more.
6. Cook the mushrooms in the remaining 1 tablespoon of butter until brown. Season with ½ teaspoon of garlic

SETTING THE SCENE:
Serve the veal chops on a bed of couscous with a ladle full of sauce drizzled over top. Garnish with chopped fresh thyme.

powder, ½ teaspoon of dried oregano, salt, and pepper. Remove them to a bowl.

7. Deglaze the skillet with the red wine. Stir to scrape up the small bits from the bottom of the pan. Reduce to about ⅓ cup of liquid.

8. Pour in the beef stock, bring to a boil, and reduce the liquid until about ¾ cup remains, about 15 minutes.

9. Stir in the mustard, half and half, and thyme sprigs. Cook for 5 minutes more.

10. Strain the sauce and return it to the pan. Add the mushrooms to the sauce.

Serves 4
Preparation time about 25 minutes

Fried Spinach

This colorful vegetable goes well with veal and beef!

1   **pound fresh spinach leaves, roughly chopped**
       Oil for frying
       Salt and freshly ground pepper

1. Thoroughly dry the chopped spinach.
2. Heat enough oil to half fill a deep pot.
3. Place spinach leaves in a Chinese basket. Carefully lower the basket into the oil. Fry for 1 to 2 minutes.
4. Raise the basket and drain the spinach on paper towels. Season to taste.

Classic Beef Stew

Make this stew early in the day and have a wonderful supper waiting for you later. Make a batch and invite friends, or save the extras as it gets better the next day.

2   pounds lean beef, cut into 1-inch cubes
2   tablespoons flour
    Salt and freshly ground pepper
½   pound bacon, diced
4   medium potatoes, cut into 1-inch cubes (about
    3 cups)
6   large carrots, peeled, cut into 1-inch pieces (about
    3 cups)
2   large yellow onions, peeled, sliced into 1-inch
    wedges (about 2 cups)
4   to 6 cloves garlic, chopped
2   cups beef stock
1   bay leaf
1   teaspoon dried thyme

Preheat the oven to 325°.
1. Place the beef cubes in a bowl. Sprinkle with flour, salt, and pepper. Toss to coat.
2. Heat a Dutch oven (or large deep pan) over medium high heat. Add the diced bacon. Cook until crisp.
3. Remove the bacon from the pan with a slotted spoon. Drain on paper towels.
4. Cook the beef cubes in the bacon drippings until brown on all sides. Remove the beef from the pan and place in a bowl.
5. Add the potatoes, carrots, onions, and garlic to the pan and cook for 3 to 5 minutes or until the vegetables just begin to brown.
6. Add the beef cubes and bacon back to the pan.
7. Pour the beef stock into the pan. Add enough water to cover the meat and vegetables.
8. Add the bay leaf and dried thyme to the pan.
9. Cover the pan and place it in the oven. Cook for

SIMPLE SUBSTITUTION:
You can add up to 1 cup of red wine (in place of some of the water used to cover the meat) to add extra flavor to the finished dish.

1½ hours or until the meat is tender. Remove the cover and cook for 30 minutes more.

Serves 6 to 8
Preparation time about 45 minutes plus simmering

Quick Biscuits

While the stew is stewing, bake a batch of these biscuits to go with it.

1¾	cups all-purpose flour
½	teaspoon salt
3	teaspoons baking powder
6	tablespoons cold vegetable shortening, cut into pieces
1	cup milk

1. In the bowl of a food processor place the flour, salt, baking powder, and shortening. Pulse to combine.
2. Add the milk to form a dough.
3. Drop by tablespoons onto a baking sheet.
4. Bake for 12 to 15 minutes until golden brown.

Makes about 2 dozen

Braised Lamb Shanks with Gramalata Garnish

The meat around the bone on the lamb shank becomes tender and juicy as it slow cooks in the liquids. The gramalata is a traditional garnish made from fresh chopped parsley, minced garlic, and a hint of citrus zest. Prepare this wonderfully aromatic dish in advance and let it simmer until you are ready to serve.

4	12- to 14-ounce lamb shanks
	Salt and freshly ground pepper
1	tablespoon olive oil
2	medium onions, diced (about 1 cup)
3	large carrots, diced (about 1½ cup)
6	to 8 cloves garlic, minced (about 3 to 4 tablespoons)
½	750-millimeter bottle red wine
1	28-ounce can tomatoes in purée
1	10¾-ounce can beef stock
1	10¾-ounce can chicken stock
3	teaspoons chopped fresh rosemary
2	teaspoons chopped fresh thyme
	Grated zest of 1 medium orange (about 2 tablespoons)
	Zest of 1 medium lemon (about 1 tablespoon)
	Zest of 1 medium orange (about 2 tablespoons)
2	cloves garlic, minced (about 1 tablespoon)
⅓	cup chopped fresh parsley

1. Season the lamb shanks with salt and freshly ground pepper.
2. In a large pot heat the oil over a medium high heat.
3. Brown the lamb shanks on all sides and transfer them to a bowl.
4. Cook the onions, carrots, and garlic in the same pot until soft, about 10 minutes.
5. Pour in the wine, tomatoes, broths, herbs, and orange zest.
6. Place the browned lamb shanks back into the pot, submerging them in the liquid and bring to a boil.

TECHNIQUE:
The cooking method used for this dish is termed braising and can be used when slow cooking a particular cut of meat is desired. The meat is first browned in the pot and then covered with liquid in which it cooks over low heat for a long period of time.

SETTING THE SCENE:
Serve the lamb shanks with yellow rice and spoon the rich sauce over all. Sprinkle the gramalata over the entire plate.

Share your favorite comfort food recipe at www.jorj.com.

7. Reduce the heat, cover, and simmer about 2 hours until the meat is cooked.

8. Uncover the pot and continue to simmer for at least 30 minutes or until the liquid is reduced to a sauce consistency.

9. In a small bowl mix together the lemon zest, orange zest, garlic, and parsley. Garnish the lamb with the gramalata.

Serves 4
Preparation time about 30 minutes plus 2½ hours to simmer

Baked Stuffed Peppers with Lentils

This versatile dish serves as an upscale starter when teamed with a lightly dressed salad or a complete meal as is. The addition of ground beef or sausage turns the stuffed pepper into updated comfort food.

6	ounces dried lentils (about 1½ cups)
2	tablespoons olive oil
1	large onion, diced
2	large carrots, diced
2	ribs celery, diced
2	large cloves garlic, minced
1	teaspoon dried oregano
½	teaspoon red pepper flakes
	Salt and freshly ground pepper
½	cup grated Parmesan cheese
4	large bell peppers
½	cup shredded mozzarella cheese

Preheat the oven to 350°.

1. In a stock pot cover the lentils in 3 cups of water. Bring to a boil, reduce the heat, and simmer until tender, about 15 to 20 minutes.
2. In a skillet heat the olive oil over medium high heat.
3. Sauté the onions, carrots, and celery in the olive oil.
4. Add the garlic and cook for several minutes more.
5. Add the lentils to the pan. Stir in the oregano and red pepper flakes. Season with salt and pepper. Turn off the heat and allow the mixture to cool slightly.
6. Stir in the Parmesan cheese.
7. Cut the tops from the peppers. Remove the seeds.
8. Stuff each pepper with lentil mixture.
9. Sprinkle mozzarella cheese on top of each pepper. Drizzle with additional olive oil.
10. Bake for 20 to 30 minutes, until the cheese melts and the peppers begin to brown.

Serves 4

Preparation time about 30 minutes plus baking

HELPFUL HINT:
Add 1 pound of cooked and crumbled sausage or ground beef to the lentil mixture before stuffing to create a filling midweek meal.

SETTING THE SCENE:
For an upscale appetizer, cool the cooked peppers slightly. Cut each one in half. In a large bowl combine 4 cups of mixed salad greens, 2 sliced medium tomatoes, and 1 sliced cucumber. Drizzle with your favorite vinaigrette. Place a handful of dressed salad on a plate. Place a pepper half on top of the greens. Drizzle with olive oil and add a sprinkle of freshly ground pepper.

Fresh from the Sea

PREPARING SEAFOOD

Fresh fish is much more abundant today than in years past thanks to farms that harvest and overnight shipping techniques that speed delivery. Many grocery stores are individualizing the fish section into smaller kiosks within the larger butcher department. Purchase fresh fish from a busy market. That way you will know that the fish is being turned over on a regular basis and not held until a customer happens to stroll into the store.

Fresh fish is firm to the touch and odorless. A whole fish has reddish gills that are not sticky. The eyes of the fish are clear and the scales shiny. A good fish monger is able to skin the fish and remove most of the bones. The few stray bones can be removed during the preparation of the dish. Feel free to ask questions about the type of fish displayed in the case. Regionally unique types of fish are being flown to stores all over the country. You may not have heard of a certain variety of fish, but that does not mean you should not try it.

The recipes in this chapter are designed to allow for substitution of various fish. Yellow tail snapper is a delicate fish that has firm flesh and is low in fat. Types of snapper vary widely and lend themselves to many different preparations. Sea bass is a white-fleshed fish that is firm and moist with moderate fat. If it is unavailable, you may easily substitute with grouper. Tuna is a member of the mackerel family and is most often cut into steaks. The flesh is much denser and oilier than most fish and is easily compared to meat. The flesh of a salmon is firm, compact and moderate to high in fat. It is the fat content that makes this fish so flavorful and why it is usually very simply prepared.

It is important to remember the basic difference between fish and poultry or meat. The distinction is that fish is basically tender before you cook it. Therefore you do not need to use a cooking process that is designed to tenderize or break down the food.

Poaching is a common manner of cooking fish and can be used on fillets, steaks, or whole fish. The fish is cooked in liquid that can be as basic as water or as complicated as fish stock. Fresh herbs, vegetables, and spices are tossed in to complete the tapestry of flavors. The fish is then submerged in the liquid that is just brought to the boiling point. Too quick a boil may damage a delicate fish. Simmering the fish allows the aroma and flavors of the liquid to infuse the fish. Champagne, white wine, chicken stock, and vegetable stock are readily available poaching liquids. The resulting fish is moist and flavorful. The remaining liquid is then ready to become a savory sauce.

The perfectly sautéed fillet begins with a nonstick pan. First, warm the pan over medium high heat. Add olive oil or butter to the pan and swirl it around until it is hot. Place the fillet, presentation side down, into the pan. Never crowd several pieces into a too small skillet. Allow 3 to 4 minutes before turning. Use a fish spatula to flip the fillet. This long-handled tool has a rectangular shape that is slightly curved. It will easily hold the fillet and reduce the chance of splintering. The fish is done when the flesh springs back after you gently press it with your finger.

Most other cooking techniques work well with fish. Bear in mind that the fish will cook faster than meat or poultry. The moment the flesh turns opaque and the fish flakes easily it is done. In all cases, personal preference determines the amount of cooking. For example, many people choose tuna that is prepared more rare than well cooked. Discriminating palates may favor salmon that is rare on the inside and flaky on the outside. A traditional rule for cooking fish is to cook it for 8 minutes for every inch of thickness.

Remove the fear of overcooking by remembering that as with other food, fish will continue cooking briefly after it is removed from the pan. It will retain the heat from whichever process you use. Therefore, it is best to slightly undercook fish. Remove it from the pan to a serving dish and cover with aluminum foil while you proceed with a terrific sauce.

Find more information about the recipes in the Fresh From the Sea chapter at www.jorj.com.

Cracked Stone Crab Claws with Dilled Mustard Sauce

Fresh stone crabs offered in the fall and winter months are a true treat. When you purchase them fresh from your fish monger or grocer, ask him to crack them for you. This eliminates the need for crackers at home and the occasional sharp piece of shell.

2   tablespoons mayonnaise
1   tablespoon sour cream
1   teaspoon mustard
1   teaspoon tarragon vinegar
1   tablespoon chopped fresh dill sprigs
     Freshly ground pepper

2   to 4 fresh, cooked stone crab claws

     Lemon wedge
     Lime wedge

1. Stir together the mayonnaise, sour cream, mustard, vinegar and chopped fresh dill in a small bowl.
2. Season with freshly ground pepper.

Serves 2 to 4
Preparation time about 10 minutes

SETTING THE SCENE:
Serve the cracked stone crab claws by placing a layer of chopped ice in a shallow bowl. Place a smaller bowl filled with mustard sauce in the center of the larger bowl. Place the stone crab pieces in a circle on top of the ice. Garnish with wedges of lemon and lime and sprigs of fresh dill.

Spicy Baked Shrimp

This is an incredibly easy dish that you can serve as an appetizer or as a simple supper over Fried Spiced Rice.

| 1 | **pound medium shrimp, peeled and deveined** |

½	**cup olive oil**
2	**cloves garlic, minced (about 1 tablespoon)**
2	**tablespoons chopped fresh cilantro**
2	**tablespoons ground chili powder**
1	**tablespoon soy sauce**
1	**tablespoon honey**
	Juice of 1 lemon (about 2 tablespoons)
¼	**teaspoon red pepper flakes**
	Salt and freshly ground pepper

Preheat the oven to 450°

1. Place the shrimp in a shallow baking dish that has been sprayed with vegetable oil spray.
2. In a small bowl mix together the olive oil, minced garlic, cilantro, ground chili powder, soy sauce, honey, lemon juice and red pepper flakes.
3. Pour the mixture over the shrimp. Season with salt and pepper.
4. Bake for 10 minutes.

Serves 4

Preparation time about 15 minutes

SETTING THE SCENE:
Serve the shrimp on toasts or bruschetta as a first course. Sprinkle with additional cilantro.

Steamed Dolphin and Veggie Packages

All of the preparation for this easy dish is in advance of the meal. The actual cooking occurs on an outside grill or in the oven in case of inclement weather.

4	6-ounce dolphin fillets
	Salt and freshly ground pepper

1	stalk broccoli, cut into florets (1 cup)
⅓	head cauliflower, cut into florets (1 cup)
1	cup snow peas
1	cup sliced mushrooms
1	medium tomato, cut into wedges
1	Vidalia onion, sliced (1 cup)

1	medium lemon
1	tablespoon olive oil
1	tablespoon fresh dill
1	tablespoon fresh cilantro
½	teaspoon red pepper flakes

1. Season each fillet with salt and pepper and place on a square of aluminum foil.
2. Divide the broccoli, cauliflower, snow peas, mushrooms, tomato, and onion into 4 parts.
3. Place the vegetables on top of the fish filets.
4. Season each serving with lemon, drizzled olive oil, fresh dill, cilantro and a sprinkle of red pepper flakes.
5. Seal the packet by joining the edges of the foil square and rolling together.
6. Grill the packages on top of an outside grill for 15 to 20 minutes or until the fish is opaque and the vegetables are crisp tender.

Serves 4
Preparation time about 30 minutes

HELPFUL HINT:
In place of grilling, you may cook the fish packets by placing them on a cookie sheet. Bake at 350° for 15 to 20 minutes or until the fish is opaque and the vegetables are crisp tender.

SIMPLE SUBSTITUTION:
The veggies are easily substituted with any that are readily available. Zucchini, yellow peppers, and carrots also work well in this recipe. In place of fresh herbs, olive oil, and lemon juice, you may drizzle each serving with bottled salad dressing for an even quicker preparation!

SETTING THE SCENE:
Open each packet and transfer the fish and veggies to a dinner plate.

Garlicky Soft Shell Crabs

Soft shell crab is a delicacy that is available only a few times a year when the warm waters coax the crabs to shed their hard shell. Buy them fresh (still waving) from the fishmonger and ask him to clean them for an absolutely decadent seafood treat.

2	**very fresh soft shell crabs**
	Juice of 1 medium lemon (about 2 tablespoons)
	Salt and freshly ground pepper
½	**cup flour for dredging**
6	**tablespoons butter**
4	**large cloves garlic, minced**
3	**to 4 green onions, sliced**

1. Season the crabs with lemon juice, salt, and pepper.
2. Dip the crab in flour on both sides. Shake off the excess.
3. Heat a medium size skillet over high heat. Reduce heat to medium high.
4. Melt the butter in the pan.
5. Add the garlic and cook for 1 minute. Be very careful not to burn the garlic.
6. Place the crabs in the hot butter. Cook for 4 to 6 minutes. Turn and cook for 4 to 6 minutes more. The crabs will be golden brown and crispy.
7. Toss the green onion into the pan and cook for 1 minute more.

Serves 2 as a first course
Preparation time about 10 minutes

SETTING THE SCENE:
Serve each crab on a small plate. Pour the garlic butter sauce over the top. Garnish with fresh lemon wedges.

Fresh Mussels Steamed In Garlic Tomato Broth

Shellfish lovers appreciate the quick preparation of this dish. The terrific thing is that it presents like you were cooking all day.

1	tablespoon olive oil
1	large shallot, chopped (about 1 tablespoon)
3	to 4 green onions, sliced (about ½ cup)
2	large cloves garlic, sliced (about 1 tablespoon)
½	cup dry white wine
4	medium plum tomatoes, chopped (about 1 cup)
½	cup chopped fresh parsley
1	medium lemon, juiced
½	cup chicken broth
	Salt and freshly ground pepper
2	pounds fresh (or fresh-frozen) mussels

1. In a deep skillet heat the olive oil over medium high heat.
2. Cook the shallots until they begin to soften, about 3 minutes.
3. Add the green onion and sliced garlic and cook until soft, about 3 to 5 minutes more.
4. Add the white wine to the pan and cook until the liquid disappears, about 5 minutes.
5. Add the chopped tomatoes, parsley, lemon juice, and chicken broth to the pan. Stir and season with salt and freshly ground pepper.
6. Place the mussels in the pan and cover with a lid. Cook until the mussels open, about 5 minutes.

Serves 2 to 4
Preparation time about 15 minutes

TECHNIQUE:
Chop the vegetables in advance for simple preparation.

HELPFUL HINT:
Choose only mussels with unopened shells. Discard any mussels that have opened.

SETTING THE SCENE:
Serve the mussels in a bowl, spooning the sauce over top. A few slices of fresh crusty bread are a perfect accompaniment for dipping in the flavorful broth.

Poached Yellowtail Snapper with Chopped Tomato and Parsley

This recipe will work with most fresh fish fillets. I suggest a snapper or sole for the first attempt because of the sturdy nature and delicate flavor of the fish.

2   4- to 6-ounce) yellowtail snapper fillets
1   to 1½ cups chicken stock
1   medium tomato, chopped (about 1 cup)
½   cup parsley, chopped
      Juice of ½ medium lemon (about 1 tablespoon)
1   tablespoon butter
      Salt and freshly ground pepper

1. Poach the fish fillets in the chicken stock for several minutes until the fish is opaque in color and firm to the touch.
2. Transfer the fish to a warm platter while the sauce is prepared.
3. Reduce the stock for several minutes over high heat.
4. Turn the temperature down to medium high. Add the chopped tomato, parsley, and lemon juice. Continue reducing until there is approximately ½ cup of liquid remaining.
5. Whisk in the butter over low heat, being careful not to break the sauce by boiling.
6. Season with salt and freshly ground pepper.

Serves 2
Preparation time about 20 minutes

HELPFUL HINT:
Place the chicken stock in a shallow pan. Place the fillets on a sheet of aluminum foil. Place the foil into the pan so that the ends of the foil hang over the sides of the pan. Cook the fish in simmering liquid. You do not want it to vigorously boil. After the fish has cooked, remove the foil with the fillets still in place, leaving the stock in the pan.

TECHNIQUE:
To chop the tomato for use in this sauce begin by removing the pulp of the tomato from the core and seeds. Trim the pulp from the top to the bottom in a curving motion (as you would cut an apple from it's core). Discard the core and seeds. Cut the pulp into thin strips and then dice into small pieces.

SETTING THE SCENE:
Divide the sauce among two dishes. Place one fillet on top of each dish. Serve with a green vegetable and roasted potatoes.

Fresh Tilapia Fillets with Sautéed Bananas

Tilapia is readily found in your local market. If you have trouble, don't worry, any seasonal fish will do. Experiment with your favorite for this dish! Rest assured that even a frozen fish fillet will be the star of the dish when served with this tropical sauce.

2	6-ounce tilapia fillets
	Salt and freshly ground pepper
½	cup all-purpose flour
1	egg, beaten with 2 tablespoons water
2	tablespoons olive oil
2	tablespoons butter (¼ stick)
4	tablespoons butter (½ stick)
2	tablespoons prepared chutney
½	cup white wine
½	large banana, sliced (½ cup)

1. Season the fish fillets with salt and freshly ground pepper.
2. Dip each one into the flour and then into the egg wash.
3. In a sauté pan melt the olive oil and butter over medium high heat.
4. Sauté the fillets until done (about 3 minutes per side for ½-inch fillets).
5. Transfer the fillets to a serving platter and keep warm while you prepare the sauce.
6. Melt the butter over medium heat in the same sauté pan.
7. Add the chutney and stir until well blended.
8. Add the white wine and reduce slightly.
9. Toss in the sliced bananas and warm through in the sauce.

Serves 2
Preparation time about 15 minutes

SETTING THE SCENE:
To serve, pour the sauce over the warm fish fillets and serve immediately.

Share your favorite fish recipe at www.jorj.com.

Seared Tuna in Oriental Marinade

This tuna is so flavorful that you will serve it again and again.

4	**6 ounces tuna steaks, about ½-inch thick**
	Ground pepper
½	**cup rice wine vinegar**
4	**tablespoons soy sauce**
2	**tablespoons sugar**
1	**tablespoon sesame oil**
1	**clove garlic, minced**
2	**tablespoons chopped green onions including tops**
1	**teaspoon grated fresh ginger**
4	**tablespoons sesame seeds**

1. Season the tuna steaks with freshly ground pepper.
2. In a small bowl whisk together the vinegar, soy sauce, sugar, sesame oil, garlic, green onions and ginger.
3. Place the steaks in a shallow dish and pour the marinade over all. Cover with plastic wrap, and chill for at least 30 minutes.
4. Warm the grill pan over high heat, and spray with a vegetable oil spray.
5. Remove the tuna from the marinade, reserving the mixture to make a sauce.
6. Sprinkle the sesame seeds on both sides of the tuna.
7. Lay the steaks onto the grill pan and sear, being careful not to burn the sesame seeds.
8. Sear the tuna, turning once, for about 2 to 4 minutes per side.
9. Remove the steaks to a platter and keep warm in an oven set on low heat or in a warming drawer.
10. Reduce the heat to medium. Pour the reserved marinade into the pan. Cook for several minutes until the marinade reduces to a syrupy sauce.

Serves 4

Preparation time about 20 minutes plus marinating

HELPFUL HINTS:
1. A grill pan enables you to sear the food over high heat, retaining the natural juices of the food. The raised portion of the pan leaves distinctive brown lines on both sides of the steak. If you do not own a grill pan, you can use a skillet.

2. The recipe calls for the tuna to be cooked rare or medium rare. If this is not your preference, simply add more cooking time on each side.

SIMPLE SUBSTITUTION:
You can easily substitute chicken breasts or a flank steak for the tuna steaks as you wish.

SETTING THE SCENE:
Slice the tuna steaks into strips and drizzle the sauce on top.

Sole with Parsley, Butter, and Caper Sauce

This is a French inspired dish. It becomes special if served with well carved, bite size vegetables that have been roasted and then finished in the sauce.

4	4- to 6-ounce fresh sole fillets
	Salt and freshly ground pepper
½	cup all-purpose flour
1	egg, mixed with 2 tablespoons water
½	cup butter (1 stick)
	Juice of 1 medium lemon (about 2 tablespoons)
¼	cup capers, drained
⅓	cup chopped fresh parsley

1. Season the fish with salt and freshly ground pepper.
2. Dredge each fillet first into the flour, second into the egg wash and finally into the flour again. Shake off the excess.
3. In a sauté pan heat the butter until it is very hot and just beginning to brown.
4. Cook the fillets turning once. (This will take only a few minutes per side.)
5. Squeeze the juice of one whole lemon over both sides of the fillets as they are cooking.
6. Remove the fillets to a platter and keep warm.
7. Add the capers and parsley to the browned butter remaining in the pan. Stir just to warm through.
9. Pour the sauce over the sole and serve.

Serves 2 to 4
Preparation time about 15 minutes

HELPFUL HINT:
To keep a dish warm while preparing the sauce you can do several things. The best way is to use a warming drawer. However a pre-warmed platter works just as well. Warm the platter in the oven on low heat (200°) for several minutes. Place the fish on the platter and cover with foil. Place the platter back into the oven and turn off the heat.

Roasted Sea Bass with Red Wine Sauce

Sea bass is a tasty fish, often prepared with a sauce that is more hardy than delicate. It is a great fish to serve for a dinner party as it holds well and is not easily overcooked.

4	6-ounce sea bass steaks
	Salt and freshly ground pepper
1	7-ounce jar sun-dried tomatoes in oil
2	large leeks including some green parts, sliced into rings (about 2 cups)
1	cup red wine
½	cup green Spanish olives
2	tablespoons capers
2	tablespoons chopped fresh tarragon
2	tablespoons butter (½ stick)

Preheat the oven to 375°.

1. Season the sea bass with salt and pepper.
2. Heat a large skillet over medium high heat. Place the sun-dried tomatoes and the oil that they are packed in into the pan.
3. Add the leek slices to the pan and cook until soft and just beginning to brown.
4. Stir in the wine and add the olives, capers, and tarragon.
5. Place the sea bass steaks in the pan with the sauce basting each piece.
6. Place the entire skillet into the oven.
7. Bake the fish for 10 to 15 minutes until firm to the touch.
8. Remove the skillet from the oven.
9. Transfer the steaks from the skillet onto a serving platter. Add the butter to the hot vegetables stirring quickly to thicken the sauce.

Serves 4
Preparation time about 35 minutes

HELPFUL HINT:
Remember to use a potholder when removing the skillet from the oven—the handle will be hot!

SETTING THE SCENE:
Spoon the sauce over the sea bass. Garnish with additional fresh tarragon.

Roasted Red Snapper with Braised Leeks

The textures are terrific in this dish. The skin of the fish is crisp and teams nicely with the brothy sauce of leeks and tomatoes.

2	tablespoons olive oil
4	8-ounce fillets of Florida snapper
	Salt and freshly ground pepper

1	tablespoon butter
4	large leeks, washed, trimmed and split
1	14½-ounce can diced tomatoes
1	shallot, minced
2	cloves garlic, minced (about 1 tablespoon)
2	tablespoons capers
1	cup chicken stock
2	tablespoons fresh basil

Preheat the oven to 400°

1. In a skillet heat the olive oil over high heat.
2. Season the fish with salt and pepper. Place the fillets skin side down in the skillet. Cook until the skin is golden. Turn the fillets over and place the pan into the oven. Cook for 5 minutes more.
3. In a skillet heat the butter over medium high heat.
4. Add the leeks, canned tomatoes, minced shallot, and cloves garlic to the skillet. Cook for 3 minutes.
5. Add the capers, chicken stock, and basil to the skillet. Reduce the heat and simmer for 8 to 10 minutes more until the leeks are soft.

Serves 4
Preparation time about 20 minutes

SETTING THE SCENE:
Carefully remove the pan from the oven. Don't forget to us a pot holder! Place a fillet of fish on each dinner platte. Spoon the braised leeks and sauce on top of the fish.

Roasted Salmon in the Grass with Cucumber Mint Sauce

The salmon is roasted with a selection of dried spices. The heat is balanced with a refreshing cucumber sauce made with fresh yogurt. Sautéed spinach makes the perfect "bedding" for the fish.

4	6-ounce salmon fillets
1	tablespoons olive oil
	Juice of ½ lemon (about 2 tablespoons)
1	clove garlic, minced
1	teaspoon brown sugar
1	teaspoon ground cumin
½	teaspoon ground coriander
½	teaspoon dried thyme
½	teaspoon ground cinnamon
½	teaspoon salt
½	teaspoon ground pepper
1	large cucumber, peeled, seeded and cut into several pieces (about 3 cups)
1	cup plain yogurt
2	tablespoons fresh mint leaves
	Salt and freshly ground pepper
1	tablespoon olive oil
1	pound fresh spinach leaves
	Juice of ½ lemon (about 2 tablespoons)

SETTING THE SCENE:
Lay the sautéed spinach on a platter. Top the spinach with the roasted salmon fillets. Serve the cool yogurt sauce on the side. Garnish with fresh lemon wedges.

Preheat the oven to 400°.

1. Brush the salmon fillets with 1 tablespoon of olive oil. Place them in a shallow baking dish that has been sprayed with vegetable oil spray, skin side down. Squeeze lemon juice over the top.
2. In a small bowl mix together the minced garlic, brown sugar, cumin, coriander, thyme, cinnamon, salt and pepper. Rub the mixture over each fillet.
3. Roast the salmon for 10 to 15 minutes.

4. In the bowl of a food processor combine the cucumber, yogurt, and mint leaves. Pulse to combine. Season with salt and pepper. Pulse.

5. Heat 1 tablespoon of olive oil in a skillet over medium high heat. Quickly cook the spinach leaves in the oil until just softened. Season with lemon juice, salt, and pepper.

Serves 4
Preparation time about 20 minutes

Veronique Sauce for Fish

Served in the best restaurants—this sauce is a snap to make at home.

1	cup chicken stock
¼	cup white wine
1	tablespoon brandy
2	to 3 green onions, finely chopped (about 2 tablespoons)
1	teaspoon cornstarch
2	tablespoons of water
½	cup heavy cream
	Salt and pepper to taste
20	seedless green grapes
2	tablespoons butter, chilled, cut into pieces

1. In a pot combine the chicken stock, wine, brandy, and green onion over medium high heat until reduced to about ½ cup. Strain and return to the pan.

2. Blend the cornstarch with the water. Stir the mixture into the reduced liquid. Cook until bubbly.

3. Stir in the cream. Bring just to boiling. Season with salt and pepper.

4. Add the grapes. Cook for 1 minute. Remove from the heat and swirl in the butter, stirring until melted and combined.

Salmon Livornese

Salmon is a favorite on many menus. It is a very durable fish and is easily broiled, baked, or poached. This recipe combines sautéing the fillet and then baking. The piquancy of the sauce produces the perfect fish entrée.

1	2-pound whole salmon fillet, skin and bones removed
	Salt and freshly ground pepper
	Juice of 1 medium lemon (about 2 to 3 tablespoons)
1	cup seasoned bread crumbs
2	tablespoons olive oil
1	bunch green onions including tops, thinly sliced (about 1 cup)
1	tablespoon olive oil, additional
1½	cups dry white wine
¼	cup capers, rinsed and drained
1	4¼-ounce can sliced black olives (about ⅔ cup)
1	tablespoons canned tomato paste
¼	cup fresh lemon juice
¼	cup fresh dill sprigs, chopped

Preheat oven to 350°.

1. Season the salmon with salt and freshly ground pepper and sprinkle each side with lemon juice.
2. Place the bread crumbs in a shallow baking dish. Coat both sides of the fillet lightly with the crumbs.
3. In a large skillet heat 2 tablespoons olive oil over medium high heat.
4. Sauté the salmon in the oil, turning once, until each side is golden brown. Remove the fillet to a large baking dish.
5. In the same skillet sauté the green onions in 1 tablespoon olive oil.
6. Add the white wine and deglaze the pan by stirring the brown bits from the bottom. Reduce the liquid to about ¾ cup.

HELPFUL HINTS:

1. If the salmon fillet is too large to fit into you pan, you may cut it into halves or thirds and then continue with the recipe.

2. The sauce will thicken as you stir in the tomato paste. You may thin it with water or with more wine.

ABOUT SALMON:

A perfectly cooked salmon fillet is opaque around the outside of the piece and a translucent pink in the center. If you prefer you fish more thoroughly cooked, test for doneness by making sure the cooked fish is firm to the touch and opaque all the way through.

7. Add the capers and black olives, and stir in the tomato paste.
8. Season the sauce with lemon juice and fresh dill.
9. Pour the sauce over the salmon. Bake for 10 to 20 minutes until the salmon is cooked through.

Serves 6 to 8
Preparation time about 45 minutes

Salmon Salad

Use leftover salmon in tomorrow's salmon salad!

1   **cup cooked salmon, flaked**
2   **stalks celery, diced (about 1 cup)**
¼   **cup mayonnaise**
1   **tablespoon chopped fresh garlic chives**
1   **tablespoon chopped fresh parsley**
    Iceburg lettuce
    Olive oil
    Lemon juice
    Freshly ground pepper

1. In a medium bowl combine the salmon, celery, mayonnaise, garlic chives, and parsley. Toss well.
2. In a separate bowl toss together lettuce, olive oil, lemon juice, and freshly ground pepper.
3. Serve the salmon mixture over the dressed lettuce.

Serves 4
Preparation time about 10 minutes

Orange Marinated Grouper with Toasted Almond Sauce

Grouper is a fish that some people shy away from because it may have a stronger flavor than a delicate fish. This dish works well on every fish, but feel free to substitute dolphin, tibia, or even fresh water trout. The sauce is a perfect accent with its blend of fresh orange and almonds.

SETTING THE SCENE:
Spoon the sauce over the fish and serve immediately. Add a roasted vegetable and a tossed salad to complete the meal.

4	**6- to 8-ounce grouper fillets**
	Juice of 2 medium navel oranges (about ⅔ cups)
	Salt and freshly ground pepper
1	**to 2 cloves garlic, minced (about 1 tablespoon)**
½	**cup slivered almonds**
1	**tablespoon snipped fresh dill sprigs**
¼	**cup butter (½ stick), cold, cut into pieces**

1. Preheat the oven to 375°.
2. Place the fillets in a shallow dish. Squeeze the juice of ½ orange over the fish. Season with salt and freshly ground pepper. Marinate for at least 15 minutes.
3. Transfer the fish to a baking dish and cook for 8 to 10 minutes in the oven.
4. Remove the fish to a serving platter and keep warm.
5. Place the baking dish on the stove top.
6. Add the juice from the remaining 1½ oranges to the pan.
7. Cook the garlic in the orange juice over medium high heat.
8. Add the almonds to the pan and cook until the orange juice is reduced and the almonds begin to brown.
9. Toss in the chopped dill.
10. Reduce the heat to low and whisk in the cold butter.

Serves 4
Preparation time about 30 minutes

Outta Hand Orange Roughy with Basil Cream Sauce

The cream sauce for this dish is definitely over the top in rich ingredients, but the texture of this fish stands up to the challenge. This dish is elegant enough for company, yet comes together quickly in just a few minutes.

1	cup all-purpose flour
2	eggs, beaten with 2 tablespoons water
1	cup seasoned bread crumbs
2	tablespoons olive oil
4	4- to 6-ounce orange roughy fillets
¼	medium white onion, finely diced (about ¼ cup)
1	cup white wine
1	cup heavy cream
½	cup finely chopped fresh basil
	Juice of ½ medium lemon (about 1 tablespoon)
	Salt and freshly ground pepper

1. Pour the flour into a shallow bowl. Beat the egg with the water in a second shallow bowl. Pour the bread-crumbs into a third shallow bowl.
2. In a skillet heat the olive oil over medium high heat.
3. Dip each fillet first into the flour. Shake off the excess. Dredge the fillets into the egg mixture, and finally into the bread crumbs.
4. Cook the fish, turning once, until the coating is golden brown, about 4 minutes per side.
5. Transfer the fish to a warm platter while the sauce is prepared.
6. Add the diced onions to the pan and cook for several minutes.
7. Pour the wine into the pan and simmer until most of the liquid evaporates.
8. Add the cream to the pan and simmer until reduced by one third. Add the chopped basil, and lemon juice.
9. Season with salt and freshly ground pepper.

Serves 4
Preparation time about 20 to 30 minutes

INTIMATE DINNER FOR FOUR

Sweet Pea Soup with Mint

Outta Hand Orange Roughy with Basil Cream Sauce

Herb Glazed Roasted Tomatoes

Simple Cinnamon Cake

Salmon Cakes with Sauce Remoulade

Fish cakes used to be a Friday night staple when I was growing up. Thankfully, the dish has evolved into a lighter, more flavorful one filled with fresh ingredients. The secret is to use fish, in this case salmon, that is fresh and delicate. Try to only use enough filler (bread or breadcrumbs) to bind the cakes together. Handle gingerly so that the cake does not become tough.

HELPFUL HINT:
You may keep the salmon cakes warm in a low oven for up to 30 minutes.

Share your favorite seafood cake recipe at www.jorj.com.

1	to 1½ pounds fresh salmon fillet, skin removed, diced
2	tablespoons chopped garlic chives
½	cup medium red bell pepper, diced (about ½ cup)
3	green onions including tops, chopped (about 3 tablespoons)
1	egg, beaten
2	tablespoons chili sauce
2	tablespoons all-purpose flour, plus flour for dipping
4	slices white bread, crusts removed, cubed (or about 2 cups fresh bread crumbs)
⅓	cup milk
	Salt and freshly ground pepper
2	tablespoons olive oil, or more
½	cup mayonnaise
1	teaspoon sweet pickle relish
1	teaspoon capers, drained
1	teaspoon ketchup
1	teaspoon fresh dill weed, chopped
1	teaspoon fresh cilantro, chopped

1. In a large bowl combine the diced salmon, chives, chopped red pepper, green onions, egg, chili sauce, and 2 tablespoons of flour. Mix well, being careful not to over stir.
2. Mix in the fresh cubed bread (or breadcrumbs) and milk. The mixture will be very wet. Season with salt and pepper.

3. Form the mixture into patties. Dip each patty into flour so that it is lightly coated on both sides. Place the patties on a baking sheet and place in the refrigerator to chill for at least 20 minutes.
4. In a skillet heat the oil over medium high heat.
5. Cook the cakes, turning once, until just brown, making sure not to crowd them in the pan, about 3 to minutes per side. Drain well on paper towels.
6. In a small bowl combine the mayonnaise, relish, capers, ketchup, and seasonings and stir thoroughly to make the sauce.

Serves 4
Preparation time 40 minutes

Tartar Sauce

This great sauce is super with all types of fish cakes.

1   **tablespoon capers**
1   **tablespoon pickle relish**
1   **tablespoon chopped fresh parsley**
1   **cup mayonnaise**
1   **teaspoon lemon juice**
     Salt and freshly ground pepper to taste

1. In a food processor combine all of the ingredients. Pulse to combine.
2. Transfer to a serving dish.

Makes 1 cup
Preparation time about 5 minutes

Vegetable Stuffed Whole Trout with Lemon Sauce

This recipe came together during a North Carolina family vacation. Trout fishing is terrific local pastime. Trout farms line the highways and the fish literally jump onto the hook—they are so well trained! If you are unable to visit a trout farm for the freshest trout available, you will find that cleaned whole trout are available fresh frozen in the supermarket.

SETTING THE SCENE:
Drizzle the lemon sauce over the trout. Garnish the platter with fresh rosemary sprigs.

4	8- to 10-ounce whole trout, cleaned
	Salt and freshly ground pepper
1	tablespoon olive oil
1	medium yellow onion, diced (about ½ cup)
1	medium zucchini, diced (about 1 cup)
4	cloves garlic, sliced (about 2 tablespoons)
1	7-ounce jar sun-dried tomato halves in oil, drained, julienned
4	rosemary sprigs
½	cup white wine
	Juice of 3 medium lemons (about ½ cup lemon juice)
2	tablespoons butter
1	bunch green onion, chopped (about 1 cup)

Preheat the oven to 350°

1. Wash the trout and pat dry. Season the inside of the trout with salt and pepper. Place into a shallow baking dish that has been sprayed with vegetable oil spray.
2. In a skillet heat the olive oil over medium high heat.
3. Add the onions and zucchini and cook until soft, about 10 minutes.
4. Add the garlic and cook for 5 minutes more.
5. Add the strips of sun-dried tomatoes and cook until warmed through. Remove the vegetables from the heat.
6. Place 2 to 3 tablespoons of vegetables into the cavity of each trout. Place a whole rosemary sprig on top of the vegetables.

7. Bake the trout for about 30 minutes. The trout is done when the flesh is pink and opaque yet still moist and the vegetables are soft and steaming. Remove the trout to a platter and keep warm.
8. Deglaze the baking dish with the white wine. Heat the dish over medium high heat. Pour in the wine, scraping up all of the brown bits from the bottom. Reduce the wine to ½ cup.
9. Pour the lemon juice into the dish and continue cooking for several minutes.
10. Reduce the heat to low. Add the butter and green onions. Cook until the butter is just melted. Season with salt and freshly ground pepper.

Serves 4
Preparation time about 20 minutes plus baking

Baked Whole Fish

You may choose to stuff the fish or not. This basic recipe will work well for most whole fish.

1   whole fish, butterflied, bones removed, head and tail removed (optional)
Salt and freshly ground pepper to taste
Lemon

Preheat the oven to 500°.
1. Place the fish on a parchment lined baking sheet.
2. Use a sharp knife to score the skin.
3. Season with salt and pepper. Drizzle with lemon juice.
4. Bake the fish for 8 minutes for every 1 inch of thickness.

Bahamian Style Conch Fritters

The original recipe for these fritters produces enough to serve most of the Islanders! I cut it down to a more manageable amount—but it still serves a bunch of your favorite party guests.

2½   pounds conch
2   red bell peppers, finely diced
2   yellow bell peppers, finely diced
1   large Vidalia onion, finely diced
6   ribs celery, finely diced
4   cups all-purpose flour
1   tablespoon baking powder
4   eggs, beaten
1   cup milk
½   to 2 teaspoons hot sauce
      Salt and freshly ground pepper
      Canola oil for frying
      Cocktail sauce

1. Dice the conch into small pieces.
2. In a large mixing bowl combine the conch and diced vegetables.
3. Add the flour and baking powder to the bowl.
4. Add the eggs and milk to the bowl and stir well.
5. Season the batter with as much hot sauce as you like and season with salt and pepper. Set aside.
6. In a large pot heat the oil over high heat.
7. Drop rounded tablespoons of batter into the pot. The fritters will drop to the bottom of the pan, and then float to the top as they begin to cook. Do not crowd the pan.
8. Remove the fritters after several minutes and drain on paper towels.

Serves a crowd
Preparation time about 30 minutes

SETTING THE SCENE:
Serve the fritters in a napkin lined basket with spicy cocktail sauce.

The "In" Bread and Breakfast

BAKING BREADS AND BRUNCH FOOD

You can't beat the aroma of fresh baking bread or the ooey gooeyness of hot-from-the-oven glazed cinnamon buns. How about the crumble of streusel muffin topping or the combination of banana and peanut butter in a quick bread? These smells and flavors and textures and goodies are all available at the quaintest rural inns. Let's not wait for the next vacation to enjoy these particular treats. With just a tiny bit of inspiration, you can turn your home into one of the best bed and breakfast inns around.

Baking bread used to be an all day, every week occurrence. Today, technology advances the process. In the blink of the flashing light on your trusty bread machine a piping hot loaf of fresh bread springs from the pan to add just the right touch to a midweek meal. Everyone needs a bread machine. It takes all of the guesswork out of bread baking. In the morning dump all of the ingredients into the bread pan, set the dial, and go on to work, school, or play. A few hours later out pops a delicious, warm, fragrant loaf. The dough cycle allows for error free bread dough that can then be used in all standard recipes. The bread machine encourages unobstructed experimentation. Bread basics are fairly simple, and the extra ingredients can be personalized to the likes and dislikes of your family and friends.

Quick breads and muffins are as diverse as the ingredients in your pantry. Make a batch and sneak an extra piece into tomorrow's lunchbox for an exceptional treat.

Brunch is a great meal that is often overlooked in our jam-packed lifestyle. We dart through the kitchen, grabbing a snack for breakfast, in order to get our engines running. We use lunch as an opportunity to conduct business meetings or we skip it altogether to run errands. Brunch is the occasion that combines both meals at a much more leisurely pace with a huge array of delicious food options.

Successful brunch for a crowd often incorporates dishes that are made in advance and easily served on a buffet table. Honeyed ham, baked egg casserole, thick French toast, and warm scones are all examples of prepared-in-advance dishes that are usually found in a traditional brunch menu. But for a laid-back Sunday brunch, simplicity is the mode. Forget the advance planning. There are no hard and fast rules to cooking at home. Your perfect Sunday brunch can be a spur of the moment inspiration. Better yet, your perfect brunch can be served at midnight on Saturday for just the two of you. After all, at your inn it's all about a personalized Bread and Breakfast!

Find more information about the recipes in The "In" Bread and Breakfast chapter at www.jorj.com.

Ricotta Bread

This bread is a great basic, rich, white bread that is best served fresh and warm. If there is any left over the next day, use it to make your favorite French toast or home-made croutons.

For inspiration, check out how Ricotta Bread pumps up lunchtime in the Peppered Steak Super Sandwich recipe on page 82.

6	tablespoons half and half
1	15-ounce container ricotta cheese
2	tablespoons butter
1	whole egg, beaten
¼	cup sugar
1	teaspoon salt
3	cups bread flour
2½	teaspoons yeast

1. Place all of the ingredients into the bread machine except the yeast.
2. Pour the yeast into the yeast compartment (or follow the specific directions for your bread machine).
3. Bake the bread on the basic, non-rapid setting for best results.

Makes 1 large loaf
Preparation time 10 minutes plus setting for bread machine

Herb and Cheese Bread

This is a really great, dense, and flavorful bread. I usually make it to serve with left-overs. You may easily substitute with any fresh herbs that you have on hand. Swiss or Fontina cheese in place of Cheddar also makes a nice alternative.

To share your favorite herb or cheese bread recipe visit www.jorj.com.

1⅓	cups water
2	tablespoons butter, cut into pieces
⅔	cup grated sharp Cheddar cheese
½	teaspoon salt
3	tablespoons honey
¼	cup grated Parmesan cheese
1	teaspoon chopped fresh dill sprigs
1	teaspoon chopped fresh basil
1	teaspoon finely diced fresh jalapeño peppers
1	cup whole wheat flour
3	cups bread flour
1	package yeast (2½ teaspoons)

1. Place all of the ingredients into the bread machine except the yeast.
2. Pour the yeast into the yeast compartment (or follow the specific directions for your bread machine).
3. Bake the bread on the basic non-rapid setting for best results.

Makes 1 loaf
Preparation time 10 minutes plus setting for bread machine

Whole Wheat Baguettes

The original recipe for whole wheat rolls came with instructions for kneading, rising, and baking in the oven. The bread machine has shortened the time considerably, making this bread a more regular addition to the weekly menu.

1	cup water
½	cup milk
2	tablespoons butter, cut into small pieces
2	tablespoons honey
1	teaspoon salt
2	cups bread flour
1½	cups whole wheat flour
1	package yeast (2½ teaspoons)
1	egg, beaten
1	tablespoon water

Preheat the oven to 450°.

1. Place the water, milk, butter pieces, honey, salt, bread flour, and whole wheat flour into the bread machine.
2. Pour the yeast in the yeast compartment (or follow the specific directions for your bread machine).
3. Set the machine on the dough setting and continue until it is completed.
4. Turn out the dough on a lightly floured surface and divide into thirds. Let the dough rest for 10 minutes.
5. Roll each third into a rectangle about 10 x 4 inches long and about ¼-inch thick using a rolling pin.
6. Use your fingers to roll the dough into a long tube. Tuck the ends underneath. Repeat with the remaining dough.
7. Place the dough seam side down on a baking sheet that has been lightly sprayed with vegetable oil cooking spray.
8. Mix the beaten egg with water. Brush the top of each roll with the mixture.

SETTING THE SCENE:
For a truly "Elvis" experience, slice the warm rolls in half. Slather peanut butter on both halves. Top each half with banana slices. Serve the open face sandwich and listen for all of the hoots and hollers.

9. Cover the dough with a dry towel (or with plastic wrap that has been sprayed with vegetable oil spray) and let rise for about 45 minutes.
10. Make 3 diagonal cuts across each roll with a sharp knife (to form a baguette shape).
11. Bake for 10 to 15 minutes, until golden brown.

Makes 12 large rolls
Preparation time 10 minutes plus setting for bread machine and baking

Flavored Butters

Flavored butters are easy to make and elegant on a brunch or dinner table. A tablespoon of chilled herb butter is a knockout on sizzling steak. Create your own home favorites.

HERB BUTTER
Mix ½ cup of softened butter with 2 tablespoons of fresh chopped herbs.

HONEY BUTTER
Mix ½ cup of softened butter with 2 tablespoons of honey.

RASPBERRY BUTTER
Mix ½ cup of softened butter with 2 tablespoons of raspberry jam.

Serve chilled or at room temperature.

Focaccia Bread

Focaccia bread is a staple on the Italian table. Serve it as an accompaniment to pasta and a tossed salad. A loaf or two completes an antipasti display.

¾	**cup water**
¼	**cup dry white wine**
3	**tablespoons olive oil**
½	**cup canola oil**
½	**teaspoon salt**
1	**teaspoon chopped fresh rosemary**
1	**tablespoon sugar**
4	**cups bread flour**
2	**teaspoons yeast**
½	**7-ounce jar sun-dried tomato halves in oil, chopped**
1	**clove garlic, minced (about 1 teaspoon)**
1	**tablespoon chopped fresh rosemary**
1	**teaspoons coarse salt**
	Black olives, sliced
	Olive oil

1. Place the water, white wine, olive oil, canola oil, salt, rosemary, sugar, and flour in the pan of a bread machine.
2. Pour the yeast into the yeast compartment (or follow the specific directions for your bread machine).
3. Complete the process for the dough setting.
4. Remove the dough from the machine and press it onto a baking sheet that has been lightly sprayed with vegetable oil cooking spray.
5. Cover and let rise for 30 minutes.
6. Preheat the oven to 375°. Spread the chopped tomatoes over the dough. Sprinkle with minced garlic, fresh rosemary, coarse salt, and black olives.
7. Drizzle with olive oil.
8. Bake for 20 to 30 minutes or until golden brown.

Yield 1 loaf
Preparation time about 20 minutes plus setting for bread machine

SIMPLE SUBSTITUTION: Vary the toppings on the focaccia just as you would on a pizza.

Some suggestions:

- Sliced olives and rosemary
- Gorgonzola cheese and thinly sliced white onion
- Prosciutto and plum tomatoes
- Vine-ripened tomatoes and anchovies

Hot Chocolate Rolls

What a treat—the marriage of warm, fresh baked bread and melting chocolate. Serve these fun rolls for a yummy snack or on a breakfast buffet.

⅓	cup sugar
¼	cup unsweetened cocoa powder
1	teaspoon salt
1	cup brewed coffee
1	egg
1	tablespoon butter, cut into pieces
3	cups bread flour
2½	teaspoons yeast

½	cup white chocolate chips

1. Place the sugar, cocoa powder, salt, coffee, egg, butter, and flour into the bread machine. Pour the yeast into the yeast compartment or follow the specific directions for your bread machine.

Preheat the oven to 400°.

2. After the dough cycle is complete, remove the dough to a lightly floured surface. Let the dough rest, covered with a clean towel for 10 minutes.
3. Use your fingers to stretch out the dough to rectangle about 10 x 8 inches.
4. Sprinkle the white chocolate chips over the dough.
5. Fold the dough over and knead for several minutes.
6. Divide the dough into 10 to 12 pieces. Roll each one into a ball.
7. Place each ball onto a baking sheet that has been sprayed with vegetable cooking spray.
8. Cover the rolls with a towel and allow to rise for 30 to 45 minutes.
9. Bake the rolls for 15 to 20 minutes in the center of the oven.

Makes 10 to 12 rolls

Preparation time about 15 minutes plus time for rising and baking

SIMPLE SUBSTITUTION:
This is such a fun recipe and it lends itself to every imaginable addition. For white chocolate chips substitute semisweet or peanut butter chips. You can glaze the rolls with vanilla glaze or sprinkle with confectioners' sugar. Chopped nuts of all kinds can be incorporated into the dough. Have fun with all the combinations that you can create.

Best Cinnamon Rolls

There is nothing better than the smell of fresh baking bread—unless of course that bread is surrounded by melting cinnamon and brown sugar and begging to be glazed with a pure vanilla frosting. The perfect early morning treat, made easy with the help of the trusty bread machine and a little adapting of a family recipe.

1	cup milk
6	tablespoons unsalted butter, chilled, cut into small pieces
3	eggs
⅓	cup granulated sugar
½	teaspoon salt
4½	cups all-purpose flour
2½	teaspoons yeast
1	cup firmly packed brown sugar
⅓	cup granulated sugar
¼	cup all-purpose flour
1	tablespoon ground cinnamon
½	teaspoon nutmeg
½	cup unsalted butter (1 stick), chilled, cut into small pieces
1	tablespoon half and half
1¼	cups confectioners' sugar
1	teaspoon light corn syrup
1	teaspoon vanilla extract
1	to 2 tablespoons half and half

Preheat the oven to 375°.

1. Place the milk, 6 tablespoons of butter pieces, 3 eggs, ⅓ cup of granulated sugar, salt, and 4½ cups of flour into the bread machine. Pour the yeast into the yeast compartment or follow the specific directions for your bread machine.

SETTING THE SCENE:
Serve these rolls for a great Sunday morning treat. Prepare them the day before and refrigerate. In the morning, bake and glaze! These should be renamed Magic Rolls—they disappear before your very eyes.

2. After the dough cycle is complete, remove the dough to a lightly floured surface. Roll out the dough to a 10 x 14-inch rectangle.

3. Place the brown sugar, ⅓ cup of granulated sugar, ¼ cup of flour, cinnamon, and nutmeg in the bowl of a food processor. Pulse to combine. Add the chilled butter pieces and pulse briefly until the mixture resembles course crumbs.

4. Spread the filling over the dough. Roll up jelly roll style starting at the narrow end. Pinch the open ends underneath the roll.

5. Slice the roll into 1-inch pieces. Arrange the slices (cut side up) into a 13 x 9 x 2-inch baking dish that has been sprayed with vegetable oil spray. Cover the dish with plastic wrap and allow to rise for at least 30 minutes or overnight in the refrigerator.

6. Brush the rolls with half and half. Bake for 25 to 30 minutes. If the rolls brown too quickly, cover with aluminum foil. Brush the rolls again with half and half after they are removed from the oven.

7. Make a glaze for the rolls by combining the confectioners' sugar, corn syrup, vanilla, and half and half in a small bowl. Drizzle the glaze over top and serve warm.

Makes 12 to 14 rolls
Preparation time 45 minutes plus time for rising and baking

Parker House Rolls

Here is an easy way to make great dinner rolls. Use the bread machine to make the dough until the point of shaping the rolls.

1⅓	**cups milk**
2	**tablespoons unsalted butter, cut into small pieces**
2	**eggs**
1	**tablespoon sugar**
½	**teaspoon salt**
3½	**cups all-purpose flour**
2½	**teaspoons yeast**

¼	**cup butter (½ stick), melted**
1	**egg, beaten**

Preheat the oven to 400°.

1. Spray a muffin tin with vegetable oil cooking spray.
2. Place the milk, butter pieces, 2 eggs, sugar, salt, and flour into the bread machine.
3. Pour the yeast into the yeast compartment (or follow the specific directions for your bread machine).
4. After the dough cycle is complete, remove the dough to a floured surface.
5. Knead the dough for 5 minutes.
6. Roll out the dough and cut out circles with a biscuit cutter or cup.
7. Brush each circle with melted butter. Fold the circles in half and place in the muffin tin. Cover the tin with a clean towel and let rise for 30 minutes.
8. Brush the tops with the beaten egg and bake for 20 to 30 minutes or until golden brown.

Makes 12 rolls
Preparation time 30 minutes plus time for rising and baking

HELPFUL HINT:
To make the rolls ahead of time, you may cover the tin with plastic wrap and refrigerate overnight or until you are ready to bake. The rolls will rise in the refrigerator.

Jalapeño Corn Muffins

The heat of the peppers in these corn muffins is blended with the sweetness of brown sugar to make a perfect go-together for black bean soup.

1	cup all-purpose flour
1	cup cornmeal
2½	teaspoons baking powder
¼	teaspoon salt
3	tablespoons butter, melted
⅓	cup firmly packed dark brown sugar
1	egg
1	cup buttermilk
½	cup canned creamed corn
1	tablespoon finely diced jalapeño pepper, seeded

Preheat the oven to 425°.

1. Prepare a muffin pan by lining it with paper cups or spraying it with vegetable oil cooking spray.
2. In a medium bowl combine the flour, cornmeal, baking powder, and salt, and set aside.
3. In the bowl of an electric mixer combine the melted butter and brown sugar, and mix well.
4. Mix in the egg and buttermilk.
5. Stir in the dry ingredients.
6. Mix in the creamed corn and jalapeño.
7. Pour the batter into the prepared muffin pan, filling the cups two-thirds full.
8. Bake for 20 to 25 minutes. Cool on racks for several minutes before removing from the muffin pan.

Makes 12 muffins
Preparation time about 20 minutes plus baking

SIMPLE SOUP SUPPER MENU

Black Bean Soup with Toasted Corn
and Rosemary

Jalapeño Corn Muffins

Key Lime Squares

Apple Streusel Muffins

Here is a perfect accompaniment to a piping hot bowl of soup. These sweet muffins are as fragrantly appealing as they are appetizing.

2½   cups all-purpose flour
1   teaspoon baking soda
½   teaspoon salt
1   teaspoon ground cinnamon
¼   teaspoon ground nutmeg
2   cups sugar
½   cup butter (1 stick), room temperature
2   eggs
1   cup applesauce
2   medium apples, peeled and finely diced (about 2 cups)

2   tablespoons all-purpose flour
¼   cup brown sugar
½   teaspoon ground cinnamon
¼   cup cold butter (½ stick)

Preheat the oven to 400°.
1. Prepare a muffin pan by lining it with paper cups or spraying it with vegetable oil cooking spray.
2. In a medium bowl combine the flour, baking soda, salt, cinnamon, and nutmeg, and set aside.
3. In the bowl of an electric mixer combine the sugar and butter and mix until creamy.
4. Add the eggs one at a time.
5. Add the applesauce, mixing well. Stir in the dry ingredients.
6. Stir in the apple pieces.
7. Pour the batter into the prepared muffin pan, filling the cups two-thirds full.
8. In a food processor combine the 2 tablespoons of flour, brown sugar, and ½ teaspoon of cinnamon.
9. Add the butter and pulse until the mixture resembles fine crumbs.

SETTING THE SCENE:
These muffins are equally good in the morning for breakfast piled into a napkin-lined basket as they are in a take-along picnic basket for a light dessert.

10. Sprinkle the mixture over the muffin batter and bake for 20 to 25 minutes. Cool on rack.

Makes 12 large muffins
Preparation time about 20 minutes plus baking

Pumpkin Apple Muffins

You can make these fun pumpkin muffins in just minutes. The aroma that comes from the oven while they bake makes everyone run to the kitchen!

2½	**cups all-purpose flour**
1	**teaspoon baking soda**
½	**teaspoon salt**
2	**cups sugar**
1	**cup canned pumpkin pie mix**
2	**eggs**
½	**cup canola oil**
1	**medium apple, peeled and finely diced (about 1 cup)**
	Confectioners' sugar

Preheat the oven to 350°.
1. Prepare a muffin pan by lining with paper cups or spraying with vegetable oil cooking spray.
2. In a medium bowl combine the flour, baking soda, and salt. Set aside.
3. In a large bowl whisk together the sugar, pumpkin pie mix, eggs, and oil until well blended.
4. Stir in the dry ingredients.
5. Stir in the apple pieces.
6. Pour the batter into the prepared muffin cups, filling two-thirds full.
7. Bake for 30 to 35 minutes or until a toothpick inserted in the center comes out clean. Cool on a rack.
8. Sprinkle the muffins with confectioners' sugar.

Makes 16 large muffins
Preparation time about 10 minutes plus baking

Zucchini Bran Muffins

The secret to a well-made muffin is the batter. For this muffin the batter should be lumpy, not too smooth and stirred only enough to mix the ingredients together.

2¾	cups bran flakes, processed (about 1 cup)
¼	cup brown sugar
½	medium zucchini, finely shredded (about ½ cup)
¾	cup sour cream
3	eggs
½	cup all-purpose flour
½	cup whole wheat flour
2	teaspoons baking powder
1	teaspoon salt
3	tablespoons butter, melted

Preheat the oven to 400°.

1. Prepare a muffin pan by lining it with paper cups or spraying it with vegetable oil cooking spray.
2. In a food processor pulse the bran flakes and the brown sugar until coarsely ground. Transfer to a bowl.
3. In a food processor shred the zucchini using the fine-shredding blade.
4. Add the sour cream and eggs to the zucchini and pulse until just combined.
5. In the bowl of an electric mixer combine the flours, baking powder, and salt.
6. Mix the ground bran flakes mixture into the dry ingredients on the slowest speed.
7. Pour the zucchini mixture into the dry ingredients. Mix until combined.
8. Add the melted butter and stir until just combined.
9. Pour the batter into the prepared muffin pan, filling the cups two-thirds full.
10. Bake for 20 to 25 minutes. Cool on racks completely before removing from the muffin pan.

Makes 12 large muffins
Preparation time about 30 minutes plus baking

TECHNIQUE:
When baking muffins, fill the tins two-thirds full. They need room to expand. If you do not have enough batter to fill every cup, put a tablespoon of water in the empty cups to keep the rest of the muffins moist.

Quick Apple Cinnamon Bread

This quick bread easily doubles as a snack cake. Bake the bread using small mini loaf pans so that you can serve one loaf on the day you bake and freeze the other loaves for use on a day when you are short on time.

1½ cups granulated sugar
1¾ cups flour
½ cup canola oil
¼ cup apple juice
3 apples, peeled and finely diced (about 1½ cups)
2 eggs
¾ teaspoon salt
1 teaspoon baking soda
¾ teaspoon cinnamon
½ teaspoon nutmeg

Preheat the oven to 350°.

1. In a large mixing bowl combine all of the ingredients. Stir to mix well.
2. Prepare four 4½ x 2¾-inch mini loaf pans by spraying first with vegetable oil spray and then dusting with flour.
3. Pour one-fourth of the batter into each loaf pan.
3. Bake for 40 to 50 minutes or until a toothpick inserted into the center comes out clean.

Makes 4 mini loaves
Preparation time about 15 minutes plus time for baking

SETTING THE SCENE
Mini loaves of quick bread are the perfect gift. Wrap each one well with plastic wrap. Use beautiful ribbon to tie each package. Place a loaf in a small basket alongside individual packages of gourmet coffee beans and a fresh, ripe apple for a thoughtful hostess gift.

Banana Peanut Butter Chip Quick Bread

You will love the combination of peanut butter and bananas in this recipe. Feel free to use it as a guideline to create your own favorite flavored homemade quick bread.

1½	cups all-purpose flour
1	teaspoons baking powder
½	teaspoon salt
6	tablespoons butter (¾ stick), room temperature
1	cup granulated sugar
4	very ripe bananas, mashed (about 1½ cups)
2	eggs
1	teaspoon vanilla extract
½	cup peanut butter chips

Preheat the oven to 350°.

1. Prepare a 9 x 5-inch loaf pan by spraying first with vegetable oil spray and then dusting with flour.
2. In a small bowl combine the flour, baking powder, and salt.
3. In the bowl of an electric mixer combine the butter and sugar until fluffy.
4. Add the bananas. Stir.
5. Add the eggs and mix well.
6. Add the vanilla and mix to combine.
7. Add the flour mixture in 3 parts, mixing after each addition.
8. Stir in the peanut butter chips.
9. Pour the batter into the prepared loaf pan and bake for 55 to 60 minutes or until a toothpick inserted into the center comes out clean.

Makes 1 loaf
Preparation time about 15 minutes plus time for baking

Basic Scones

Scones are the rich relative to the everyday biscuit—rich because of the addition of cream and eggs. Upscale bakeries are adding everything to scones from dried cranberries to sugared pecans. The batter can be flavored with pumpkin or chocolate, for example. It's really all up to you.

1½   cups all-purpose flour
2   teaspoons baking powder
1   tablespoon granulated sugar
½   teaspoon salt
¼   cup butter (½ stick), chilled, cut into pieces
2   eggs
⅓   cup cream

2   tablespoons granulated sugar

Preheat the oven to 450°.
1. In the bowl of a food processor combine the flour, baking powder, 1 tablespoon of sugar, and salt.
2. Add the butter pieces. Pulse until the dough resembles small crumbs.
3. In a small bowl beat the eggs. Measure out about 2 tablespoons of the egg mixture. Set this aside for later.
4. Pour the rest of the beaten eggs into the crumbled mixture with the cream. Pulse until the dough comes together.
5. Pour the dough onto a floured surface. Roll out the dough to about ¾-inch thickness.
6. Use a pastry cutter to cut the dough into 6 squares. Cut each square into 2 triangles.
7. Place each triangle on a baking sheet that has been sprayed with vegetable oil spray.
8. Brush each triangle with the reserved beaten egg and sprinkle with extra granulated sugar.
9. Bake for 12 to 15 minutes or until golden brown.

Makes about 12 scones
Preparation time about 15 minutes plus baking

TECHNIQUE:
If the dough is a little sticky, add a bit more flour to make it easier to handle.

SIMPLE SUBSTITUTION:
Now that you have the basics down, feel free to experiment with lots of fun additions. Add chocolate bits to make chocolate chip scones. Flavor the scones with dried fruit, chopped nuts, and a touch of pumpkin or maple syrup. There is no limit to the fun you will create.

Fluffy Egg And Cheese Casserole

This dish works well amid holiday meal preparations because you can make it the day before and pop it into the oven when you are ready to bake. It has the fluffiness of a soufflé and the staying power of a quiche.

10	slices white bread
8	large eggs
3	cups milk
3	tablespoons chopped garlic chives
1	tablespoon prepared mustard
	Salt
	Dash hot pepper sauce
2	cups shredded sharp Cheddar cheese
3	tablespoons diced green onions

Preheat oven to 325°.

1. Trim the crusts from the bread and discard. Cut the bread slices into 1-inch cubes.
2. In a large bowl whisk together the eggs, milk, chives, and mustard.
3. Season with as much salt and hot pepper sauce as you like.
4. Stir the bread cubes, Cheddar cheese and green onion into the egg mixture.
5. Pour the mixture into an ungreased baking dish.
6. Bake the casserole for about 1 hour or until the center is just set and the edges begin to brown.

Serves 6 to 8
Preparation time about 20 minutes plus baking

HELPFUL HINT:
To prepare the dish for baking the next morning, cover it with plastic wrap and refrigerate after step 5.

SIMPLE SUBSTITUTION:
Personalize this brunch casserole for one of your "new traditions" recipes by adding one or more of the following ingredients just before baking:
- 1 cup cooked chopped spinach, well drained
- 2 cups cooked shrimp or crabmeat
- 1 cup cooked sausage, drained
- 1 cup cooked, crumbled bacon

Thick Cinnamon French Toast

Use thick slices of day old bread (Ricotta Bread, page 236, works well) for this dish. For a brunch buffet, you can make the toast up to 30 minutes in advance and keep warm until you are ready to serve.

4	eggs
½	cup milk
½	cup heavy cream
2	tablespoons maple syrup
2	tablespoons vanilla extract
1	teaspoon ground cinnamon
½	teaspoon ground nutmeg
½	cup (or more) canola oil for frying
8	1-inch thick slices bread

Confectioners' sugar
Warm maple syrup
Toasted pecans or almonds (optional)

1. In a shallow bowl whisk together the eggs, milk, cream, maple syrup, vanilla, cinnamon, and nutmeg.
2. In a skillet heat 1 inch of canola oil over medium high heat. The oil should be very hot but not smoking.
3. Dip one slice of bread in the egg mixture, turning once so that it is coated well but not soggy.
4. Cook the bread in the oil, turning once, until golden brown on both sides.
5. Remove the toast to a dish lined with paper towels. Keep warm. Repeat with the remaining bread.

Serves 4
Preparation time about 15 minutes

SETTING THE SCENE:
Place the toast on a warm platter. Sprinkle with confectioners' sugar. Place a pitcher of warm maple syrup nearby. Top the toast with toasted pecans or almonds for a totally upscale twist on French toast.

Dicey Potato Casserole

This easy make-ahead brunch casserole uses pre-diced frozen potatoes to give it a jump start on preparation time. Make it for a crowd and serve the leftovers for days afterwards.

1	32-ounce bag frozen diced potatoes, defrosted
3	to 4 green onions, chopped (about ½ cup)
½	medium red bell pepper, diced (about ½ cup)
½	medium green bell pepper, diced, about ½ cup
¾	cup butter (1½ stick), melted
1	10¾-ounce can cream of celery soup
1	cup sour cream
	Salt and freshly ground pepper
2	tablespoons finely chopped fresh garlic chives
1	cup crushed corn flake crumbs

Preheat the oven to 350°.

1. In a large mixing bowl stir together the potatoes, onions, and peppers.
2. Stir in ½ cup of melted butter.
3. Mix in the soup and sour cream.
4. Season with salt and pepper and toss in the chopped chives.
5. Pour the mixture into a 13 x 9-inch baking dish that has been sprayed with vegetable cooking spray.
6. Sprinkle the corn flake crumbs on top of the casserole. Drizzle the remaining ½ cup butter over the top.
7. Bake the casserole for about 45 minutes or until it is bubbling and the top begins to brown.

Serves 8 to 10
Preparation time about 10 minutes plus baking.

HELPFUL HINT:
To prepare the dish for baking the next morning, cover it with plastic wrap and refrigerate after step 6.

Sautéed Ham Steaks and Candied Bacon

A sweet treatment of breakfast meats adds a neat twist to a brunch buffet. These staples take on an updated look in these two recipes.

¼	cup butter (½ stick)
2	tablespoons brown sugar
2	4- to 6-ounce ham steaks, 1-inch thick
1	pound thick cut bacon
1	cup firmly packed brown sugar

FOR HAM:
1. In a skillet melt the butter over medium high heat.
2. Stir in the sugar until melted.
3. Cook the ham steaks, one at a time, in the sauce until heated through.
4. Serve the ham steaks on a warm platter. Pour the extra sauce over top.

FOR BACON:
Preheat the oven to 200°.
1. Cut each bacon slice in half.
2. Place the brown sugar in a shallow bowl.
3. Dip each slice of bacon into the brown sugar, coating both sides. Shake off the excess.
4. Place the bacon slices onto a baking sheet.
5. Cook the bacon for 2 to 3 hours. It will be browned and candy like.
6. Cool the bacon. Serve in stacks and sprinkle chopped parsley over top.

Serves 4
Preparation time about 15 minutes plus baking

TECHNIQUE:
Nonstick sheets, called Silpats, work well when slow cooking sticky stuff like candied bacon.

Scrambled Eggs with Diced Smoked Salmon

Here is an new twist on the favorite scrambled eggs and ham breakfast served at the local diner. Serve this dish for a midnight supper with a chilled glass of champagne.

4	**eggs**
2	**tablespoons fresh chives, diced**
1	**tablespoon half and half**
1	**tablespoon butter**
1	**shallot, finely diced**
4	**ounces smoked salmon, finely diced**
1	**teaspoon capers, drained**

1. In a small bowl whisk together the eggs, chives, and half and half.
2. In a skillet melt the butter over medium high heat.
3. Cook the shallot in the butter until golden brown.
4. Reduce the temperature to medium. Add the egg mixture to the pan. Stir until the eggs are just fluffy but still wet.
5. Stir in the salmon. Cook until the eggs are just done.

Serves 2
Preparation time about 15 minutes

SETTING THE SCENE:
Divide the eggs onto 2 plates. Place ½ teaspoon of capers over the top of each portion. Garnish with whole chives. Serve with mini bagels and whipped cream cheese.

The After Work Pub

MAKING FAST APPETIZERS

"TGIF" is the battle cry for most of us at the end of a hectic work week. Casual Fridays have set the tone for casual Friday evenings filled with after work get-togethers. What better place to convene than at the local pub. Cool beverages, plenty of nibbles, and inspired conversation take place at every turn. The After Work Pub inspires laid-back entertaining at home with coworkers dropping by for the feet-on-the-table type of gathering that breaks the rigor of a frenzied work week.

Drive-by buddies set the tone for the recipes in this chapter: quick, fun snacks that you can make in just a few moments and have ready to eat while the party builds. Make-ahead nibbles jump out of the freezer ready to warm as the celebration begins to heat up.

Read about Foods to Keep on Hand in the first chapter, Getting Started. You'll find a huge selection of simple ingredients that can be combined to produce rustic salsas, smooth dips, and funky snacks. Innovation is key here and substitution is your pal. Missing fresh cilantro for your salsa? Substitute basil or dill. No ground beef for your spicy nachos? Try ground turkey or black beans. Missing smoked white fish for you fish dip? Experiment with canned tuna or leftover salmon. The more people that gather unexpectedly, the better you become at innovation.

Remember—the key is casual. The fun is in the gathering, and your participation is crucial. Spend your time with your guests. Invite them to help out when preparing fun snacks. Maybe, with just a little leadership, the After Work Pub might move from your house to his or hers or theirs. Now, isn't that a fun plan!

Find more information about the recipes in The After Work Pub chapter at www.jorj.com.

Black Bean and Toasted Corn Salsa

This salsa is a terrific example of a great spur of the moment dish you can pull together with just a few of the items stored in your pantry.

	Olive oil
1	16-ounce can corn, drained
1	16-ounce can black beans, drained
1	16-ounce can diced tomatoes
1	to 2 tablespoons chopped jalapeño peppers
½	medium red onion, diced
1	teaspoon dried cilantro
1	tablespoon lime juice
¼	cup olive oil
2	tablespoons red wine vinegar
	Salt and freshly ground pepper

1. In a small skillet heat a small amount of olive oil over medium high heat.
2. Place the drained corn in the skillet and cook until the kernels just begin to brown. Cool to room temperature.
3. In a large bowl combine the drained black beans, diced tomatoes, chopped jalapeño, onion, cilantro, and toasted corn.
4. Drizzle the salsa with lime juice, olive oil, and vinegar.
5. Season with salt and freshly ground pepper.
6. Toss and chill until ready to serve.

Serves a crowd
Preparation time 15 minutes

SIMPLE SUBSTITUTIONS:
Feel free to use fresh or left over ingredients in this salsa. Use left over corn on the cob in place of canned corn. Substitute 2 whole fresh jalapeño peppers that have been seeded and diced in place of canned. Fresh herbs can be substituted for dried. Try 2 tablespoons of fresh, chopped cilantro, or basil. A squeeze of fresh lime juice will work well in place of bottled juice. Make up your own combinations by marrying the items that you have stocked in your pantry with fresh veggies and herbs.

SERVING SUGGESTIONS:
You don't have to limit yourself to tortilla chips to enjoy this terrific and simple dish. Salsa is a great accompaniment to breakfast scrambled eggs or a juicy backyard burger. Serve it as a relish alongside simply sautéed fish or wrapped inside a flank steak fajita. Make a big batch of salsa and enjoy the results for days and days.

Roasted Peppers with Anchovies and Roasted Garlic

Roasted bell peppers and roasted garlic are a real treat. They stand alone as an appetizer or as an accent to a favorite dish. When you add some cubed cheese and salami and toss around a few steamed asparagus spears, you have the beginning of a great antipasti dish.

1	large red bell pepper
1	large yellow bell pepper
6	to 8 flat anchovy fillets, drained
1	tablespoon balsamic vinegar
	Salt and freshly ground pepper

3	large garlic bulbs
1	tablespoon olive oil
1	teaspoon dried oregano
	Salt and freshly ground pepper

Blue cheese

1. Roast the peppers.
2. Remove the black skin from the pepper. Discard the stem and seeds. Slice into strips.
3. In a medium size bowl place the sliced peppers, anchovies, and balsamic vinegar. Toss.
4. Season with salt and freshly ground pepper.
4. Marinate for at least 30 minutes.
5. Roast the garlic.

Serves a crowd
Preparation time about 10 minutes plus roasting

TECHNIQUE:
To roast a pepper place it on a broiler pan at the top of the oven. Set the temperature on the broil. Turn the pepper one quarter turn as the skin blackens. When you are roasting a large quantity of peppers use may use an outside barbecue grill. Char the skin of the pepper until it is black. Place the pepper in a large brown bag to steam for at least 10 minutes. Remove the pepper from the bag. Peel away the black skin and remove the inside pulp. Continue with the recipe.

SETTING THE SCENE:
To serve, drain the pepper mixture. On a colorful platter, alternate strips of red and yellow pepper with anchovy fillets. Place the warm garlic bulbs alongside. Add a wedge of blue cheese nearby. A roasted green veggie and some bite-size slices of bread complete the presentation.

Super Nachos Two Ways

You can make these nachos two ways. Combine all of the ingredients in a layered casserole and serve tortilla chips on the side, or make the nachos individually on a large platter smothered with melted cheese. You choose!

1	tablespoon olive oil
1	medium yellow onion, chopped (about ½ cup)
¾	pound lean ground beef
1	to 2 drops hot pepper sauce
1	package tortilla chips, use whole round chips for individual nachos
1	10¾-ounce can refried beans
½	cup prepared tomato salsa
1	to 2 cups shredded sharp Cheddar cheese
1	to 2 medium jalapeño peppers, thinly sliced (about 2 to 4 tablespoons)

Sour cream, optional
Guacamole, optional

FOR INDIVIDUAL NACHOS:

1. In a skillet cook the onion until soft in the olive oil over medium high heat.
2. Add the ground beef and brown. Season with hot sauce. Remove the mixture from the heat and set aside.
3. Lay out tortilla chips on a microwave safe platter.
4. Spread a small amount of refried beans on each chip.
5. Place a spoonful of the beef mixture on top of the refried beans.
6. Spoon the salsa over the top.
7. Sprinkle the entire platter with the cheese and dot with sliced jalapeño pepper.
8. Microwave on high for several minutes or until the cheese melts.
9. Top each nacho with sour cream and guacamole.

HELPFUL HINT:
Substitute leftover taco meat in this recipe for a quick start.

SETTING THE SCENE:
Serve the warm nacho casserole in a earthenware baking dish. Place fiesta patterned linen around the dish. Serve a basket of tricolored chips on the side.

FOR SUPER NACHO CASSEROLE:

Preheat the oven to 350°.

1. Prepare the beef as stated above.
2. Spread the refried beans in the bottom of a casserole dish.
3. Cover the beans with the beef mixture.
4. Pour the salsa over top and cover with cheese and jalapeño peppers.
5. Bake for 20 to 30 minutes until cooked through and the cheese melts.
6. Garnish the top with sour cream and guacamole.
7. Serve warm with plenty of chips for dipping.

Serves a crowd
Preparation time about 20 minutes

Simple Tomato Salsa

Tomato salsa is the basic on many after-work pub tables. This one can be spiced up or down depending on the amount of chilies you add. The perfect salsa should have the consistency of a wet salad with just enough liquid to cover the diced veggies—not drown them!

2   jalapeño peppers, seeded and diced
1   green bell pepper, seeded and diced
1   medium onion, diced
2   to 4 medium plum tomatoes, seeded and diced (pulp only)
4   cloves garlic, minced
3   tablespoons fresh cilantro, chopped
1   to 2 tablespoons fresh lime juice
    Salt and freshly ground pepper to taste

1. In a medium bowl combine all of the ingredients. Stir to mix.
2. Season with salt and freshly ground pepper.
3. Store in an airtight container for up to 1 week.

Bruschetta with Three Toppings

Bruschetta is grilled bread often served in rustic soups or as an appetizer slathered with wonderful antipasto toppings. The secret is to use a good quality bread and fresh, fragrant ingredients. Here are three bruschetta toppings that can be prepared in advance and assembled at the last moment.

¼	cup olive oil
1	teaspoon garlic powder
1	loaf crusty bread, sliced
1	7-ounce jar jar sun-dried tomato halves in oil, drained and chopped
8	ounces mozzarella cheese, sliced
	Fresh oregano leaves
6	to 8 plum tomatoes, seeded and chopped (about 2 cups)
⅓	cup chopped fresh basil
1	clove garlic, minced (about 1 teaspoon)
1	tablespoon olive oil
1	tablespoon balsamic vinegar
	Salt and freshly ground pepper
8	to 10 flat anchovy fillets
10	to 12 green olives
1	tablespoon fresh cilantro

Preheat the oven to 350° or heat a grill or grill pan over high heat.

1. In a small bowl combine the olive oil and garlic powder.
2. Lightly brush each side of the bread slices with the olive oil mixture.
3. Bake the bread on a baking sheet, turning once, for several minutes on each side until lightly toasted. Do not overbake. As an alternative grill the bread on both sides over a hot grill.

HELPFUL HINT:
If you are preparing appetizer portions, use a small loaf of French bread or cut slices from a larger loaf into triangles before grilling.

SETTING THE SCENE:
A platter of bruschetta with all three toppings is a delicious and attractive start to any party. Decorate the platter with whole plum tomatoes and a head of roasted garlic. Add a bouquet of basil on the side.

MOZZARELLA AND SUN-DRIED TOMATO TOPPING:

1. In a food processor chop the sun-dried tomatoes.
2. Spoon a small amount of the tomato on the bruschetta and place on a baking sheet.
3. Top with a slice of mozzarella.
4. Bake at 350° for several minutes or until the cheese is just melted. Remove from the oven.
5. Top with a leaf of oregano.

BASIL AND CHOPPED TOMATO TOPPING:

1. In a small bowl combine the tomatoes, basil, and garlic.
2. Drizzle the olive oil and vinegar over all and toss.
3. Season with salt and freshly ground pepper.
4. Marinate in the refrigerator for at least 30 minutes.
5. Drain the tomato mixture. Place a generous spoonful on a bruschetta slice.

ANCHOVY AND OLIVE PESTO TOPPING:

1. In a food processor combine the anchovies, olives, and cilantro. Pulse to form a paste that is not quite smooth.
2. Spread a spoonful of the pesto on top of a bruschetta slice and serve.

SIMPLE SUBSTITUTION:
Experiment by substituting easily made bruschetta for croutons in soups and salads.

Herbed Toast

This is another great spin on the fun bruschetta.

⅓   **cup olive oil**
1   **tablespoon chopped fresh parsley**
1   **tablespoon chopped fresh basil**
1   **clove garlic, minced**
8   **slices bread, 1-inch thick**

Preheat the broiler.

1. In a small bowl combine the olive oil, parsley, basil, and garlic.
2. Place the bread on a baking sheet and brush with the oil mixture. Cut each slice in half diagonally.
3. Broil for 2 to 4 minutes until brown.

Bruschetta with Goat Cheese

Goat cheese adds a highbrow image to the easy to make bruschetta. Assemble the dish in advance but broil just before serving for a starter that is both sharp and rich in taste.

HELPFUL HINT:
Feel free to save some time and use red peppers from a jar for this recipe. Drain well before placing the pepper strips in the food processor.

1	loaf crusty French bread, sliced
¼	cup olive oil

8	ounces goat cheese
½	cup pitted black olives
½	cup roasted red pepper
4	green onions, chopped

Preheat the oven to 350° or heat a grill or grill pan over high heat.

1. Lightly brush each side of the bread slices with olive oil.
2. Bake the bread on a baking sheet, turning once, for several minutes on each side until lightly toasted or use a grill pan to grill the bread slices on both sides.

Preheat the oven to broil.

1. Place the goat cheese in a mixing bowl to soften.
2. In the bowl of a food processor place the black olives and red pepper. Pulse to mince the ingredients.
3. Add the minced olives, peppers, and chopped green onion to the goat cheese. Mix well using a potato masher.
4. Spread a generous amount of the goat cheese mixture on each slice of bruschetta. Place each one on a baking sheet.
5. Broil the pieces under a broiler for several minutes or until the goat cheese begins to turn brown and bubble.

Makes about 1 dozen bruschetta
Preparation time about 10 minutes

Roasted Red Pepper, Garlic, and Eggplant Dip

This is an easy to make appetizer that works well as a top-ping on bruschetta and wrapped in a leaf of endive. Alter the vegetables to experiment with your favorite flavors.

1	medium eggplant, peeled and chopped into cubes (about 4 cups)
2	large red bell peppers, chopped (about 2 cups)
1	large Spanish onion, chopped (about 2 cups)
1	medium jalapeño pepper, seeded and diced (about 1 tablespoon)
	Fresh rosemary sprigs
2	whole heads garlic, roasted, cloves removed
2	tablespoons olive oil
1	tablespoon prepared chili sauce
1	tablespoon fresh cilantro leaves
	Salt and freshly ground pepper

Preheat the oven to 400°.
1. In a large bowl toss together the eggplant, peppers, onion, and jalapeño.
2. Drizzle the olive oil over the top. Toss well.
3. Place the vegetables on a baking sheet.
4. Place the rosemary sprigs around the vegetables.
5. Roast the vegetables for 45 minutes to 1 hour. They will be soft and beginning to brown.
6. Roast the garlic heads with a drizzle of olive oil.
7. Cool the vegetables and discard the rosemary sprigs.
8. In the bowl of a food processor place the vegetables.
9. Add the chili sauce and fresh cilantro. Season with salt and freshly ground pepper.
10. Pulse until the mixture becomes a course dip.

Makes 1 to 2 cups
Preparation time about 1 hour

HELPFUL HINT:
The more you pulse, the smoother the dip will become. If you prefer a chunkier spread, pulse briefly.

SETTING THE SCENE:
Variations of this dish are considered the "poor man's caviar" because of the similarity in texture. Serve this dip in a caviar dish surrounded by toast points, chopped egg, sour cream and capers for a fun treat. For a more casual presentation, serve the dip at room temperature with breadsticks or chunks of fresh bread for dipping.

Warm Artichoke and Crab Dip

For a fun presentation of this rich dip, purchase a large round loaf of bread. Cut off the top of the bread, and hollow out the inside. Serve the warm dip in this "bread bowl." Cut the inside bread into cubes and toast for dipping.

1	14-ounce can artichoke hearts, drained
8	ounces imitation crab
1	cup sour cream
1	cup mayonnaise
4	ounces goat cheese
½	cup grated Parmesan cheese
	Dash hot pepper sauce
1	tablespoon fresh parsley
	Salt and freshly ground pepper

Celery sticks
Carrot sticks
Breadsticks

Preheat the oven to 350°.

1. Place the artichoke hearts, crab, sour cream, mayonnaise, goat cheese, Parmesan cheese, hot pepper sauce and parsley in the bowl of a food processor.
2. Pulse to combine.
3. Season with salt and pepper.
4. Pour the mixture into a baking dish. Bake for 20 to 30 minutes.

Makes: 2 to 3 cups
Preparation time about 10 minutes plus baking

SETTING THE SCENE:
Serve the dip in a bread bowl or right out of the casserole dish. Use carrot sticks, celery sticks, and bread sticks for dipping alongside the toasted bread cubes.

Baked Spinach and Artichoke Dip

This is a favorite dip served with fresh tortilla chips and salsa for dipping. It comes together in minutes and can be made in advance if friends are dropping by.

1	10-ounce package frozen spinach, thawed, squeezed dry
1	14-ounce can artichoke hearts, drained and chopped
2	8-ounce packages cream cheese, room temperature
½	cup sour cream
4	cloves garlic, minced
2	cups shredded mozzarella cheese
¼	cup grated Parmesan cheese
	Salt and freshly ground pepper

Tortilla chips
Salsa
Sour cream
Fresh cilantro

Preheat the oven to 350°.

1. In a large bowl place the spinach, chopped artichoke hearts, cream cheese, sour cream, and cloves garlic. Mix well.
2. Add 1½ cups of mozzarella cheese and half of the Parmesan cheese.
3. Season with salt and pepper.
4. Pour the mixture into a baking dish.
5. Sprinkle the remaining ½ cup of mozzarella and the remaining Parmesan cheese over the top.
6. Bake for 30 minutes or until the top begins to brown and the casserole is bubbling.

Makes about 5 cups
Preparation time about 10 minutes plus baking

TECHNIQUE:
Thaw the frozen spinach using the microwave oven. Place the thawed spinach in a colander. Press down on the spinach with paper towels to force out most of the moisture.

SETTING THE SCENE:
Serve the dip in a crock. Serve a second crock filled with salsa. A third crock holds sour cream topped with fresh cilantro. A basket of tri-color tortilla chips completes the dish.

Chopped Chicken Liver Spread

I remember standing in my grandmother's kitchen helping her to make this dish. She used a heavy metal meat grinder that was clamped to her kitchen counter. By hand, we took turns grinding the eggs and sautéed chicken livers into a huge earthenware bowl. The smells were fabulous. Today, I use the meat grinder attachment to my Kitchen Aid mixer. It does the job nicely, with much less wear and tear on the arm.

1	tablespoon olive oil
1	tablespoon butter
1	medium onion, coarsely chopped (about 1 cup)
4	whole cloves garlic, minced (about 2 tablespoons)
1½	pounds chicken livers
¼	cup sherry
	Salt and pepper
6	eggs, hard-boiled and peeled
3	tablespoons mayonnaise

1. In a large skillet heat the olive oil and butter.
2. Add the onion and cook until just beginning to brown (but not burned).
3. Add the garlic and cook for a few minutes more.
4. Place the chicken livers in the pan and cover. Cook for about 15 minutes, checking frequently.
5. Remove the lid of the pan when the chicken livers are cooked through. Add the sherry. Cook the liver until the pan juices are reduced, but not totally dry. Season with salt and pepper.
6. Using a food grinder (or food processor), alternate spoonfuls of liver and egg until all of the ingredients are ground into a large bowl. Adjust the seasonings.
7. Mix in enough mayonnaise to combine the ingredients without overpowering the mixture. The spread should be coarser than a pâté and easily moldable.

Makes about 2 cups—serves a crowd
Preparation time about 30 minutes

SETTING THE SCENE:
Place the chopped chicken liver spread into a plastic lined mold or casserole dish. You can refrigerate for as little as 2 hours or overnight. Unmold onto a decorative platter and serve with pumpernickel and rye rounds.

Smoked Fish Dip

Here is an easy fish dip that you can mix together in minutes. Experiment with different varieties of smoked fish such as salmon or tuna for an interesting fish dip twist.

½ pound smoked marlin, bones and skin removed

⅓ cup sour cream

1 3-ounce package cream cheese, room temperature

2 teaspoons prepared horseradish

Juice of ½ fresh lemon (about 1 tablespoon)

1 whole shallot, finely diced, about 1 tablespoon

Dash hot pepper sauce

Dash Worcestershire sauce

Salt and freshly ground pepper.

Crackers

1. In a medium mixing bowl break apart the fish using a fork.
2. Add the sour cream, cream cheese, horseradish, lemon juice, diced shallot, hot pepper sauce, and Worcestershire. Season with salt and pepper. Mix well.
3. Serve the fish dip with crackers.

Makes about 1 cup dip
Preparation time about 10 minutes

HELPFUL HINT:
If smoked marlin is unavailable, feel free to substitute smoked white fish or even smoked trout. You can adjust the seasonings to spice up the dip if you choose!.

Simple Salmon Spread

This spread has a fresh, tangy taste due to the squeezed lemon juice and freshly snipped dill. For a large crowd, use a fish mold to turn out the mock salmon onto a decorated platter garnished with wedges of lemons and limes. For a small group, prepare individual portions and pass them around to your pals.

1   15-ounce can salmon
1   8-ounce package cream cheese, room temperature
1   package ranch salad dressing seasoning mix
1   green onion, chopped (about 2 tablespoons)
    Juice of 1 lemon (about 2 tablespoons)
1   teaspoon Worcestershire sauce
1   whole clove garlic, minced
1   teaspoon prepared mustard
¼   cup finely chopped fresh parsley
¼   cup finely chopped fresh dill weed
    Salt and freshly ground pepper

1. Line a fish mold (or small bowl) with plastic wrap.
2. Drain the salmon through a colander and remove all of the bones and skin from the fish.
3. In a food processor combine the cream cheese, salad dressing mix, green onion, lemon juice, Worcestershire sauce, garlic, and mustard. Pulse until the mixture is smooth and creamy.
4. Add the salmon, parsley, and dill to the bowl. Pulse until just mixed. Season with salt and freshly ground pepper.
5. Place the mixture into the prepared mold and refrigerate for at least 4 hours or overnight.

Makes about 2 cups
Preparation time 10 minutes plus refrigeration

TECHNIQUE:
For consistent results, spray the mold lightly with vegetable oil spray. Line it with plastic wrap, and then very lightly spray the plastic wrap. The plastic will not stick to the bowl or mold and the food will not stick to the plastic.

SETTING THE SCENE:
Serve the salmon spread with crackers. Decorate the fish mold with thinly sliced cucumbers representing fish scales. Garnish with lemon wedges.

For an alternate presentation serve the salmon by layering a thinly sliced cucumber piece on top of a round cracker and topping it with a spoonful of the salmon spread. Top each round with a touch of fresh dill.

Crab and Artichoke Balls with Key Lime Butter

These creamy bites must be cooked at the last moment and served hot. Grab a pal for a little help on this one, to serve while you pop more into the pan to cook.

1	12-ounce jar artichoke hearts, drained
12	ounces cream cheese, room temperature
1	pound crab meat, chopped
2	tablespoons Dijon mustard
2	eggs beaten with 1 tablespoon water
1	to 2 cups crushed corn flake crumbs
½	cup or more canola oil for frying

¼	cup unsalted butter (½ stick), melted
	Juice of 3 to 4 key limes (about ¼ cup)

1. In the bowl of a food processor place the drained artichokes. Pulse to rough chop.
2. Use an electric mixer to combine the chopped artichokes, cream cheese, crab meat, and mustard. Refrigerate for at least 30 minutes.
3. In a shallow bowl beat the eggs with a little water. Place the corn flake crumbs in another shallow bowl.
4. Remove the crab mixture from the refrigerator. Place a tablespoon of the mixture in your hand and form into 1-inch balls (smaller than a golf ball).
5. Place each ball first into the egg mixture and then roll it in the corn flake crumbs. Place on a baking sheet. Repeat until all of the mixture is used. Refrigerate until ready to serve or for at least 30 minutes.
6. In a deep skillet heat 2 inches of canola oil over medium high heat. Place the balls one at a time into the hot oil.
7. Remove the balls with a slotted spoon. Drain on a paper towel.
8. In a small saucepan melt the butter. Add the fresh key lime juice.

Makes about 2 dozen 1-inch balls
Preparation time about 30 minutes plus chilling and frying

HELPFUL HINT:
You can purchase crushed cornflake crumbs. The crumbs are processed and the result is similar to purchased bread crumbs. To make your own corn flake crumbs, use a food processor to completely process corn flakes to this consistency.

TECHNIQUE:
Gently drop the balls into the oil at the far side of the pot to avoid splashing. Do not crowd them in the pan. Cook only a few at a time. The crabmeat balls are done when they turn golden brown, in just a few minutes.

SETTING THE SCENE:
Serve the crab and artichoke balls next to a bowl full of key lime butter dipping sauce.

Make Ahead Nibbles

In an effort to get a head start on drop by guests, make either of these when you have some extra time. They both freeze well and are quickly heated when needed.

HELPFUL HINT:
Make these appetizers days ahead of a great party. Prepare extra and store in the freezer for up to 2 months.

ENGLISH CRABBIES

1	7-ounce jar process Cheddar cheese spread (like Old English Cheddar)
½	cup butter (1 stick), room temperature
¼	cup mayonnaise
12	ounces imitation crab
½	teaspoon salt
½	teaspoon garlic powder
1	loaf party pumpernickel bread

BACON CHEDDAR BITES

½	pound bacon, cooked, drained and crumbled
2	cups grated sharp Cheddar cheese
15	pitted black olives
1	tablespoon fresh parsley
½	medium onion
2	tablespoons prepared mustard
3	tablespoons mayonnaise
½	cup butter (1 stick), room temperature
1	loaf party rye rounds

FOR ENGLISH CRABBIES:

1. In the bowl of a food processor place the cheese spread, butter, mayonnaise, chopped crab, salt and garlic powder. Pulse to combine.
2. Spread a spoonful of the crab mixture onto each pumpernickel slice. Place each one on a baking sheet and freeze for at least 15 minutes.
3. Place the crabbies between sheets of plastic wrap in an airtight container and freeze until needed.
4. Place the crabbies on a baking sheet. Bake at 350° for about 10 minutes or until brown and bubbling.

FOR BACON CHEDDAR BITES:

1. In the bowl of a food processor place the cooked bacon, cheese, olives, parsley, onion, mustard and mayonnaise. Pulse to combine.
2. Lightly butter both sides of each bread slice.
3. Spread a spoonful of the bacon cheese mixture on top of each slice of bread. Freeze for at least 15 minutes.
4. Place the Cheddar bites between sheets of plastic wrap in an airtight container and freeze until needed.
5. Place the bites on a baking sheet. Bake at 350° for about 10 minutes or until brown and bubbling.

Makes several dozen
Preparation time about 20 minutes plus baking

Quick and Cheesy Appetizer

For a right-out-of-the-cabinet quick appetizer try this simple combination.

1	16-ounce jar spreadable Cheddar cheese
1	12-ounce jar prepared chutney
	Crackers

1. Mound the cheese onto a serving platter.
2. Pour the chutney over the top.
3. Surround the platter with crackers.
   How quick is that?!

Ham and Asparagus Pinwheels Old and New

A bowl of these clever pinwheels is like a bowl full of peanuts—you just keep popping them in your mouth. A true example of everything old is new again, the updated version of these pinwheels pop just as nicely!

1	8-ounce package cream cheese, room temperature
½	pound lean baked ham, sliced ⅛-inch thick
1	10¾-ounce can asparagus spears

10	flour tortilla shells
1	pound country ham, shredded
2	cups shredded Cheddar cheese
½	pound fresh asparagus spears, blanched
	Salt and freshly ground pepper
1	tablespoon olive oil

CLASSIC PINWHEELS

1. Spread a generous layer of cream cheese onto a slice of ham.
2. Place one asparagus at the small end of the ham.
3. Roll the ham and cheese around the asparagus. Trim the ends. Slice into 1-inch pinwheels.
4. Repeat with all of the ingredients. Refrigerate until ready to serve.

UPDATED PINWHEELS

Preheat the oven to 325°

1. Lay one tortilla shell on the work surface.
2. Spread a layer of shredded ham on top.
3. Spread a layer of cheese on top of the ham.
4. Place 1 to 2 blanched asparagus spears at one end of the tortilla.
5. Season the asparagus with salt and pepper.
6. Roll the tortilla around the asparagus tightly. Place the rolled tortilla seam side down in a baking dish.
7. Repeat with all of the ingredients.
8. Brush each tortilla with olive oil. Bake for 10 to 15 minutes until the cheese begins to melt.

9.. Remove the pan from the oven. Cool slightly. Trim the ends from each tortilla. Slice into 1-inch pinwheels. Serve with salsa.

Makes about 2 dozen each
Preparation time about 20 minutes plus baking

Quick Crab Starter

You need only 4 ingredients and 4 minutes to prepare this easy appetizer.

1	**8-ounce package cream cheese**
8	**ounces fresh crab meat**
½	**cup prepared cocktail sauce**
	Crackers

1. On a decorative platter, place the cream cheese.
2. Cover with crab meat and then cocktail sauce.
3. Serve with crackers.

SIMPLE SUBSTITUTION:
Feel free to substitute imitation crab meat.

Scallop Topped Zucchini Cakes

The zucchini cakes can be made a day in advance. Sauté the scallops at the last moment and serve with a dollop of spicy salsa for a new twist on an old "Southern" favorite.

2	large zucchini, shredded (about 3 to 4 cups)
1	cup buttermilk baking mix
1	small yellow onion, finely chopped (about ½ cup)
1	cup shredded sharp Cheddar cheese
3	tablespoons chopped fresh parsley
1	to 2 teaspoons hot pepper sauce
1	clove garlic, minced
½	cup olive oil
4	eggs, beaten
	Salt and freshly ground pepper
1	tablespoon olive oil
10	to 12 medium to large scallops
	Prepared salsa

Preheat the oven to 350°.

1. In a large mixing bowl mix together the shredded zucchini, baking mix, onion, cheese, parsley, hot pepper to taste, minced garlic, olive oil and eggs.

2. Season with salt and pepper.

3. Pour the mixture into a shallow jelly roll baking pan that has been sprayed with vegetable oil spray.

4. Bake for 20 to 30 minutes or until the top just begins to brown. Cool completely. Use a glass to cut out 10 to 12 circles from the cake.

5. Heat 1 tablespoon of olive oil in a skillet over medium high heat. Season the scallops with salt and pepper. Quickly sear the scallops in the hot oil until just beginning to brown on both sides, about 4 to 5 minutes depending on the size of the scallop. Drain on paper towels before placing on top of the cakes.

Makes about 10 to 12 hors d'oeuvres
Preparation time about 20 minutes plus baking

TECHNIQUE:
Use a medium shred disk of a food processor to finely shred the zucchini.

SIMPLE SUBSTITUTION:
For a totally upscale appetizer, make the zucchini cake and cool. Use a small shot glass to cut out two dozen or more small circles. Top each one with a thin slice of hard boiled egg, a dollop of sour cream, and a small amount of terrific caviar. Garnish with finely diced red onion. Serve on a silver tray with cold champagne close by.

SETTING THE SCENE:
Place a zucchini cake circle on a small appetizer plate. Serve a seared scallop on top of each zucchini circle. Garnish with a dollop of salsa.

Margarita Madness

Everyone has a favorite recipe for this popular after work cocktail. The secret is to use a quality brand of tequila.

1	lime sliced into 5 wedges
	Salt for dipping
4	ounces tequila
4	ounces Cointreau
4	ounces fresh lime juice
	About 2 cups crushed ice

1. Moisten each glass with one wedge of lime.
2. Dip the glass into a small dish of salt.
3. Pour the tequila, Cointreau, and lime juice into a pitcher. Add the crushed ice.
4. Let the mixture stand for 5 minutes. Pour into each glass. Garnish with the remaining 4 lime wedges.

Makes 2 to 4 cocktails each
Preparation time about 10 minutes

LEMON LIME MARGARITA:
Combine the juice from 1 lime and 1 lemon in a small bowl. Add the zest from both the lime and lemon. Add $\frac{1}{4}$ cup of sugar. Cover the bowl and allow this mixture to sit overnight or for at least 4 hours. Combine 4 ounces tequila and 4 ounces of Triple Sec in a large pitcher. Add in 2 cups crushed ice. Strain the lemon lime mixture into the pitcher. Stir until well chilled, about 1 minute. Pour into 4 glasses that have been dipped in salt.

STRAWBERRY MARGARITA:
In a food processor puree 1 cup of fresh strawberries, the juice from 1 lime and 1 lemon, and $\frac{1}{4}$ cup sugar. In a large pitcher combine 4 ounces of tequila, 2 ounces of Triple Sec, and 2 ounces of strawberry liqueur. Add 2 cups of crushed ice. Strain the strawberry mixture into the pitcher. Stir until well chilled, about 1 minute. Pour into 4 glasses that have been dipped in salt.

FROZEN MARGARITA:
Blend $1\frac{1}{2}$ ounces Tequila, $\frac{1}{2}$ ounce Triple Sec, and 1 ounce fresh lime juice with 1 cup of crushed ice in a blender for 1 to 2 seconds to combine. Blend on high speed until firm. Pour into a glass and garish with a slice of lime.

Coffee, Mint Tea, and Lemonade

Choose your favorite brands and spend just a few extra minutes on the presentation of these beverages to impress your friends.

Coffee
Cinnamon
Granulated sugar
Salt
Cinnamon sugar
Cream
Cinnamon sticks

Iced tea
Lemon, sliced into pinwheels
Lime, sliced into pinwheels
Fresh mint sprigs

Lemonade
Granulated sugar
Fresh raspberries or blueberries

FOR COFFEE PRESENTATION:

1. Use your favorite flavored fresh ground coffee beans, or add a dash of cinnamon, sugar, and salt to the coffee grounds just before you brew. Brew the coffee just before you serve. Coffee will keep its fresh flavor and aroma for a limited amount of time.
2. Add a clear (crystal) salt shaker filled with cinnamon sugar to the coffee service. This extra dash of flavor adds a nice touch.
3. Complete the coffee service with a pitcher of fresh cream, a bowl of sugar cubes, and a small vase filled with cinnamon sticks.

FOR ICED TEA PRESENTATION:

1. Fill a large pitcher halfway with ice cubes. Add the cold tea to the pitcher.

HELPFUL HINT:
Prepare cinnamon sugar by combining 4 parts sugar to 1 part cinnamon.

TECHNIQUE:
To make raspberry lemonade place 2 cups of raspberries and ½ cup of sugar in a blender. Pulse to combine. Place 3 cups of water and 2 cups of fresh lemon juice in a pitcher. Strain the raspberries through a colander into a small bowl. Add the strained raspberries to the pitcher. Stir well. Add ice cubes.

2. Float the lemon and lime circles in the pitcher.
3. Place fresh mint sprigs in the glasses or in a small bowl next to the pitcher.

FOR LEMONADE PRESENTATION:
1. Fill a large pitcher halfway to the top with ice cubes. Add the cold lemonade
2. Dip the rims of the lemonade glasses first in water and then in a shallow bowl of sugar.
3. Place a fresh raspberry or blueberry in each glass before you pour.

PEOPLE IN AND OUT ALL DAY MENU

Some occasions call for food that is easily interchanged on an all-day buffet: a home meeting, a business networking session, or an all-day conference, for example. Presentation is the key—and dishes with staying power.

Coffee Presentation
Lemonade Presentation
Iced Tea Presentation
❧

Quick and Cheesy Appetizer
❧

Simple Salmon Spread
❧

Fresh Fruit Salad
with Raspberry Yogurt Sauce
❧

Pasta Salad
with Southwestern Vinaigrette
❧

Sour Cream Coffee Cake
❧

Apple Streusel Muffins

The Perfect Martini

This is the famous recipe for a bond-like martini. Feel free to substitute gin for vodka or add a touch of fruit juice to create your favorite martini fun.

2	ounces Vodka
¼	ounce dry vermouth
3	to 4 ice cubes
	Twist of lemon peel, olive, or cocktail onion

1. Combine the Vodka, dry vermouth and ice in a cocktail shaker and shake to chill.
2. Strain the martini into a well chilled glass and garnish with either a lemon peel, olive, or cocktail onion.

Makes 1 cocktail each
Preparation time about 5 minutes

SWEET MARTINI:
Combine 1½ ounces of gin, ½ ounce of dry vermouth, ½ ounce of sweet vermouth, and 3 to 4 ice cubes in a cocktail shaker. Shake to chill. Strain the martini into a well chilled glass. Garnish with an olive.

The Dessert Cafe

BAKING TECHNIQUES

The art of baking a scrumptious dessert rests in the accuracy of the recipe directions, ingredient measurements, and prescribed equipment. Substitution in a dessert recipe will not automatically produce consistent results. The difference between butter and margarine does not simply rest in the calorie count. Substituting one for the other will alter the results of homemade cookies.

This fact also holds true for baking pans and cooking times. The dessert recipe is timed by the size of the pan. The batter poured into a 9-inch cake pan will bake faster than a cake cooking in an 8-inch round pan. A baking sheet full of two-inch cookies will cook more rapidly than a sheet holding one that is jumbo sized. The batter for a ten-inch cheesecake will not fit into a nine-inch spring form pan. The results will be lopsided and uncooked.

While these little nuances may make baking a touch more challenging, they are only points that need to be mastered and not overlooked. Substitution of ingredients in baking works well with the tasty treats in the recipe like the chocolate sandwich cookies, or the peanut butter candies, rather than in the foundation of the recipe, the butter, eggs, and flour.

Review the terms to learn in the first chapter, Getting Started, to familiarize you with baking terms such as *mixing, whipping* and *folding.* Review your equipment to make sure that you have the correct pan for the recipe that you choose to prepare. Read the recipe thoroughly and have all of the ingredients on hand. Now you are on your way to foolproof dessert baking that will be relished by your family and friends.

Enjoy the Dessert Café in your home by taking a few extra minutes to include a special treat in your weekly meal plan.

Find more information for all of the recipes in The Dessert Bar chapter at www.jorj.com.

Key Lime Squares

I adapted this recipe from one given to me by a friend who swears that her lemon squares are the easiest and best ever. The change from lemon to lime is refreshing and interesting. Use fresh squeezed juice from key limes if you have them. A good quality bottled lime juice can be substituted.

HELPFUL HINT:
Use a zester—a nifty kitchen gadget—to grate the green peel from a lime. If a zester is missing from your drawer, a hand-held grater works well.

2½	cups flour
1	cup butter (2 sticks), chilled and cut into small pieces
½	cup confectioners' sugar
½	cup shredded sweetened coconut
1½	cups sugar
3	eggs
⅓	cup lime juice (about 3 medium limes)
½	teaspoon baking powder
1	teaspoon fresh lime zest (about ½ medium lime)
	Confectioners' sugar

Preheat the oven to 350°.

1. Spray a 13 x 9-inch baking pan with vegetable oil cooking spray.
2. In a food processor combine 2 cups of the flour with all of the butter, confectioners' sugar, and coconut until the mixture forms a dough.
3. Press the dough into the bottom of the pan using your fingertips or the back side of a fork.
4. Bake for 25 minutes until the edges are golden brown.
5. In the bowl of an electric mixer combine the sugar, eggs, lime juice, baking powder, lime zest, and remaining ¼ cup of flour. Mix until smooth.
6. Pour the filling onto the crust and bake for 25 minutes more. The center should be firm and the edges just beginning to turn brown.
7. Cool completely Cut into squares and dust with confectioners' sugar.

Makes approximately 3 dozen 1-inch bars
Preparation time about 20 minutes plus baking

Lemon Coconut Macaroons

A quick and simple cookie recipe for any day of the week. Serve half of the cookies for dessert, and freeze half for later.

1½	cups all-purpose flour
1½	teaspoons baking powder
¼	teaspoon salt
⅔	cup sugar
6	tablespoons butter (¾ stick), room temperature
4	ounces cream cheese, room temperature
2	eggs
1	teaspoon vanilla extract
1	tablespoon lemon juice (about ½ medium lemon)
½	teaspoon ground lemon peel
1	10-ounce package shredded sweetened coconut (about 3 cups)

Preheat the oven to 300°.

1. Prepare a baking sheet by spraying it with vegetable oil cooking spray.
2. In a medium bowl combine the flour, baking powder, and salt and set aside.
3. In the bowl of an electric mixer combine the sugar, butter, and cream cheese and beat together until fluffy.
4. Beat in the eggs, vanilla, lemon juice, and ground lemon peel.
5. Add the dry ingredients and mix until just combined.
6. Mix in the coconut.
7. Drop heaping teaspoons of the batter onto the cookie sheet, leaving at least 1 inch between each cookie.
8. Bake for 18 to 25 minutes until the cookies puff and the coconut begins to brown on the top.
9. Transfer to a rack to cool completely.

Makes about 3 dozen cookies
Preparation time about 20 minutes plus baking

Iced Orange Treats

The cookie dough can be made in minutes before you leave the house in the morning. When you return, slice and bake the cookies. While they are cooling, make the orange icing. A helper may suddenly appear to finish the treats.

HELPFUL HINT:
If the mixture is too dry add more orange juice. If it is too wet add more confectioners' sugar.

1	cup vegetable shortening
½	cup confectioners' sugar
1	teaspoon ground orange peel
2	teaspoons orange extract
2½	cups all-purpose flour
1	cup cornstarch

6	tablespoons vegetable shortening
1½	cups confectioners' sugar
2	tablespoons orange juice
1	teaspoon orange extract

Preheat the oven to 350°.

1. In the bowl of an electric mixer combine 1 cup of vegetable shortening with ½ cup of confectioners' sugar. Use a paddle attachment to cream together the ingredients until fluffy.
2. Add the ground orange peel and orange extract and mix thoroughly.
3. Add the flour and corn starch and combine until the mixture begins to attach itself to the paddle to form a dough.
4. Divide the dough in half and roll each half into 1½-inch logs. Wrap each log in plastic wrap and refrigerate for at least 2 hours.
5. Remove one log from the refrigerator. Remove the plastic wrap. Slice into ¼-inch slices and place each on a cookie sheet, spacing at least 1 inch apart.
6. Bake for 8 to 10 minutes or until the cookie is firm to the touch. They will not turn brown.
7. Transfer the cookies to a rack and allow to cool completely.

8. In the bowl of an electric mixer combine the remaining vegetable shortening and confectioners' sugar. Use a whisk attachment to whisk until fluffy.
9. Add the orange juice and orange extract and mix until the consistency is that of a frosting.
10. Frost each cooking with a dollop of the orange frosting. Store in an air tight container.

Makes approximately 5 dozen cookies
Preparation time about 30 minutes plus refrigeration and baking

Crescent Cookies

These updated classic cookies get a makeover with the addition of mini chocolate chips instead of ground nuts.

1	**cup butter (2 sticks), room temperature**
½	**cup confectioners' sugar (plus more for sprinkling)**
2	**teaspoons vanilla extract**
2	**cups all purpose flour**
1	**cup miniature semisweet chocolate chips**

Preheat the oven to 350°.
1. In the bowl of an electric mixer blend the butter and sugar until fluffy.
2. Stir in the vanilla, flour, and chocolate chips. The dough will be stiff.
3. Shape into crescents by hand. Place on an ungreased cookie sheet.
4. Bake for 30 minutes.
5. Roll the cookies in confectioners' sugar while they are still warm.

Makes about 2½ dozen
Preparation time about 20 minutes plus baking

Peanut Butter and White Chocolate Chip Cookies

These are rich, crumbly, nutty tasting cookies. Perfect with a big glass of milk.

1½   cups all-purpose flour
½   teaspoon baking soda
½   teaspoon salt
¼   cup butter (½ stick)
¼   cup margarine (½ stick)
½   cup firmly packed brown sugar
½   cup confectioners' sugar
1   large egg
1   cup peanut butter
½   teaspoon vanilla extract
½   cup chopped peanuts
½   cup white chocolate chip pieces

Preheat the oven to 375°.

1. Prepare baking sheets by spraying with vegetable oil cooking spray.
2. In a medium bowl combine the flour, baking soda, and salt and set aside.
3. In the bowl of an electric mixer combine the butter, margarine, and sugars, and mix until fluffy.
4. Add the egg, peanut butter, and vanilla extract. Mix until smooth.
5. Mix in the dry ingredients on slow speed.
6. Stir in the peanuts and white chocolate pieces on slow speed just until blended.
7. Drop the dough by rounded teaspoons on the cookie sheet. Flatten each round with the back side of a fork 2 times (making a cross pattern).
8. Bake for 10 to 12 minutes. Remove to a rack and cool.

Makes 4 dozen cookies
Preparation time about 30 minutes

HELPFUL HINT:
Before you add an egg to anything that you are making, break the shell and open it in a small bowl. This way, you will avoid shell pieces in your batter.

Oatmeal Chocolate Chip Cookies

This is a fun variation on the standard. The white choco-
late chips and hint of cinnamon add an interesting twist. I
like to blend margarine and butter for a chewier cookie.

2½	cups all-purpose flour
1	teaspoon baking soda
¾	teaspoon salt
½	teaspoon cinnamon
½	cup margarine (1 stick), room temperature
½	cup unsalted butter (1 stick), room temperature
1	cup firmly packed brown sugar
½	cup granulated sugar
2	eggs
1	teaspoon vanilla extract
¾	cup old-fashioned rolled oats
¾	cup white chocolate chips
¾	cup semisweet chocolate chips

Preheat the oven to 350°. Prepare a large baking sheet by
spraying it with vegetable oil cooking spray.

1. In a medium bowl combine the flour, baking soda,
   salt, and cinnamon, and set aside.
2. In the bowl of an electric mixer combine the margarine and butter and mix until creamy.
3. Stir in both sugars and blend well.
4. Add the eggs one at a time, mixing well after each
   addition.
5. Stir in the vanilla.
6. Add the flour mixture in 3 parts, scraping down the
   bowl after each addition.
7. Stir in the oatmeal and both the white and semisweet
   chocolate chips using the slow speed.
8. Drop the cookie batter by rounded teaspoons onto the
   prepared baking sheet. Bake for 10 minutes or until
   slightly browned and firm to the touch. Cool on baking racks for several minutes.

Makes 5 dozen cookies
Preparation time about 20 minutes

SIMPLE SUBSTITUTION:
For another fun chip cookie eliminate
the cinnamon. Substitute peanut butter chips and/or chocolate mint
chips for the white or dark chocolate
chips. You may add ½ cup of
chopped walnuts or pecans for a
nutty taste.

To share your favorite cookie recipe
visit www.jorj.com.

Iced Chocolate Cake Cookies

These cookies have the consistency of dense chocolate cake. The icing is divine and can be flavored by substituting a great tasting liqueur in place of brewed coffee.

2½   **cups all-purpose flour**
½   **teaspoon baking soda**
½   **teaspoon salt**
½   **cup butter (1 stick)**
2   **ounces unsweetened chocolate, chopped into pieces**
1   **cup firmly packed dark brown sugar**
1   **egg**
½   **cup sour cream**
1   **teaspoon vanilla extract**

2   **ounces semisweet chocolate, cut into pieces**
3   **to 4 tablespoons brewed hot coffee**
2   **cups confectioners' sugar**
2   **tablespoons corn syrup**

Preheat the oven to 350°.
1. Prepare baking sheets by spraying with vegetable oil cooking spray.
2. In a medium bowl combine the flour, baking soda, and salt, and set aside.
3. In a small saucepan melt together the butter and unsweetened chocolate over medium low heat, being careful not to burn the chocolate. The result should be a smooth and shiny mixture. Remove the pan from the heat and cool slightly.
4. In the bowl of an electric mixer combine the chocolate mixture and the brown sugar, and mix until blended. Add the egg and mix well.
5. Add the dry ingredients in batches until well mixed. Stir in the sour cream and vanilla.
6. Drop the cookie batter by rounded tablespoons onto the baking sheets allowing 1 inch between each cookie. Bake for about 10 to 12 minutes. The cookies should feel firm when touched. Place the cookies on racks over waxed paper to cool.

7. In a saucepan melt together the semisweet chocolate and coffee over medium low heat, being careful not to burn the chocolate.

8. Remove the mixture from the heat when it is smooth. Pour the chocolate into the confectioners' sugar. Add the corn syrup to make a shiny icing.

9. Drizzle the icing over the cookies in a decorative pattern, letting the excess run off onto the waxed paper. Allow the icing to set for several minutes before serving.

Makes 2½ dozen cookies
Preparation time about 30 minutes plus baking

Snowflake Cookies

This is a great recipe for bite size butter cookies sprinkled with colored sugar.

A cookie press is a great kitchen gadget that allows you to create many different cookie shapes. The hand pump version is fine—but I prefer an electric cookie press.

1	cup shortening
3	ounces cream cheese
1	cup sugar
1	egg yolk
1	teaspoon vanilla extract
1	teaspoon grated orange peel
2½	cups all-purpose flour
½	teaspoon salt
¼	teaspoon cinnamon

Preheat the oven to 350°.

1. In the bowl of an electric mixer combine all of the ingredients. Mix well.

2. Chill the dough for at least 1 hour.

3. Use a cookie press to press the cookies onto an ungreased cookie sheet. Sprinkle with colored sugar.

4. Bake for 10 to 12 minutes or until the edges just begin to turn brown.

Makes about 2½ dozen
Preparation time about 20 minutes plus baking

Simple Cinnamon Cake

This snack cake takes no time to whip up. It is great for breakfast or a fast dessert with a scoop of ice cream.

1½   cups all-purpose flour
¾   cup firmly packed brown sugar
¾   teaspoon ground cinnamon
½   teaspoon ground ginger
⅛   teaspoon salt
½   cup butter (1 stick), cut into pieces
½   teaspoon baking powder
½   teaspoon baking soda
¾   cup buttermilk
1½   teaspoon vanilla extract
1   large egg
½   cup pecan pieces (optional)
    Confectioners' sugar

TECHNIQUE:
Feel free to change the size of the pan to a circular cake pan or a square pan. Just watch the cooking time—you may have to adjust a bit.

Preheat the oven to 350°.

1. Prepare a 10 x 8-inch baking dish by spraying it with vegetable oil spray.
2. In the bowl of a food processor combine the flour, sugar, cinnamon, ginger, salt, and butter. Pulse several times until the mixture resembles crumbs.
3. Add the baking powder, baking soda, buttermilk, vanilla, and egg. Pulse again until the mixture becomes a batter.
4. Stir in the nuts with one or two pulses.
5. Pour the batter into the prepared pan.
6. Bake for 20 to 25 minutes or until a toothpick inserted into the cake comes out clean.
7. Cool the cake. Cut into pieces and dust with confectioners' sugar and a sprinkle of cinnamon.

Makes 12 to 18 squares
Preparation time about 35 minutes

Sour Cream Coffee Cake

This simple snack cake serves equally well as an eye opener with morning coffee or as the sweet with afternoon tea.

1	cup butter (2 sticks), room temperature
1	cup sugar
2	eggs
1	teaspoon vanilla extract
½	teaspoon salt
1	teaspoon baking soda
2	cups all-purpose flour
1	cup sour cream
⅓	cup firmly packed brown sugar
¼	cup sugar
1	teaspoon cinnamon
1	cup chopped walnuts

Preheat the oven to 350°.

1. Prepare a 13 x 9-inch baking dish by spraying with vegetable oil cooking spray and lightly dusting with flour.
2. In the bowl of an electric mixer combine the butter and sugar and mix until creamy.
3. Mix in the eggs and vanilla.
4. Add in the salt, baking soda, and flour. Mix well.
5. Beat in the sour cream. Set the batter aside.
6. In a food processor place the brown sugar, sugar, cinnamon, and nuts. Pulse until the mixture resembles course crumbs.
7. Place half of the batter in the prepared pan. Sprinkle with half of the nut mixture.
8. Top with the remaining batter. Sprinkle the remaining nut mixture over the top.
9. Bake for 35 minutes. Cool and cut into squares.

Makes 12 to 18 squares
Preparation time about 10 minutes plus baking

Pumpkin Brownies with Cream Cheese Frosting

These brownies blend the tastes of pumpkin pie and rich spice cake. If you don't have time to ice them, serve them warm with a scoop of vanilla ice cream.

2	cups all-purpose flour
2	teaspoons baking powder
1	teaspoon ground cinnamon
1	teaspoon ground ginger
¼	teaspoon ground cloves
½	teaspoon salt
¾	cup butter (1½ sticks), room temperature
1½	cups firmly packed brown sugar
2	eggs
2	teaspoons vanilla extract
1	15-ounce can pumpkin

Cream Cheese Frosting (recipe follows)
Candy Corn

Preheat the oven to 350°.

1. Prepare a 13 x 9-inch baking pan by spraying it with vegetable oil spray and dusting with flour.
2. In a medium bowl combine the flour, baking powder, cinnamon, ginger, cloves, and salt, and set aside.
3. In the bowl of an electric mixer combine the butter and sugar and cream together until smooth and fluffy.
4. Add the egg and mix.
5. Stir in the vanilla extract and canned pumpkin.
6. Add the dry ingredients and mix thoroughly.
7. Spread the batter into the pan and bake for 20 to 25 minutes or until a toothpick inserted into the middle of the brownies comes out clean.
8. Cool the brownies and spread the frosting on top. Cut into squares and sprinkle with candy corn to serve.

Makes 12 to 18 brownies
Preparation time about 15 minutes plus baking

Cream Cheese Frosting

This is an easy and fun-to-make frosting that will blend with all types of brownies and cakes.

1   **8-ounce package cream cheese**
¾   **cup confectioners' sugar**
1   **tablespoon cream**
¼   **teaspoon ground cinnamon**

1. In the bowl of an electric mixer combine the cream cheese, sugar, cream, and cinnamon, and mix until fluffy.

Chocolate-Peanut Butter Frosting

For a change try this fun frosting on your next batch of brownies or cake.

16   **ounces semisweet chocolate**
½   **cup butter (1 stick), cut into pieces**
1½   **cups peanut butter**
2   **tablespoons cream**

1. In the top of a double boiler over simmering water melt the chocolate, stirring until smooth.
2. Remove the pan from the water. Whisk in the butter, peanut butter, and cream.
3. Place the pan in a larger bowl filled with ice. Stir until the frosting becomes thick and spreadable.

Chocolate Cookie Cheesecake Bars

Cheesecake meets cookie and everyone wins with this dessert. Dip whole chocolate cookies in melted chocolate to decorate a platter full of cheesecake bars.

40	chocolate sandwich cookies
¼	cup butter (½ stick), melted
3	8-ounce packages cream cheese, room temperature
¾	cup sugar
4	eggs
1	cup sour cream
1	teaspoon vanilla extract
2	cups sour cream
¼	cup confectioners' sugar
1	teaspoon vanilla extract

HELPFUL HINT:
Place the cookies in a plastic bag. Gently pound the bag with a rolling pin or meat mallet to produce chunks instead of crumbs.

Preheat the oven to 350°.

1. Prepare a 13 x 9-inch baking dish by spraying with vegetable oil spray.
2. Place 25 of the cookies in a food processor. Pulse until finely crumbled. Add the melted butter and pulse again.
3. Press the mixture into the bottom of the dish using the back of a fork.
4. Break the remaining 15 cookies into chunks.
5. In the bowl of an electric mixer combine the cream cheese and sugar and beat until fluffy. Add the eggs one at a time. Mix in the sour cream and vanilla extract.
6. Stir in the chocolate sandwich cookie pieces.
7. Pour the batter on top of the crust. Bake for 45 minutes or until the center is set.
8. Mix together the sour cream, sugar, and vanilla.
9. Remove the cheesecake from the oven. Pour the sour cream mixture over the top. Return to the oven for 5 more minutes.

10. Remove the cake from the oven to a wire rack and cool. Cover the dish with plastic wrap. Chill in the refrigerator for at least 4 hours or overnight.

To serve cut into 2-inch squares and place on a platter dusted with cocoa powder.

Makes 12 bars
Preparation time about 1 hour plus refrigeration

Chocolate Sandwich Cookies Dipped in Chocolate

How fun is this? More ways to add chocolate to your life!

8   ounces semisweet chocolate
2   dozen cream-filled chocolate sandwich cookies

1. In the top of a double boiler over simmering water melt the chocolate, stirring until smooth.
2. Dip each cookie into the melted chocolate.
3. Place on a wire rack and allow to cool.
4. Refrigerate for 10 minutes.

Makes 2 dozen
Preparation time about 20 minutes

Loaded Chocolate Brownies

You can make brownies from a mix. However, this recipe is so easy, that you can make them from scratch faster than it takes to make a trip to the store.

1	cup unsalted butter (2 sticks)
16	ounces semisweet chocolate
6	ounces unsweetened chocolate
6	eggs
3	tablespoons instant coffee powder
1	cup firmly packed dark brown sugar
⅔	cup sugar
2	tablespoons vanilla extract
1	cup all-purpose flour
1	tablespoon baking powder
1	teaspoon salt
12	ounces semisweet chocolate chips

Preheat the oven to 350°.

1. Prepare a 12 x 8-inch jelly roll pan by spraying it with vegetable oil cooking spray and dusting with flour.
2. In a saucepan melt together the butter, 16 ounces of semi sweet chocolate, and unsweetened chocolate until smooth and shiny.
3. Cool the chocolate mixture.
4. In a large bowl stir together the eggs, coffee, sugar, and vanilla.
5. Add the chocolate mixture and stir well.
6. Mix in the flour, baking powder, and salt.
7. Stir in the chocolate pieces.
8. Pour the batter into the prepared pan. Bake for 30 to 40 minutes or until a toothpick inserted into the center comes out clean. Cool before cutting.

Makes 2 dozen large brownies
Preparation time about 20 minutes plus baking

HELPFUL HINT:
You can melt chocolate in a double boiler over medium heat. Remember to stir frequently. You may also melt chocolate using a microwave oven. The microwave can be tricky. I suggest that you place the butter and chocolate in a bowl and loosely cover with plastic wrap. Microwave on low heat for 30 seconds at a time until both the butter and chocolate are melted. Remove and stir the mixture thoroughly.

SIMPLE SUBSTITUTION:
For the nut lover, feel free to add 1 to 2 cups of chopped walnuts or pecans to the batter before baking. For an even chocolatier brownie, frost with black walnut frosting (see the frosting recipe with Chocolate Mahogany Cake on page 358).

SETTING THE SCENE:
Serve the brownie with a scoop of chocolate ice cream topped with warm chocolate sauce.

My Favorite Cheesecake

Whipped egg whites incorporated into the batter at the last moment make this cheesecake a fluffier version than most others. Lightly sweetened berries are the perfect accompaniment.

1½	**cups graham cracker crumbs**
½	**cup granulated sugar**
¼	**cup butter (½ stick), melted**

2	**8-ounce packages cream cheese**
1	**cup sugar**
4	**egg yolks**
1	**teaspoon vanilla**
1	**cup sour cream**
4	**egg whites, whipped**

Preheat the oven to 350°.

1. Prepare a 9-inch round spring form pan by spraying it with a vegetable oil cooking spray. Wrap the outside of the pan with aluminum foil.
2. In a food processor combine the graham cracker crumbs, sugar, and butter.
3. Press the crumb mixture into the bottom of the pan using your fingertips or the back side of a fork.
4. In the bowl of an electric mixer combine the cream cheese and sugar.
5. Add the egg yolks one at a time. Mix thoroughly, scraping down the sides of the bowl.
6. Add the vanilla and sour cream. Mix well until totally combined. Pour the batter into a large bowl.
7. In the bowl of an electric mixer whip the egg whites until they are fluffy and not too dry.
8. Fold the egg whites into the batter.
9. Pour the batter into the prepared pan.

Serves 8 to 10

Preparation time about 30 minutes plus baking and refrigeration

TECHNIQUE:
Fold egg whites into the batter by gently sliding the spatula across the bottom of the bowl and then upward, turning the bowl, until the batter is just blended. This is done so that the air that has been incorporated into the whipped ingredient is not released.

HELPFUL HINT:
Place the pan into a larger baking pan that contains about 1 inch of hot water. This water bath will insure even cooking for the cheesecake. The aluminum foil will make sure that the hot water does not enter the pan. Bake for 1 hour and 10 minutes in the lower third of the oven. The top of the cheesecake will brown and look puffy. I may not be set in the center. Carefully remove the cheesecake from the water bath. Remove the aluminum foil. Cool on a rack for 30 to 30 minutes. Run a knife around the inside edge of the pan. Cover with plastic wrap and chill in the refrigerator for at least 4 hours.

SETTING THE SCENE:
Serve a slice of cheesecake with a spoonful of berries that are in season and have been lightly sugared. The taste combination is deliciously decadent.

Peanut Butter Cup Cheesecake

This is a most delicious, rich, and velvety cheesecake. The peanut butter in the batter blends decadently with the chocolate peanut butter candies. You can have some fun with your favorite candy bars using this recipe as a guideline.

HELPFUL HINT:
To serve the cheesecake, remove it from the refrigerator. Release the sides of the pan. Cut the cheesecake into wedges.

1½ cups chocolate wafer cookies
½ cup peanuts
3 tablespoons firmly packed brown sugar
1 tablespoon unsweetened cocoa powder
5 tablespoons butter, melted (about ⅓ cup)

4 8-ounce packages cream cheese, room temperature
1½ cups firmly packed brown sugar
½ cup peanut butter
1 teaspoon vanilla extract
4 eggs
⅓ cup whipping cream
2½ cups chocolate covered peanut butter candy, chopped

2 cups sour cream
¼ cup sugar
½ teaspoon vanilla extract

Preheat the oven to 375°.
1. Spray a 12-inch springform pan with vegetable oil cooking spray.
2. In a food processor combine the chocolate wafer cookies, peanuts, brown sugar, and cocoa powder. Pulse until combined. Add the melted butter and pulse briefly.
3. Press the crumb mixture into the bottom and up the sides (about ½ inch) of the pan using the back of a fork. Bake for 8 to 10 minutes. Remove from the oven and cool. Reduce the oven temperature to 325°.
4. In the bowl of an electric mixer combine the cream cheese and brown sugar. Beat until fluffy.

5. Add the peanut butter and vanilla and mix until combined. Stir in the eggs one at a time.

6. Add the whipping cream and beat until the mixture is smooth. Stir in the candy chunks.

7. Pour the batter into the pan. Bake for 50 to 60 minutes. The cheesecake will puff and may crack on the sides. The center does not have to be set.

8. In the bowl of an electric mixer combine the sour cream, sugar, and vanilla, and heat until smooth.

9. Spoon the topping over the warm cheesecake and return to the oven for an additional 5 minutes.

10. Remove the cheesecake from the oven. Cool on a rack. Run sharp knife around the inside of the pan. Cover with plastic wrap and refrigerate overnight.

Serves 12 to 16
Preparation time about 15 minutes plus baking and refrigeration

Decorating Desserts

Turn your everyday desserts into Cafe fare by using a few tricks to decorate them.

❦ Sprinkle cheesecake with toasted almonds, pecans, cashews, hazelnuts, or macadamias.

❦ Drizzle a cake slice with strawberry, blackberry, or raspberry purée.

❦ Crown a scoop of ice cream with chocolate shavings, cocoa powder, white chocolate chips, crumbled fudge brownies, pieces of chocolate chip cookies, or chocolate wafers.

Share your favorite dessert decoration at www.jorj.com.

Chocolate Shortcake with Strawberries and Chocolate Sauce

This is a chocolate twist on a family favorite. If you don't have time to make the chocolate biscuits, a store bought pound cake will suffice.

1½	cups all-purpose flour
½	cup unsweetened cocoa
½	cup firmly packed brown sugar
1	tablespoon baking powder
½	teaspoon baking soda
½	teaspoon salt
1	cup buttermilk
3	tablespoons butter (⅓ stick), melted
2	tablespoons vanilla extract
1	pound fresh strawberries, hulled and halved
	Chocolate Sauce (recipe follows)
	Vanilla ice cream

Preheat the oven to 425°.

1. Prepare a baking sheet by spraying it with vegetable oil cooking spray.
2. In a medium bowl place the flour, cocoa powder, brown sugar, baking powder, baking soda, and salt.
3. Pour in the buttermilk, melted butter, and vanilla extract.
4. Use a fork to mix the batter together until just blended. Do not over mix or biscuits will be dry.
5. Drop the dough by rounded tablespoons on the baking sheet 1 to 2 inches apart. Bake for 10 to 12 minutes.

Serves 8
Preparation time about 40 minutes

SETTING THE SCENE:
To serve the dessert, slice the biscuits in half horizontally. Place one half of the biscuit at the bottom of a serving dish. Top with a spoonful of strawberries. Stack the top half of the biscuit on top. Place a scoop of vanilla ice cream on the biscuit. Mound more strawberries on top of the ice cream. Drizzle the Chocolate Sauce on top.

Chocolate Sauce

Way better than the stuff in the plastic squeeze bottle. This sauce served warm dresses up everyday ice cream—into Sunday's sundae.

1	**tablespoon butter**
½	**cup unsweetened cocoa**
¼	**cup confectioners' sugar**
1	**cup dark corn syrup**
1	**tablespoon whipping cream**

1. In a saucepan combine the butter, cocoa powder, sugar, and corn syrup over medium heat. Blend until smooth, being careful not to burn.
2. Stir in the whipped cream. The chocolate sauce should be smooth and shiny. Remove from heat.

Serves 8
Preparation time about 10 minutes

Apple Strawberry Cobbler

Fresh fruit is topped with a dark, rich oatmeal topping that has a toffee-like quality in this summer dessert.

6	**Granny Smith apples, peeled, cored and sliced (about 4 cups)**
2	**pints fresh strawberries, sliced**
	Juice of ½ medium lemon
¼	**cup sugar**
¼	**cup firmly packed brown sugar**
1	**teaspoon cinnamon**
2	**tablespoon flour**
1	**cup oatmeal**
¾	**cup sugar**
¾	**cup firmly packed dark brown sugar**
1½	**cups all-purpose flour**
2	**teaspoons cinnamon**
1	**teaspoon nutmeg**
¼	**teaspoon salt**
1	**cup butter (2 sticks)**

Vanilla ice cream, optional

Preheat oven to 350°.

1. Place the apples and strawberries in the bottom of a 15 x 10 x 3-inch baking pan. Drizzle with lemon juice.
2. Sprinkle the sugar, brown sugar, cinnamon, and flour over the fruit.
3. In a food processor combine the oats, sugar, brown sugar, flour, cinnamon, nutmeg, and salt. Pulse to mix.
4. Cut the butter into small pieces and place in the food processor bowl. Process until the mixture resembles small crumbs.
5. Sprinkle the crumb mixture over the fruit.
6. Bake for 45 minutes to 1 hour or until the top browns and the fruit is bubbling.

Serves 10 to 12
Preparation time about 20 minutes plus baking

SIMPLE SUBSTITUTION:
You may substitute with many different types of fruit. I like to blend the tartness of the apples with the sweetness of the strawberries.

HELPFUL HINT:
To prevent the apple slices from turning brown while you are preparing the recipe, squeeze a few drops of lemon juice over top and toss gently.

SETTING THE SCENE:
Serve the cobbler warm in a pottery bowl or an oversized mug. Offer a spoonful of vanilla ice cream on top.

Share your favorite fruit dessert at www.jorj.com.

Chocolate Bread Pudding with Cinnamon Vanilla Sauce

This is a terrific dish to place on a dessert buffet. Feel free to make the pudding the day before, and bake just as your guests arrive. Serve warm with the delicious vanilla sauce over the top.

SETTING THE SCENE:
Spoon a generous amount of bread pudding into a dessert bowl. Offer the cinnamon vanilla sauce from a gravy boat with a ladle. Top with a dollop of whipped cream and a sprinkle of cinnamon sugar.

16	ounces French bread, cut into 1-inch cubes
3¼	cups milk
5	eggs
1½	cups chocolate syrup
¾	cup brown sugar
2	teaspoons vanilla extract
4	ounces semisweet chocolate chips
4	ounces white chocolate chips

Cinnamon Vanilla Sauce (page 305)

Preheat the oven to 350°.
1. Place the bread cubes in a large baking dish.
2. In a small bowl whisk together the milk, eggs, syrup, brown sugar, and vanilla.
3. Toss the semisweet and white chocolate chips into the bread cubes.
4. Pour the milk and egg mixture over the bread. Press the cubes down into the mixture to make sure they absorb the liquid. Set aside for 20 to 30 minutes.
5. Bake for 50 minutes or until the center is puffy.

Serves 10 to 12
Preparation time about 20 minutes plus baking

Cinnamon Bread Pudding with Bourbon Sauce

*This is a delicious way to end a meal and begin the rest of
the evening. Serve the bread pudding warm from the
oven.*

8	slices cinnamon bread
1	cup whipping cream
½	cup milk
¼	cup sugar
2	egg yolks
1	egg
¼	teaspoon ground cinnamon
1	teaspoon vanilla extract

Bourbon Sauce (recipe follows)
Whipped cream for topping

Preheat the oven to 350°.

1. Trim the crusts from the cinnamon bread and cut the
   slices into cubes.
2. Toast the cubes on a baking sheet for 5 to 10 minutes
   until they are just beginning to brown. Remove from
   the oven and cool. Place the cubes into a medium size
   baking dish.
3. In a saucepan combine the whipping cream, milk, and
   sugar over medium high heat. Stir together until the
   sugar is dissolved.
4. Whisk in the egg yolks and the egg and continue to
   cook for several minutes.
5. Stir in the cinnamon and vanilla until well blended.
6. Pour the custard mixture over the bread. Make sure
   that each bread cube is gently pushed down into the
   sauce. Cover the dish and bake for 30 minutes.
   Uncover and bake for 10 minutes more or until the top
   of the bread pudding begins to brown.

Serves 6 to 8
Preparation time about 20 minutes plus baking

SIMPLE SUBSTITUTION:
Substitute any thick day old bread
for the cinnamon bread. My favorite
is to use 4 whole croissants smothered with the rich custard sauce.

SETTING THE SCENE:
Spoon a generous amount of the
bread pudding into a dessert bowl.
Offer the bourbon sauce from a
gravy boat with a ladle. Top with a
dollop of whipped cream.

Bourbon Sauce

½ cup whipping cream
1 tablespoon sugar
1 teaspoon vanilla extract
1 to 2 tablespoons bourbon whiskey

1. In a saucepan reduce the whipping cream over medium high heat, stirring constantly, until it begins to thicken.
2. Add the sugar and vanilla and stir until the sugar is dissolved.
3. Add the bourbon to the whipping cream and cook for several minutes.

Cinnamon Vanilla Sauce

1⅓ cups heavy cream
⅔ cup milk
2 cinnamon sticks
⅓ cup sugar
4 egg yolks
1 teaspoon vanilla extract

1. In a saucepan combine the cream, milk, and cinnamon sticks. Bring to a boil over medium high heat. Remove from the heat and let sit for 1 hour.
2. Place ice cubes in a large bowl. In a medium bowl stir together the sugar, egg yolks, and vanilla.
3. Remove the cinnamon sticks from the cream mixture. Heat the cream to a boil.
4. Pour the hot mixture into the egg yolks, whisking briskly. Place the bowl containing the egg yolk mixture in the larger bowl of ice. Continue whisking on and off for 30 minutes. This will cool and thicken the sauce.

Warm Apple Tart with Almond Crème and Classic Caramel Sauce

This dessert comes together quickly yet looks like you fussed all day. It can be prepared an hour or two ahead of cooking and kept warm in a warming drawer until ready to serve.

½	cup toasted almonds
2	tablespoons all-purpose flour
2	tablespoons unsalted butter, room temperature
¼	cup confectioners' sugar
1	egg
¼	teaspoon almond extract

1	puff pastry sheet, thawed
1	Granny Smith apple, peeled, cored and sliced into thin pieces
1	teaspoon sugar
⅛	teaspoon ground cinnamon

Cinnamon vanilla ice cream (optional)

Preheat the oven to 400°.

1. In the bowl of a food processor place all but 1 teaspoon of the toasted almonds. Pulse until the almonds become a powder.
2. Add the flour, butter, and sugar to the almonds. Pulse to combine.
3. Add the egg and the almond extract. Pulse until the mixture has a creamy consistency.
4. Unfold the puff pastry sheet and roll out slightly. Cut two pieces from the sheet by using the top of a small bowl and a knife to cut around the edge to form circles.
5. Place the circles onto a cookie sheet that has been sprayed with vegetable oil cooking spray.
6. Pierce the dough with a fork several times to prevent uneven rising. Spread the almond crème evenly over both circles of dough.

SETTING THE SCENE:
Serve the tart by removing it from the cookie sheet and placing it on a dessert plate. Drizzle the warm caramel sauce over top. Add a scoop of cinnamon vanilla ice cream and another drizzle of sauce to complete the dish.

7. Place the apple slices over the almond crème in a circular pattern. Sprinkle the sugar and cinnamon over the apples slices. Top with the reserved almonds.
8. Bake the tarts for 20 to 25 minutes.

Serves 2
Preparation time about 20 minutes plus baking

Classic Caramel Sauce

Take particular care when making this sugary sauce, because the sugar mixture gets hot quickly and bubbles up when you add the cream.

1	**cup water**
1½	**cups sugar**
½	**cup heavy cream**

1. In a saucepan combine the water and sugar over high heat and bring to a boil. Continue cooking until the sugar dissolves and begins to darken to a caramel color.
2. Very carefully add the cream to the hot mixture. It will bubble up instantly. Continue to stir until the sauce begins to thicken. Reduce the heat and keep warm.

Lime Buttery Cake

There are many versions of rich butter cake. Here, the addition of zesty key limes makes all the difference.

3	**cups cake flour**
3	**teaspoons baking powder**
½	**teaspoon salt**
1	**cup unsalted butter (2 sticks), room temperature**
1½	**cups sugar**
4	**eggs**
1	**cup milk**
3	**tablespoons fresh key lime juice, about 3 to 4 key limes**
2	**tablespoons key lime zest**
2½	**cups confectioners' sugar**
½	**teaspoon vanilla**
½	**cup fresh key lime juice, about 6 to 8 key limes**

Preheat the oven to 325°.

1. In a small bowl combine the flour, baking powder and salt and set aside.
2. In the bowl of an electric mixer cream the butter until fluffy.
3. Add the sugar and mix on medium speed, scraping down the sides of the bowl, for several minutes.
4. Add the eggs, one at a time, stirring well after each addition.
5. Stir in one-third of the flour mixture followed by one-third of the milk. Repeat until both ingredients are incorporated into the batter.
6. Stir in the key lime juice.
7. Pour the batter into a Bundt cake pan (or other decorative cake pan) that has been sprayed with a vegetable oil cooking spray. Bake for 40 to 50 minutes (depending on the pan) or until the cake springs back when touched.
8. Cool on a rack for several minutes. Then, invert the cake and remove it to the rack.

HELPFUL HINT:
Piercing the cake will allow some of the glaze to seep into the cake keeping it moist and full of key lime flavor.

SIMPLE SUBSTITUTION:
Substitute lemons or oranges for a must have buttery, citrus cake.

SETTING THE SCENE:
Garnish with fresh berries.

9. Whisk together the key lime zest, sugar, vanilla and key lime juice.
10. Use a skewer to pierce the cake several times. Brush the glaze over the top and sides of the warm cake. Pour the leftover glaze that has collected on the waxed paper onto the cake. Repeat until all of the glaze is used—about 3 times.

Serves 10 or more
Preparation time about 15 minutes plus baking

THE DESSERT BUFFET TABLE

Key Lime Buttery Cake
Served with whipped cream and
fresh strawberries

Chocolate Bread Pudding
Served with a ladleful of warm
Chocolate Sauce

Peanut Butter Cup Cheesecake
sliced into wedges

Mixed Fresh Berries
with Zabaglione Sauce

Peach Pie Y'all

There's nothing like the aroma of a fresh-from-the-oven baked fruit pie. This one is a family favorite. Feel free to substitute with your favorite fresh fruit like apple, blueberry, cherry, or a combination of them all.

2	cups all-purpose flour
1	teaspoon salt
¼	cup confectioners' sugar
4	tablespoons butter (½ stick), chilled, cut into pieces
3	tablespoons shortening, chilled, cut into pieces
5	tablespoons ice water

5	ripe peaches, sliced, about 5 cups
½	cup firmly packed brown sugar
⅛	teaspoon salt
1½	tablespoons cornstarch
½	teaspoon cinnamon
1	tablespoon butter, cut into small pieces
1	tablespoon cream

Preheat the oven to 450°.

1. In the bowl of a food processor combine the flour, salt and confectioners' sugar.
2. Add the butter and shortening to the bowl. Pulse until the mixture resembles tiny crumbs.
3. Add the ice water and pulse until a dough forms. (You may use more or less of the water.)
4. Remove the dough from the bowl and form it into two rounds. Wrap each in plastic wrap and refrigerate for at least 30 minutes.
5. In a large bowl combine the sliced peaches, brown sugar, salt, cornstarch, and cinnamon and toss to coat.
6. Roll out the first dough round into a circle about ¼-inch thick. Place it into the bottom of a 9-inch pie plate.
7. Place the filling into the pie. Dot the filling with small pieces of butter. Top with the second dough round that has been rolled out to ¼-inch thickness. Crimp the edges together.

HELPFUL HINT:
A foolproof way to roll out dough is between two floured pieces of plastic wrap. Remove the top piece from the dough and use the bottom piece to lift the dough into the pie plate.

8. Make slits in the top of the crust with the pointed end of a knife. Brush the crust with cream.
9. Bake the pie for 10 minutes at 450°. Reduce the oven temperature to 350° and bake for 35 to 45 minutes more or until golden brown.

Serves 6
Preparation time about 20 minutes plus baking

Whipped Cream

Much better than the stuff that squirts out of a red-topped can—homemade whipped cream is made in minutes.

1   **pint heavy whipping cream**
¾   **cup confectioners' sugar**

1. In the bowl of an electric mixer, using the whisk attachment, beat the cream on high speed for several minutes.
2. Add the sugar and whip until soft peaks form. Too much whipping will turn your cream into butter!

HELPFUL HINT:
Guarantee great results by making sure the cream is chilled before you begin. Place the mixing bowl and whisk attachment in the freezer for 5 to 10 minutes.

SIMPLE SUBSTITUTION:
For an upscale flavor add a table-spoon or two of your favorite liqueur lake Amaretto or Kahlua as you begin to whip.

Perfect Pumpkin Pie

Pie crusts can be a challenge. The secret is to use very cold butter and ice cold water. It also helps to chill the dough before you roll it out. The best clue that I have picked up over the years is to roll the dough between two pieces of plastic wrap. This makes moving the dough into the pie dish a snap.

2	cups all-purpose flour
¾	cup confectioners' sugar
½	cup butter (1 stick), chilled, cut into pieces
3	to 4 tablespoons ice water
¾	cup firmly packed light brown sugar
1	tablespoon cornstarch
2	teaspoons cinnamon
¾	teaspoon ginger
¼	teaspoon salt
1	16-ounce can pumpkin purée
¾	cup whipping cream
½	cup sour cream
3	eggs, beaten
¼	cup apricot preserves

Preheat the oven to 350°.

1. In a food processor pulse the flour, sugar, and chilled butter pieces, until the mixture resembles small clumps. Add enough water to just bring the clumps together.
2. Pour the dough onto a floured surface and form into a ball. Flatten the ball into a disk, cover with plastic wrap and chill for at least 30 minutes.
3. Roll out the dough between two floured plastic sheets. Transfer the dough to a pie pan (removing the plastic). Form a decorative crust with the overhang. Freeze for 15 minutes.
4. Line the crust with foil that has been lightly sprayed with vegetable oil cooking spray (sprayed side down). Place pie weights (or dried beans) on top of the foil. Bake the pie shell for 10 minutes.

SETTING THE SCENE:
Serve the pie at room temperature with whipped cream flavored with a touch of apricot brandy.

5. Remove the foil and the pie weights and bake for an additional 10 minutes or until the crust just begins to brown. Remove the pie from the oven. Reduce the oven temperature to 325°.

For filling:
6. Using an electric mixer and a whisk attachment, blend the brown sugar, cornstarch, cinnamon, ginger, and salt with the canned pumpkin.
7. Add to the bowl the whipping cream, sour cream and beaten eggs. Mix thoroughly.
8. Use a pastry brush to spread the apricot preserves over the bottom of the pie crust.
9. Pour the filling into the crust. Bake until the filling puffs up and the center is almost set (about 55 minutes).

Serves 8
Preparation time about 30 minutes plus baking

Pie Crust Decorations

To decorate a pumpkin pie, cut out maple leaf (or other fall shapes) from the extra pie crust dough. Place the shapes on a baking sheet. Sprinkle with granulated sugar. Bake for 5 to 10 minutes or until golden brown. Cool. Place the baked shapes onto the top of the pumpkin filling as the pie is cooling.

Chocolate Pudding Pie

This pie is the favorite with all the little ones during the holidays. There are never any leftovers in the dish—but there are plenty of little faces and fingers that will require wiping.

1½	**cups graham cracker crumbs**
¾	**cup chocolate wafer cookies, ground into crumbs**
2	**tablespoons firmly packed brown sugar**
¼	**cup butter (½ stick), melted**
2	**ounces unsweetened chocolate**
½	**cup sugar**
3½	**cups milk, divided**
¼	**teaspoon salt**
5	**tablespoons cornstarch**
2	**teaspoons vanilla extract**

For crust:
1. Preheat the oven to 350°.
2. In the bowl of a food processor combine the cracker crumbs, chocolate wafer crumbs, and brown sugar.
3. Add the melted butter.
4. Place the crumb mixture into a pie pan and push down firmly (using the back of a fork) on the bottom and up the sides.
5. Bake for 5 minutes. Set aside to cool.

For filling:
1. In a double boiler melt the unsweetened chocolate.
2. Stir in the sugar, 3 cups of milk, and salt.
3. Combine the cornstarch with the remaining ½ cup of milk.
4. Slowly stir in the cornstarch when the chocolate mixture has reached the boiling point. Cook over boiling water until thickened.
5. Remove from heat and continue stirring until the pudding begins to cool.

6. Stir in the vanilla. Pour the pudding into the prepared pie crust.
7. Chill at least 4 hours.

Serves 6 to 8
Preparation time about 30 minutes plus 4 hours to chill

Make Your Own Sundaes

Here's another fun dessert to share with little ones.

* Use an ice cream scoop to place balls of various ice creams into a large bowl. Try vanilla, chocolate, mint, butterscotch, strawberry, and any other favorites.

* Freeze the bowl full of ice cream balls.

* Serve the bowl buffet-style surrounded by any and all of your favorite toppings.

SOME TOPPING SUGGESTIONS:

- Chocolate sauce
- Caramel sauce
- Whipped cream
- M & M candies
- Toasted coconut
- Chopped nuts
- Crumbled cookies
- Red licorice pieces
- Kiwi and raspberries with sprigs of fresh mint
- Sliced nectarines and blueberries
- Sliced peaches

Sautéed Fruit with Walnut Shortbread

Summer season's freshest berries star in this simple but stunning dessert. Easily prepared in advance and assembled at the last minute, it works well for dinner parties.

1	cup all-purpose flour
½	cup chopped walnuts
½	cup oatmeal
¼	teaspoon salt
2	tablespoons firmly packed brown sugar
½	cup butter (1 stick)
¼	cup orange juice

1	pint fresh raspberries
1	pint fresh quinberries
1	pint fresh strawberries, sliced
1	banana, sliced
1	tablespoon butter
¼	cup orange juice

Preheat the oven to 350°.

1. In a food processor combine the flour, chopped walnuts, oatmeal, salt, and brown sugar until well blended.
2. Add the butter and orange juice and pulse until a dough is formed,
3. Spread the dough between two sheets of parchment paper on a cookie sheet using your hands or a rolling pin. The dough should be ¼ inch thick.
4. Bake the dough for 6 to 10 minutes. Allow to cool and then slice into triangles or rounds.
5. Sauté the fruit in the butter for 1 to 2 minutes.
6. Add the orange juice and cook for several minutes more.

Serves 6
Preparation time about 45 minutes

SETTING THE SCENE:
Serve the warmed fruit in a shallow dessert bowl on top of a scoop of ice cream. Place a piece of shortbread on top.

Crunchy Chocolate Fudge

This is a foolproof recipe for a great chocolatey treat. You can cut the fudge into small squares and place into individual candy cups so that you can share a bunch with your friends.

2   8-ounce packages semisweet chocolate
1   14-ounce can sweetened condensed milk
¼   teaspoon salt
½   teaspoon vanilla extract
2   cups chopped pretzel pieces

1. Spray a 13 x 9-inch baking dish with vegetable oil cooking spray. Line the sprayed pan with waxed paper.
2. In the top of a double boiler melt the chocolate with the condensed milk over medium high heat. Stir until smooth.
3. Stir in the salt and vanilla.
4. Remove the double boiler pan from the water. Stir in the pretzel pieces.
5. Spread the fudge into the lined baking dish. Chill in the refrigerator for at least 2 hours.
6. Remove the dish from the refrigerator and invert it onto a cutting board. Peel off the waxed paper. Cut the fudge into squares.

Makes approximately 2 dozen pieces
Preparation time about 20 minutes plus refrigeration

HELPFUL HINT:
To chop the pretzel pieces place them in a mini food processor or hand chopper. Pulse quickly. Pour the pretzel pieces into a colander and shake out any powder residue.

To share your favorite fudge recipe visit www.jorj.com.

Chewy Caramels

As a kid we used to hide hands full of these chewy caramels in our pockets and steel away to a corner to eat them. This recipe makes a big batch—perfect for deep pockets. Or you can store them in a tin for days and days.

2	**cups dark corn syrup**
1	**cup milk**
2	**cups sugar**
½	**cup butter (1 stick)**
2	**tablespoons vanilla extract**
8	**ounces unsweetened chocolate**

Confectioners' sugar

1. Place all of the ingredients into a large deep pan.
2. Heat over medium high heat stirring constantly.
3. Remove the caramel mixture from the heat. Cool to room temperature.
4. Spray a 13 x 9-inch baking dish with vegetable oil cooking spray. Line the sprayed pan with waxed paper. Spray the waxed paper. Pour the caramel mixture into the pan. Let the caramels continue to cool until they are firm.
5. Turn out the caramels onto a cutting board. Remove the waxed paper.
6. Use poultry sheers to cut the caramels into ½ inch squares and drop them into a bowl of powdered sugar.
7. Wrap each one in waxed paper twisting the ends.

Makes approximately 3 pounds of caramels
Preparation time about 30 minutes

HELPFUL HINT:
The mixture will bubble up while cooking and then begin to cook down. Make sure that you are using a very deep pot. The caramels will reach about 250° on a candy thermometer or a wooden spoon drawn across the bottom of the pan will leave a track that doesn't fill immediately. Do not overcook as the chocolate may burn.

TECHNIQUE:
If you use a knife instead of poultry sheers, dip the knife in powdered sugar or ice water to prevent sticking. If the caramels are too firm, place them in the microwave for a few seconds.

Upscale Dining Made Easy

PUTTING IT ALL TOGETHER

Whew! You have created your own fresh salads, stirred up some fabulous soups, taken advantage of seasonal veggies and mastered both indoor and outdoor grilling. You can swim with the fish and drive by the take out window. You alternately dine alfresco and bask in the complexities of comfort food. You have breakfast at midnight just as easily as you have friends in for nibbles. Dessert is a treat that regularly works it's way into your menu plan. There is nothing that you can't do. So, it's time for a little upscale entertaining.

The dinner party is the culmination of all of your skills and the best gift that you can give to friends, coworkers, and family. All that's needed is a little organization and a foolproof plan. Here are some suggestions for a countdown to a great party.

- Place pen in hand to produce the guest list and choose invitations.
- Choose the fare to create an interesting menu.
- Take inventory of china, glassware, serving pieces, placemats and napkins.
- Organize the bar and make wine selections.
- Decide on a table theme for centerpieces and serving tables.
- Write down a shopping list that is sorted by grocery store departments.
- Make a cooking schedule. Be sure to make ahead foods like desserts and terrines.
- Identify guests that you can call upon to help during the party with serving and clearing.

You will find some inspirational ideas for terrific menus in the Upscale Dining Made Easy chapter. There are impressive first courses, elegant entrées and show stopper desserts. But don't stop here. Use your creativity and talent to devise terrific dinner party menus and then remember to share them with your friends at www.jorj.com.

Find more information about the recipes in the Upscale Dining Made Easy chapter at www.jorj.com.

Eggplant Stuffed with Goat Cheese and Black Bean Sauce

Serve this dish as an upscale starter for a sit down feast or as a staple on your buffet party table. Either way the dish is easily made in advance and baked just before serving.

2	large eggplants
	Salt
2	tablespoons olive oil
	Freshly ground pepper
8	ounces goat cheese, softened
1	teaspoon dried oregano

Black Bean Sauce (recipe follows)

Preheat the oven to 350°.

1. Cut the eggplant lengthwise into ¼-inch slices. Season each slice with salt.
2. Place the slices into a colander and allow to drain for 1 hour.
3. Place the eggplant slices on a baking sheet.
4. Brush both sides with olive oil and sprinkle with freshly ground pepper.
5. Roast the eggplant for 5 to 8 minutes on each side. (The eggplant will be pliable but not mushy.) Cool to room temperature.
6. In an electric mixer or food processor combine the goat cheese with the dried oregano.
7. Spread each eggplant slice with the goat cheese mixture. Roll the eggplant from the small end jelly roll fashion. Place each roll seam side down into a baking dish that has been sprayed with a vegetable oil spray.
8. Bake at 350° for about 20 minutes until the eggplant is cooked through.

Serves 6
Preparation time about 45 minutes

HELPFUL HINT:
The salt will help to take away the extra moisture in the eggplant. Some cooks also feel that the salt reduces some of the eggplant's bitterness.

HELPFUL HINT:
The dish can be made through step 7 and refrigerated refrigerated until you are ready to bake.

SETTING THE SCENE:
To serve place one to two eggplant rolls on a small plate. Drizzle the black bean sauce over top. Garnish with additional chopped cilantro.

Black Bean Sauce

This sauce is great served over grilled pork tenderloin or simple baked sea bass.

2	tablespoons olive oil
1	large shallot, finely diced (about 1 tablespoon)
1	15-ounce can black beans, drained
¼	cup sherry
1	cup chicken stock
3	to 4 medium cup plum tomatoes, diced (about 1 cup)
1	tablespoon chopped fresh cilantro
	Salt and freshly ground black pepper

1. In a medium skillet heat the olive oil over medium high heat.
2. Toss the shallots into the pan a cook until just golden.
3. Add the black beans and cook for 5 minutes more.
4. Add the sherry and reduce until there is only a very little liquid remaining in the pan.
5. Add the chicken stock and reduce the liquid by half.
6. Remove 2 tablespoons of the black beans and mash using the back of a spoon. Return the mashed beans to the pan to thicken the sauce.
7. Add the diced tomatoes and cilantro and cook for several minutes. Season with salt and freshly ground pepper.

Serves 4

HELPFUL HINT:
The sauce can be made in advance and refrigerated in an airtight container for several days.

UPSCALE MENU

Eggplant Stuffed with Goat Cheese
and Black Bean Sauce

Veal Cutlets with Dill and Sage
Cream Sauce

Yam Pudding

Chocolate Mahogany Cake

Spinach and Goat Cheese Ravioli with Hazelnut Butter Sauce

The ravioli are striking on as simple dish served with the toasted hazelnut butter sauce as an elegant first course.

6	slices bacon, chopped
1	clove garlic, minced (about 1 teaspoon)
2	cups chopped fresh spinach leaves
6	ounces goat cheese, room temperature
	Salt and freshly ground pepper
1	6-ounce package wonton wrappers
1	egg white, beaten with 1 tablespoon water

Hazelnut Butter Sauce (recipe follows)
Parmesan cheese, shaved
Fresh chives

1. In a large skillet cook the chopped bacon over medium high heat until crisp. Remove the bacon using a slotted spoon and drain on paper towels.
2. Remove all but 1 tablespoon of the bacon drippings from the pan. Add the minced garlic and cook until soft.
3. Toss the spinach into the pan and cook until just wilted. Place the spinach mixture into a large bowl.
4. Add the bacon and goat cheese to the spinach. Stir to combine. Season with salt and pepper.
5. Use wonton wrappers to create spinach-filled ravioli as directed in the Technique sidebar.
6. Bring water to a boil in a deep saucepan. Add 1 teaspoon salt. Drop the ravioli into the water and cook for about 3 to 4 minutes until done. Remove the ravioli using a slotted spoon. Drain in a colander.

Serves 4
Preparation time about 40 minutes

TECHNIQUE:
To form the ravioli lay out the wonton wrappers side by side working with two at a time. Brush the edge of one wonton wrapper with the egg white mixture. Place a spoonful of the filling in the center of the square. Brush the edges of the second wonton wrapper with the egg white. Place the second wonton wrapper on top of the first. Press the wet edges together to seal the filling inside. At this point you can seal the edges with the back side of a fork. You may also use a glass to cut the ravioli into circles. Once the circle is formed, use the back of a fork to seal the edges. It is important that the filling is well sealed in the ravioli and not leaking out. Do not over stuff!! Place the ravioli on a baking sheet. Repeat with remaining wrappers and filling.

SETTING THE SCENE:
On a small plate serve 2 to 3 ravioli. Place a spoonful of hazelnut butter sauce on top. Shave curls of Parmesan cheese onto the ravioli. Garnish with whole fresh chives.

Hazelnut Butter Sauce

The combination of toasted hazelnuts and butter is terrific over everyday pasta.

1	**cup hazelnuts**
½	**cup butter (1 stick)**

1. Toast the hazelnuts until just golden brown.
2. Place the nuts in the bowl of a food processor. Pulse briefly to roughly chop. Melt the butter in a small sauce pan over medium heat. Cook the chopped nuts in the butter for several minutes. Keep the sauce warm while the ravioli cook.

HELPFUL HINT:
Hazelnuts have a skin. To toast place them on a baking sheet. Bake for several minutes at 350°. Remove the hazelnuts from the oven and place them onto a clean kitchen towel. Rub the nuts in the towel until most of the skins are removed.

ELEGANT DINNER MENU

Spinach and Goat Cheese Ravioli
with Hazelnut Butter Sauce

Herb Crusted Rack of Lamb

Corn Soufflé Casserole

Sticky Toffee Pudding
with Caramel Sauce

Spicy Black Bean Cakes with Chili Cream Sauce

Here is an interesting veggie dish that can be used as an appetizer, side dish, or sophisticated midday entrée. Feel free to alter the amount of seasonings to create as much spice as you want!

1	medium yellow onion, diced (about ½ cup)
2	cloves garlic, minced (about 1 tablespoon)
2	green onions, chopped (about 2 tablespoons)
1	jalapeño pepper, seeded and diced (about 1 tablespoon)
1	tablespoon olive oil
1	teaspoon chili powder
¼	teaspoon ground cumin
1	15-ounce can black beans, drained
1	tablespoon chopped fresh cilantro
	Juice of ½ lime
	Salt and freshly ground pepper
4	large shrimp, cooked
	Chili Cream Sauce (recipe follows)

1. In a large skillet cook the onion, garlic, green onion, and jalapeño in the olive oil over medium high heat until softened.
2. Add the chili powder, cumin, black beans, cilantro, and lime juice. Cook for several minutes until the liquid disappears from the bottom of the pan. Season with salt and freshly ground pepper.
3. Use a potato masher to mix together all of the ingredients. Transfer the bean mixture to a bowl, cover, and chill for at least 30 minutes.

Preheat the oven to 350°.

4. Form the mixture into 4 cakes the size of silver dollar pancakes. Place on a baking sheet. Bake for 10 to 15 minutes.

Serves 4
Preparation time about 30 minutes plus baking

SETTING THE SCENE:
Place one spicy bean cake onto a small plate. Top with one cooked shrimp. Drizzle the chili cream sauce over all. Garnish with a spring of fresh cilantro.

Chili Cream Sauce

Try this sauce over roasted salmon!

1	**tablespoon butter**
2	**shallots, minced**
½	**cup white wine**
1	**cup whipping cream**
¼	**cup unsalted butter (½ stick), chilled**
1	**tablespoon prepared chili sauce**

1. In a large skillet cook the shallots in 1 tablespoon of butter over medium high heat until softened.
2. Add the wine to the skillet and cook until the liquid disappears.
3. Add the cream to the pan and cook until it is reduced to half.
4. Turn down the heat and whisk the butter into the sauce 1 tablespoon at a time. Be careful to not let the sauce boil.
5. Add the chili sauce to the pan and stir.

Makes about 1½ cups
Preparation time about 30 minutes

HIGH-STYLE DINNER MENU

Spicy Black Bean Cakes
with Chili Cream Sauce

Beef Tenderloin
Stuffed with Roasted Peppers,
Spinach, and Goat Cheese
served with Port Wine Sauce

Sautéed Green Beans
with Caramelized Pearl Onions

Strawberry Cake
with Cream Cheese Frosting

Lobster Burrito with Cilantro Cream Sauce

Look what happens when we use lobster medallions, stir-fry veggies, and delicate phyllo dough to update an everyday favorite. The combination of flavors is unique. This first course is rich and deserves to be savored. Make sure that you plan ahead to have everything ready before you begin!

1	medium red bell pepper, finely julienne (about 1 cup)
1	medium yellow bell pepper, finely julienned (about 1 cup)
1	medium leek, mostly white part, washed, cut into very thin strips (about 1 cup)
1	jalapeño pepper, seeded and finely julienned (about 1 tablespoon)
1	tablespoon olive oil
1	teaspoon lime zest
1	teaspoon chopped fresh cilantro
1	cloves garlic, minced (about 1 tablespoon)
6	phyllo dough sheets
¼	cup unsalted butter (½ stick), melted
1	cup canned black beans, drained
1	pound lobster meat, cooked and cut into medallions
4	ounces Monterey Jack cheese
2	whole shallots, minced (about 2 tablespoons)
1	teaspoon olive oil
¼	cup tequila
1	cup whipping cream
½	cup chopped fresh cilantro
¼	teaspoon nutmeg
	Salt and ground white pepper
1	cup Black Bean and Toasted Corn Salsa (page 258)

TECHNIQUE:
Read about cleaning leeks on page 64 and fresh lime zest on page 282.

Remember to thaw the phyllo dough before you begin the recipe. Phyllo dough thaws in the refrigerator overnight or on the counter for several hours. Use leftover lobster meat or purchase cooked lobster meat to save time.

SETTING THE SCENE:
Place a spoonful of sauce on a warm salad plate. Use a spatula to carefully lift the burrito onto the plate. Garnish with a spoonful of salsa and a sprig of fresh cilantro.

Preheat the oven to 375°.

1. In a large skillet cook the red and yellow bell pepper, leeks, and jalapeño pepper in the olive oil over medium high heat until softened.

2. Add the lime zest, cilantro, and garlic. Cook for 1 minute more and set aside.

3. Remove the phyllo sheets from the package and cover with a clean damp towel to keep moist.

4. Brush 1 sheet of phyllo lightly with butter. Cover with a second sheet and brush again. Cover with a third sheet and brush with butter again. Cover the remaining sheets with the clean damp towel.

5. Place the phyllo sheets with the narrow end facing you. Cut the sheets in half.

6. Place one-eighth of the vegetable mixture on the top third of the first half of a phyllo sheet. Place ¼ cup of black beans on top. Top the beans with lobster meat. Place one-eighth more of the vegetable mixture on top of the meat. Sprinkle one-fourth of the cheese over top.

7. Roll up the phyllo dough burrito style using melted butter to seal the edges as you work. Place on an ungreased baking sheet, covered with a clean towel and chill until all of the burritos are assembled. Repeat the above process on the second half of the layered phyllo sheets. Then continue with the next 3 sheets.

8. Remove the burritos from the refrigerator. Brush lightly with melted butter. Bake for about 10 to 15 minutes until the filling is warmed through and the burrito is golden brown.

9. Prepare the sauce by cooking the shallots in olive oil until soft. Add the tequila to the pan and reduce until no liquid remains. Pour the cream into the pan and reduce to ½ cup. Add the cilantro to the sauce. Season with nutmeg, salt, and ground white pepper.

Serves 4
Preparation time about 1 hour plus baking

TECHNIQUE:
Burrito style means covering the filling with the edge of the layered phyllo sheet. Carefully roll it over once. Fold the outer edges in and over the roll. Brush with butter. Continue to roll until all of the phyllo is in place.

UPSCALE DINNER MENU

Lobster Burrito
with Cilantro Cream Sauce
❧

Pasta Stuffed Eggplant
and Pork Medallions
❧

Flourless Chocolate Torte

Portabella Mushrooms Stuffed with Goat Cheese and Sun-Dried Tomatoes served with Mixed Greens

This combination of roasted portabella and melting goat cheese not only looks appetizing, but also is a delightful accompaniment to a tart fresh green salad.

4   whole portabella mushrooms
2   ounces goat cheese, softened
1   10-ounce jar sun-dried tomatoes packed in oil, drained chopped
1   tablespoon olive oil
      Salt and freshly ground pepper

Mixed Greens Dressed with Oriental Vinaigrette (recipe follows)

Preheat the oven to 350°.
1. Remove the stems from the mushrooms. Clean well with a mushroom brush. Slice each in half horizontally.
2. Spread one-fourth of the goat cheese on the bottom half of each mushroom.
3. Cover the cheese with a layer of chopped sun-dried tomatoes. Place the top half of the mushroom on top of the cheese tomato layer.
4. Place the mushrooms on a baking sheet that has been sprayed with a vegetable oil spray. You may make the mushrooms to this point, cover with plastic wrap and chill for up to 2 hours in advance of roasting.
5. Drizzle the top of the mushrooms with olive oil and season with salt and freshly ground pepper.
6. Roast for 10 minutes or until the cheese begins to melt.

Serves 4
Preparation time about 20 minutes

SETTING THE SCENE:
Mound one fourth of the dressed greens on a chilled salad dish. Slide a whole stuffed portabella onto the side of the mounded greens. Drizzle the dish with additional olive oil and pepper.

Mixed Greens Dressed with Oriental Vinaigrette

This lightly dressed fresh salad is the perfect accompaniment to roasted portabella.

4	**cups mixed greens**
1	**teaspoon sugar**
2	**teaspoons soy sauce**
1	**tablespoon rice wine vinegar**
1	**clove garlic**
1	**teaspoon fresh basil**
¼	**cup olive oil**

1. Place the greens in a bowl.
2. In the bowl of a food processor combine the sugar, soy sauce, rice wine vinegar, garlic, and basil. Pulse to combine. With the blade running, slowly add the olive oil.
3. Coat the greens with the dressing. Drain the salad in a colander, so the leaves are just lightly flavored with the vinaigrette.

Serves 4
Preparation time about 10 minutes

DRESSED-UP DINNER MENU

Portabella Mushrooms
Stuffed with Goat Cheese and
Sun-Dried Tomatoes
served with Mixed Greens

Roasted Pork Tenderloin
with Jack Daniels Peppercorn Sauce

The Overachiever's Twice Baked
Potatoes

Mixed Fresh Berries
with Zabaglione Sauce

Roasted Vegetable Terrine

For a first course this starter is easily made days in advance and then breezily presented. Your guests will oooh and aaah over these colorful and tasty marinated veggies.

2	large eggplants
4	large zucchini
4	large yellow squash
2	tablespoons olive oil
	Salt and freshly ground pepper
2	large yellow bell peppers
2	large red bell peppers
1	bunch fresh basil (about 1 cup)
2	to 3 cloves garlic
1	tablespoon olive oil
4	ounces goat cheese, crumbled

Preheat the oven to 350°.

1. Peel the eggplant, and cut lengthwise into ¼-inch long slices. Cut the zucchini and yellow squash lengthwise into ¼-inch long slices. Place the vegetables on a baking sheet. Brush each side with a small amount of olive oil and season with salt and pepper.
2. Roast the vegetables, turning once, for about 15 to 20 minutes until soft and just beginning to brown.
3. Roast the peppers, steam, and remove the charred skin. Cut into 1-inch strips.
4. Place the basil, garlic, and 1 teaspoon olive oil in a food processor. Pulse to combine.
5. Spray an 8 x 4 x 3-inch loaf pan with vegetable oil spray. Line the pan with plastic wrap and spray again.
6. Begin with a layer of eggplant on the bottom and up the sides of the loaf pan. The eggplant will lay over the top of the pan and be used to seal the terrine. Overlap the eggplant slices on the bottom and sides of the pan.

SETTING THE SCENE:
To serve the terrine, remove it from the refrigerator. Remove the heavy cans, the aluminum foil and plastic wrap. Invert the terrine onto a serving platter and pull the bottom plastic wrap. The loaf will slide out of the pan. Peel off the plastic wrap and slice into ¾ inch pieces. Garnish with fresh basil and roasted tomatoes.

7. Place a layer of zucchini over the eggplant and squash over the zucchini. Place the roasted peppers on top of the squash.
8. Sprinkle half of the basil garlic mixture over the peppers. Crumble half of the goat cheese mixture on top of the basil.
9. Continue layering eggplant, zucchini, squash, peppers, basil mixture, and cheese. The last layer should be eggplant, zucchini, squash, and peppers. Fold the eggplant pieces over the top.
10. Cover the loaf pan with plastic wrap and then aluminum foil. Place the terrine on a baking dish. Place several heavy cans on top of the terrine to weight it down. Refrigerate for at least 24 hours or up to 3 days.

Serves 6 to 8
Preparation time about 40 minutes plus refrigeration

UPSCALE DINNER MENU

Roasted Vegetable Terrine

Outta Hand Orange Roughy with Basil Cream Sauce

Stuffed Baked Potatoes

Gingerbread with Poached Pears

Roasted Yellow Pepper Soup with Avocado Salsa and Sautéed Scallop Garnish

You can easily make this soup days in advance of serving. Prepare the salsa hours ahead and sauté the scallops at the last moment. The presentation is totally worth all of the work.

1	tablespoon olive oil
1	medium yellow onion, chopped (about 1 cup)
2	medium carrots, peeled and diced (about ½ cup)
2	cloves garlic, minced
1	whole jalapeño pepper, seeded and diced (about 2 tablespoons)
5	large yellow bell peppers, roasted, charred skin removed, seeded
4	cups chicken stock
¼	cup sherry
⅛	teaspoon turmeric
	Salt and ground white pepper

2	medium plum tomatoes, seeded and diced
1	jalapeño pepper, seeded and finely diced (about 2 tablespoons)
1	small ripe avocado, diced (about 1½ cups)
1	clove garlic, minced
5	to 6 green onions, sliced (about 1 cup)
2	tablespoons chopped fresh basil
2	tablespoons chopped fresh cilantro
	Juice of 1 lime (about 2 tablespoons)
1	tablespoon balsamic vinegar

6	medium scallops
1	tablespoon butter
1	cup heavy cream
1	cup milk
	Sour cream
	Fresh cilantro

HELPFUL HINT:
Read about roasting peppers (page 259).

SETTING THE SCENE:
To serve the soup remove it from the refrigerator. Add the milk and the cream to the soup. Stir well. Drain the salsa in a colander. Remove the scallops from the pan, drain on paper towels. Ladle the soup into 6 shallow soup bowls. Swirl in a dollop of sour cream. Place a heaping table-spoon of salsa in the center of the soup. Place a scallop on top of the salsa. Place a fresh cilantro sprig on top of the scallop.

1. In a large soup pot cook the onion in olive oil over medium high heat.
2. Add the carrots, minced garlic, and 1 diced jalapeño pepper. Cook for 5 minutes.
3. Pour the chicken stock into the pot.
4. Cut the roasted peppers into wide strips and add to the pot.
5. Bring the soup to a boil. Reduce the heat and simmer for 20 minutes or until the carrots are soft.
6. Purée the soup in the pot using either an immersion blender or process the soup in batches using a food processor.
7. Add the sherry and turmeric to the soup, and season with salt and pepper. Simmer for 5 minutes. Remove the soup from the heat. Cover and chill for at least 2 hours.
8. Prepare the salsa by combining the diced plum tomatoes, 1 diced jalapeño, diced avocado, minced garlic, green onions, fresh basil, and cilantro in a bowl.
9. Pour in the lime juice and balsamic vinegar. Toss and season with salt and pepper. Chill for at least 30 minutes.
10. Season the scallops with salt and pepper on both sides. Cook in 1 tablespoon of butter over medium high heat until golden brown. Turn and cook until done, about 5 minutes altogether.

Serves 6
Preparation time about 45 minutes plus chilling

UPSCALE LUNCHEON MENU

Roasted Yellow Pepper Soup
with Avocado Salsa
and Sautéed Scallop Garnish
❧

Lobster Burrito
with Cilantro Cream Sauce
❧

Hazelnut Heart Cookies

Roasted Pork Tenderloin with Jack Daniels Peppercorn Sauce

The secret to this great tasting dish is the marinade. It doubles as the base for a terrific sauce.

3	whole pork tenderloins
¼	cup molasses
¼	cup olive oil
¼	cup balsamic vinegar
¼	cup Jack Daniels whiskey
1	teaspoon whole peppercorns, crushed
	Fresh rosemary sprigs
1	cup beef stock
¼	cup Jack Daniels whiskey
¼	cup heavy cream
2	tablespoons butter
	Salt

Preheat the oven to 350°.

1. Place the tenderloins in a shallow baking dish.
2. In a small bowl combine ¼ cup of molasses, olive oil, balsamic vinegar, Jack Daniel's whiskey, and peppercorns. Pour this marinade over the tenderloins. Place fresh rosemary sprigs around the tenderloins. Cover and refrigerate for several hours or overnight.
3. Remove the tenderloins from the marinade. Reserve the marinade for later use.
4. Heat a skillet over medium high heat. Brown the tenderloins on all sides. Remove to a rack in a roasting pan.
5. Roast the tenderloins for about 25 to 30 minutes until cooked. Use a meat thermometer to determine doneness. Allow to rest for 5 minutes before slicing.
6. Pour the reserved marinade into a saucepan. Bring to a boil over medium high heat. Cook until the liquid is reduced to ¼ cup.

HELPFUL HINT:
The sauce is flavorful and not overpowering. It's consistency is more like au jus. To thicken it—like gravy—add a small amount of flour mixed with cold water. Cook over medium high heat for several minutes.

SETTING THE SCENE:
Slice the tenderloins on the diagonal into 1-inch medallions. Serve with a spoon full of sauce and garnish with fresh rosemary. The Overachiever's Twice Baked Potato (page 336) make a delightful compliment for this dish.

7. Add the whiskey to the pan. Boil for 5 minutes. Add the beef stock to the pan, and boil for 5 minutes more.
8. Add the cream to the pan. Cook for about 10 minutes more. The sauce will reduce and thicken slightly.
9. Reduce the heat to low and stir in the butter until just dissolved. Season with salt.

Serves 6 to 8
Preparation time about 30 minutes plus roasting

Herb Crusted Rack of Lamb

The flavorful herb crusts seals in the natural juices of the lamb and adds a sassy flavor. Feel free to use it on beef tenderloin or salmon fillet if lamb is scarce.

¼   cup fresh parsley
2   tablespoon fresh thyme
4   cloves garlic
1   tablespoon Dijon style mustard
2   tablespoons olive oil
2   whole racks of lamb, trimmed
    Salt and freshly ground pepper

HELPFUL HINT:
Ask the butcher to prepare the lamb by trimming the fat from the long bones. Before broiling, cover the bones with aluminum foil to prevent burning.

SETTING THE SCENE:
Remove the foil from the bones. Cut between each one to produce an herb crusted lamb chop. Place 2 to 3 chops on a plate. Serve with Sautéed Green Beans with Caramelized Pearl Onions (page 341).

Preheat the oven to 500.
1. In the bowl of a food processor combine the parsley, thyme, garlic, mustard, and olive oil. Pulse to combine.
2. Season the lamb with salt and freshly ground pepper.
3. Smooth the herb paste onto the lamb meat. (Not onto the bones.)
4. Place the lamb rack bones up bracing each other in a baking dish.
5. Roast for 20 minutes for rare chops. Let the lamb racks sit for 5 minutes before carving.

Serves 4
Preparation time about 30 minutes

The Overachiever's Twice Baked Potato

This dish not only combines the great taste of white potatoes with sweet potatoes, but it is also easily made in advance of your dinner party. The presentation is fun and dramatic.

3	**large baking potatoes**
3	**medium sweet potatoes**
6	**strips bacon, diced**
½	**medium red onion, diced**
½	**teaspoon sugar**
1	**teaspoon balsamic vinegar**
3	**tablespoons butter**
⅓	**cup cream**
	Salt and freshly ground pepper
3	**tablespoons butter**
½	**cup sour cream**
2	**tablespoons fresh garlic chives**
2	**tablespoons butter cut into small pieces**

Preheat the oven to 350°.

1. Roast the white and sweet potatoes until soft, about 45 minutes for the white potatoes, about 30 minutes for the sweet potatoes.
2. In a medium skillet cook the bacon over medium high heat until crisp. Remove the bacon and drain on paper towels. Pour off all but 1 tablespoon of the drippings.
3. Cook the diced onion in the bacon drippings until just beginning to turn brown. Add the sugar and vinegar to the pan. Stir. The onions will turn brown and syrupy. Remove the pan from the heat.
4. Peel the sweet potatoes. Use an electric mixer to mix together the peeled potatoes, 3 tablespoons of butter, and ⅓ cup of cream. Season with salt and pepper. Add the caramelized onions and crisp bacon to the sweet potatoes. Stir to combine. Set aside.

5. Remove all but a ¼-inch edge from the baked white potatoes, leaving the shells. Place the white potato shells onto a baking sheet.
6. Use an electric mixer to combine the inside part of the white potato, 3 tablespoons butter, and sour cream. Season with salt and pepper. Add the chives. Mix to combine.
7. Place a tablespoon of the sweet potato mixture in the center of the white potato shell. Place a spoonful of white potato mixture in both ends of the shell. Continue until all of the potato shells are filled. You can cover the potatoes with plastic wrap and refrigerate at this point. Remove the potatoes from the refrigerator and bring to room temperature when you are ready to continue.
8. Dot the tops of the potatoes with small pieces of butter.
9. Bake the potatoes for 30 to 45 minutes or until the tops begin to brown and they potatoes are cooked through.

Serves 6
Preparation time about 30 minutes plus roasting and reheating.

Veal Cutlets with Fresh Dill and Sage Cream Sauce

The veal medallions are pounded so that they cook quickly. The sauce is a classic reduction with the addition of savory herbs. The dish comes together quickly and impressively.

4	veal cutlets (about 1½ pounds total)
1	tablespoon olive oil
1	tablespoon butter
1	medium shallot, finely diced
1	cup heavy cream
1	tablespoons fresh dill sprigs, snipped
2	tablespoons fresh sage leaves, cut into thin julienne
	Salt and freshly ground pepper

1. Pound the veal cutlets between 2 pieces of waxed paper until very thin.
2. In a large skillet heat the olive oil and butter over medium high heat.
3. Cook the veal in the butter and olive oil until just brown on both sides, about 4 to 6 minutes.
4. Remove the veal to a platter and keep warm.
5. Place the diced shallots in the same pan. Cook until just softened.
6. Add the cream to the pan. Bring to a boil and reduce to ½ cup.
7. Toss the fresh herbs into the cream reduction. Season with salt and freshly ground pepper.

Serves 4
Preparation time about 20 minutes

SIMPLE SUBSTITUTION:
The addition of sautéed wild mushrooms to the sauce adds a great earthy dimension to the dish.

SETTING THE SCENE:
Place a cutlet on each dinner plate. Pour a spoonful of sauce over top. Garnish with fresh whole sage leaves. Serve with Yam Pudding (see page 339).

Yam Pudding

*One usually only remembers the yam at holiday dinners.
But the yam can be dressed up for any occasion. The aroma
of this pudding is as welcoming as your invitation to dine.*

HELPFUL HINT:
This dish can be made in advance
and baked as your guests arrive.

1	large yam, peeled, cut into pieces
⅓	cup cornmeal
1	cup milk
2	tablespoons unsalted butter
1	tablespoon brown sugar
½	cup water
1	teaspoon vanilla extract
¾	teaspoon ground cinnamon
½	teaspoon salt
¼	teaspoon nutmeg
¼	teaspoon ground cloves
1	tablespoon flour
2	tablespoons honey
2	eggs
½	cup heavy cream

Preheat the oven to 350°.

1. In a large pot boil the yam pieces in water to cover until soft, about 15 minutes.
2. In a saucepan stir the cornmeal, milk, butter, brown sugar, and water over medium high heat until thickened, about 15 minutes.
3. Season the cornmeal mixture with vanilla, cinnamon, salt, nutmeg, and ground cloves. Remove from the heat and let cool to room temperature.
4. Pour the cooled cornmeal mixture into a food processor. Add the yam pieces and pulse to combine. Add the flour, honey, eggs, and cream. Pulse until mixed.
5. Pour the pudding into a baking dish that has been sprayed with vegetable oil spray.
6. Bake for about 35 to 45 minutes until the top of the pudding is just golden brown and the center is set.

Serves 4 to 6
Preparation time about 30 minutes plus baking

Fresh Kingsklip Fillets with Braised Cabbage and Leeks

Feel free to use any fresh fish fillet for this recipe. The accompanying braised cabbage adds a colorful and nutritious presentation.

4	6-ounce kingsklip fillets
	Salt and freshly ground pepper
1	medium lemon
½	cup flour for dredging
2	tablespoons olive oil
2	tablespoons olive oil
2	leeks, white part only, cleaned and julienned into 4-inch strips
½	small red cabbage, sliced into thin strips
½	cup chicken stock
1	tablespoon fresh dill, chopped
2	tablespoons balsamic vinegar

1. Season the fish fillets with salt, freshly ground pepper, and a sprinkle of fresh lemon juice.
2. Dip each one in the flour. Shake off the excess.
3. In a sauté pan heat 2 tablespoons of olive oil over medium high heat.
4. Cook the fillets until lightly brown on each side, about 3 minutes per side for ½-inch thick fillets.
5. Transfer the fillets to a serving platter and keep warm.
6. In the same sauté pan heat 2 tablespoons of olive oil over medium heat.
7. Add the leeks and cabbage to the pan. Cook until just beginning to brown, about 5 minutes.
8. Add the chicken stock and cook until the vegetables soften, about 5 minutes more.
9. Toss in the dill and season with balsamic vinegar, salt, and pepper.

Serves 4
Preparation time about 20 minutes

SETTING THE SCENE:
To serve, place the cabbage on the bottom of a serving platter. Place the fish fillets on top. Season with more black pepper. Wild rice pilaf and baked apples are a great addition to this easy entrée.

Sautéed Green Beans with Caramelized Pearl Onu...

The miniature onions found in the produce department are called "pearl onions." It takes a little work to peel them, but the caramelized results are well worth the effort.

36	pearl onions, peeled
3	tablespoons butter
3	tablespoons brown sugar
1	tablespoon balsamic vinegar
	Salt and freshly ground pepper
1	pound fresh green beans, washed
1	tablespoon olive oil
1	clove garlic, minced

1. Place the peeled onions in a skillet and pour in enough water to just cover.
2. Boil over high heat for about 10 minutes.
3. Add the butter and sugar and continue to boil until all of the water is evaporated and the onions begin to cook down.
4. Reduce the heat to medium. Continue to cook until the onions brown and the sauce reaches a syrupy consistency.
5. Add the balsamic vinegar and continue to cook until it evaporates. Season with salt and pepper. The onions can be placed in a bowl, covered and refrigerated at this point. Warm them before serving.
6. Place the green beans in a microwave safe dish. Pour about 1 inch of water into the bottom of the dish. Microwave on high for 5 to 6 minutes. The beans should be bright green and just crisp tender.
7. In a skillet heat the olive oil over medium high heat. Add the garlic and cook for 1 minute.
8. Add the green beans to the skillet and toss to coat. Season with salt and pepper.

Serves 6 to 8
Preparation time 25 minutes

TECHNIQUE:
Peel the pearl onions by slitting the root bottom of each one with a sharp knife. Drop the onions into boiling water for two minutes. Remove them and place directly into a bowl of ice water to stop the cooking process. The skins will come off easily.

SETTING THE SCENE:
To serve, place the green beans on a platter. Make a well in the center. Place the warm caramelized onions in the well.

Beef Tenderloin Stuffed with Roasted Peppers, Spinach, and Goat Cheese served with Port Wine Sauce

This is a terrific entrée to serve for a dinner party. You can prepare the tenderloin hours in advance. Brown the beef before your guests arrive, and roast just before you serve. Your guests will be dazzled with your easy manner in preparing such a sophisticated dish.

SETTING THE SCENE:
Cut the stuffed beef tenderloin into 1-inch slices. Pour the port wine sauce onto a dinner plat. Place a slice of tenderloin on top of the sauce. Garnish with fresh basil leaves.

1	3- to 4-pound beef tenderloin, center cut
1	10-ounce package frozen chopped spinach, thawed
8	ounces goat cheese, room temperature
1	tablespoon chopped fresh rosemary
1	tablespoon chopped fresh thyme
1	12-ounce jar roasted red peppers, drained
	Salt and freshly ground pepper
1	bunch fresh basil leaves
2	tablespoons olive oil
2	shallots, minced
½	cup port wine
1	cup beef stock
1	tablespoon cornstarch dissolved in ¼ cup beef stock
⅓	cup tomato paste
1	teaspoon fresh rosemary
¼	cup more beef stock
2	tablespoons butter, cold, cut into pieces

1. Butterfly the beef tenderloin by cutting the beef lengthwise down the center about two-thirds of the way through the beef. Open the beef. Use a meat mallet to pound the meat to ¾-inch thickness.
2. Place the spinach in a colander and squeeze out as much of the moisture as possible.
3. Mix together the spinach, goat cheese, fresh rosemary, and thyme in a large bowl.

4. To stuff and roll the tenderloin season the flattened beef with salt and freshly ground pepper. Place the red peppers on top of the beef leaving a 1-inch border. Place the fresh basil leaves on top of the red peppers.

5. Spread the cheese mixture on one end of the peppers and basil. The cheese will be at the center of the rolled beef. Roll the beef around the cheese end in a tight cylinder. Continue rolling jelly roll fashion. Use butcher string or bamboo skewers to secure the beef roll. Refrigerate for at least one hour or until ready to serve.

Preheat the oven to 375°

6. Heat 2 tablespoons olive oil in a large roasting pan over medium high heat. Add the tenderloin roll to the pan and quickly brown on all sides. Place the tenderloin on a rack in a roasting pan. Roast for 30 to 40 minutes. Use a meat thermometer to determine doneness.

7. Cook the shallots over medium high heat in the pan used to brown the beef. Cook until just soft.

8. Add the port wine to the pan and cook until the liquid is reduced by half.

9. Add 1 cup beef stock and bring to a boil. Add the dissolved cornstarch and stir until thickened. Add the tomato paste and fresh rosemary. Season with salt and pepper.

10. Remove the stuffed beef tenderloin from the pan and allow to rest for at least 10 minutes.

11. Remove the rack from the roasting pan. Place the roasting pan over medium high heat. Add ¼ cup of beef stock to the roasting pan to deglaze. Stir to loosen the brown bits from the bottom of the pan.

12. Add the port wine sauce to the roasting pan. Simmer for 2 minutes. Reduce the heat. Stir in the cold butter until just combined.

Serves 6
Preparation time about 30 minutes plus refrigeration and roasting

HELPFUL HINT:
When using a meat thermometer to determine doneness, make sure that you insert it into the meaty section and not in the filling.

Pasta Stuffed Eggplant and Pork Medallions

One Sunday evening, my creative pal, Bill, was perusing the leftovers he had stuffed into his fridge. What came next was a treat of stackable medallions.

1	cup (or more) canola oil
2	eggplants, cut into ½-inch slices
3	eggs, beaten
1	cup (or more) seasoned bread crumbs
2	pork tenderloins, butterflied, pounded to ¼-inch, sliced into medallions
2	cups Basic Marinara Sauce (page 160)
1	bunch fresh basil leaves
1	pound mozzarella cheese, sliced
1	cup (or more) Parmesan cheese
1	pound angel hair pasta, cooked
3	pounds fresh spinach leaves
4	cloves garlic, minced
1	tablespoon olive oil
	Salt and freshly ground pepper

1. Place a small amount of canola oil into a skillet over medium high heat.
2. Dip the eggplants slices first into the beaten egg, and then into the breadcrumbs. Cook for several minutes on each side. Drain well on paper towels.
3. Dip the pork tenderloin medallions first into the beaten egg, and then into the breadcrumbs. Cook for several minutes on each side.
4. Drain well on paper towels.
5. Spread a layer of marinara sauce on the bottom of a shallow baking dish.
6. Place the pork medallions onto the sauce. Stack each medallion with a layer of fresh basil leaves, a slice of Mozzarella cheese, a sprinkle of Parmesan cheese, a scoop of cooked pasta, a slice of cooked eggplant, another slice of mozzarella cheese, another dash of Parmesan cheese, a dollop of marinara sauce, and a final basil leaf.

7. Bake the stacks at 350° for 15 to 20 minutes until the cheese just begins to melt.

8. In a skillet sauté the fresh spinach and minced garlic in 1 tablespoon of olive oil, being careful not to burn the garlic. Season with salt and pepper.

9. To assemble the dish, place the sautéed spinach on a serving platter. Place the stacks on top of the spinach. Season with a drizzle of olive oil and grating of freshly ground pepper.

Serves a crowd
Preparation time 45 minutes

Corn Soufflé Casserole

This Southern inspiration is a perfect buffet dish. It acts like a soufflé but is a tad sturdier. You can make it ahead and bake just before serving.

4	**eggs**
2	**cups milk**
2	**tablespoons butter, melted**
½	**teaspoon nutmeg**
2	**tablespoons fresh parsley, finely chopped**
1	**teaspoon fresh thyme, finely chopped**
¼	**teaspoon cayenne pepper**
¼	**cup sugar**
2	**cups corn kernels**
6	**slices white bread, crusts removed**
	Salt

Preheat the oven to 350°.

1. Spray a casserole dish with a vegetable oil cooking spray.
2. In the bowl of an electric mixer beat the eggs.
3. Add the milk and melted butter and stir to combine.
4. Add the nutmeg, parsley, thyme, cayenne pepper, sugar, and corn. Mix together.
5. Cut the bread into 1-inch cubes and toss into the mixture. Use a large spoon to stir the bread into the corn mixture. Season with salt.
6. Pour the mixture into the prepared dish. You may put the casserole into the refrigerator at this point and keep chilled for several hours until ready to bake.
7. Place the casserole dish in a large roasting pan filled half way to the top with hot water.
8. Bake until the center is set about 45 to 50 minutes.

Serves 10 to 15
Preparation time about 15 minutes plus baking

TECHNIQUE:
This manner of cooking is called baking in a water bath. The mixture will cook more uniformly by using this technique. The trick is that as the water gets hotter and simmers, it will expand. Make sure that you only put water half way to the top of the casserole so that it does not spill into the pudding.

Mixed Fresh Berries with Zabaglione Sauce

This sauce is traditionally made with Marsala wine and is a delicious upgrade from whipped cream. Use the freshest, ripest berries available and display the dessert in your best crystal bowl or champagne glass.

1	pint strawberries, hulled and halved
1	pint blueberries
1	pint raspberries
4	egg yolks
¼	cup granulated sugar
¼	cup Marsala wine
½	cup heavy cream

1. Wash the berries, place in a large bowl and chill.
2. Whisk the egg yolks and sugar together in the top part of a double boiler over medium high heat.
3. Whisk in the wine.
4. Continue beating until the sauce has doubled. It will thicken, become fluffy and turn pale yellow.
5. Remove the top of the double boiler to a large bowl filled with ice. Continue whisking the sauce until it cools.
6. Place the heavy cream in the chilled bowl of an electric mixer. Beat until the cream forms peaks. (Do not overbeat or you will end up with butter!)
7. Fold the whipped cream into the Zabaglione sauce. Chill until ready to serve.

Serves 6 to 8
Preparation time about 30 minutes

HELPFUL HINT:
The water in the bottom part of the double boiler should be just simmering—not boiling.

TECHNIQUE:
Don't be afraid to use an immersion blender to beat the sauce. It will save on arm strength!

SETTING THE SCENE:
For a dramatic presentation, layer the bottom of a dessert plate with a spoon full of sauce. Place a circle of raspberries around the outside of the plate. Place a circle of blueberries inside the raspberries. Mound the strawberries in the center. Top with another drizzle of sauce and a fresh mint leaf.

Flourless Chocolate Torte

This cake is best served at room temperature when the center is rich and gooey like melting fudge. The shiny ganache that tops the torte is reminiscent of a smooth chocolate candy bar. The combination of both is too good to pass up.

1½	cups light corn syrup
1	cup granulated sugar
2½	cups semisweet chocolate (20 ounces)
2	teaspoons vanilla extract
2	sticks unsalted butter (1 cup)
10	whole eggs
½	cup whipping cream
1	cup semisweet chocolate (for ganache)

Preheat the oven to 350°.

1. In a medium saucepan melt the corn syrup and sugar until it reaches a boil. Immediately reduce the heat and continue to cook for several minutes until the sugar is dissolved.
2. In a double boiler over simmering water melt 2½ cups of semisweet chocolate. Be careful not to burn the chocolate.
3. Stir the butter into the chocolate. Add the vanilla. Set aside.
4. With an electric mixer, beat the eggs until fluffy.
5. Pour the syrup mixture into the eggs and mix together.
6. Pour the chocolate mixture into the egg mixture and mix.
7. Pour the batter into a 10-inch springform pan that has been sprayed with vegetable oil cooking spray.
8. Wrap the bottom and outside of the pan with plastic wrap and then with aluminum foil. Do not cover the pan.
9. Place the now waterproof pan into a larger ovenproof pan and add hot water half way to the top. Bake for 50 to 60 minutes.

HELPFUL HINTS:

1. Use good quality chocolate for this recipe. The better the chocolate, the better the torte.

2. The secret to smooth and shiny melted chocolate is to avoid all contact with water. Be careful that not even a drop enters the melted mixture.

3. An alternate method to melting chocolate is to use the microwave oven. Place the chocolate in a bowl. Heat on the medium high setting stirring every 30 seconds to prevent burning.

TECHNIQUE:

For a flawless presentation, dip the cake server into a bowl of warm water between slices.

10. When the cake is done, remove it from the oven and then from the pan holding the water. Remove the aluminum foil and the plastic wrap, being careful not to drip water into the torte. Cool the cake completely, about 1 hour.
11. Run a sharp knife around the inside edge of the pan and refrigerate the torte for at least 4 hours or overnight.
12. Make the ganache by heating the whipping cream in a small pot over medium high heat.
13. Stir in the remaining chocolate until it begins to melt.
14. Remove the pan from the heat and continue to stir the mixture until it is smooth and shiny. Cool slightly.
15. Remove the sides of the mold.
16. Pour the warm ganache over the top and sides of the torte. Finish the presentation with shaved white chocolate or finely chopped nuts.

Serves 12
Preparation time about 90 minutes plus cooling the cake

Sticky Toffee Pudding with Caramel Sauce

This dessert is the specialty of the house at one of Fort Lauderdale's most established restaurants, Burt and Jack's. It has English roots and keeps you coming back for more and more. Here is my home cook's version.

6	ounces pitted dates
	Water to cover
1	teaspoon baking soda
½	cup butter (1 stick), room temperature
1	cup firmly packed brown sugar
2	large eggs
2	teaspoons dark molasses
1¼	cups all-purpose flour
2	teaspoons baking powder

Vanilla ice cream

SETTING THE SCENE:
Slice the cake into 8 wedges. Slice each wedge in half. Place ½ wedge on the bottom of a dessert plate. Top with a spoonful of warm sauce. Place a spoonful of ice cream on top of the cake. Top with the second wedge of cake. Pour more warm sauce over the top.

Preheat the oven to 325°.

1. Spray a 12-inch Bundt pan with vegetable oil spray.
2. In a small saucepan cover the dates with water. Bring the water to a boil. Reduce the heat to low. Cover and simmer the dates for 25 minutes or until the liquid is completely gone and the dates are mushy.
3. Stir the baking soda into the dates and let the mixture cool to room temperature.
4. Place the butter and brown sugar in the bowl of an electric mixer. Beat until fluffy. Add the eggs to the bowl one at a time. Stir in the molasses, flour, and baking powder. Stir in the dates. Mix to combine thoroughly.
5. Pour the batter into the prepared pan. Bake on the center rack in the oven for 25 to 30 minutes. The cake is done when the top is firm to the touch. Cool on a wire rack for 5 to 10 minutes. Invert the cake onto a rack to cool completely.

Serves 8
Preparation time about 30 minutes plus baking

Caramel Sauce

This shiny sauce is terrific over a scoop of ice cream, too!

½   **cup butter (1 stick)**
1   **cup firmly packed dark brown sugar**
1   **cup heavy cream**
1   **tablespoon dark rum**
2   **teaspoons molasses**

1. Prepare the sauce by melting the butter in a saucepan over medium high heat.
2. Add the sugar and stir until dissolved.
3. Stir in the cream, rum, and molasses. Bring to a boil and remove from the heat.

Makes about 1½ cups
Preparation time about 10 minutes

HELPFUL HINT:
This sauce has great staying power. Store in an airtight container for up to 2 weeks.

Gingerbread with Poached Pears

Although gingerbread reminds us of winter, when blended with ripe pears it's a refreshing treat even in the heat of July! This dessert is perfect for a luncheon.

2½	cups all-purpose flour
1½	teaspoons baking soda
1	teaspoon ground cinnamon
2	teaspoons ground ginger
¼	teaspoon allspice
½	teaspoon salt
½	cup firmly packed brown sugar
½	cup butter (1 stick), melted
1	egg
½	cup dark molasses
½	cup honey
½	cup brewed coffee
½	cup buttermilk

2	to 4 Poached Pears (recipe follows)
	Whipped cream, optional

Preheat the oven to 350°.

1. Prepare a 13 x 9 x 2-inch pan by spraying with vegetable oil cooking spray and dusting with flour.
2. In a medium bowl combine the flour, baking soda, cinnamon, ginger, allspice, and salt, and set aside.
3. In the bowl of an electric mixer combine the brown sugar with the melted butter and mix until creamy.
4. Add the egg and mix well.
5. Beat in the molasses and honey.
6. Mix in half of the dry ingredients with the coffee. Stir.
7. Mix in the remaining dry ingredients with the buttermilk. Blend thoroughly.
8. Pour the batter into the prepared dish. Bake for 30 minutes or until a toothpick inserted in the middle comes out clean. Cool on a rack.

Makes 12 to 18 squares
Preparation time about 20 minutes plus baking

SETTING THE SCENE:
To serve the dish, cut the gingerbread into small squares and arrange on a platter. Lay several slices of pear atop each square. Drizzle some syrup over the pear slices and top with a dollop of whipped cream.

Poached Pears

Poaching the pears give them a uniquely rich flavor and a robust color. Use ripe pears to insure a sweet result.

HELPFUL HINT:
You can prepare the pears the day before you need them and refrigerate overnight.

4	ripe pears
¼	cup lemon juice, mixed into a large bowl of water (about 2 medium lemons)
2	cups port wine
½	cup granulated sugar
1	tablespoon fresh ginger, peeled and sliced
1	cinnamon stick
1	teaspoons vanilla extract

1. Peel the pears. Place each one into the water mixed with lemon juice. Leave the stem intact at the top. Use a paring knife or melon baller to remove the core from the bottom.
2. In a large stockpot combine the port wine, sugar, ginger, cinnamon stick, and vanilla. Bring to a boil to dissolve the sugar and form a syrup, about 10 minutes.
3. Drain the pears from the water. Place each one in the syrup, cover, and cook until soft (about 20 minutes). Turn the pears in the syrup halfway through the cooking time.
4. Transfer the pears, standing upright, to a dish.
5. Continue cooking the syrup for 20 minutes more until reduced to ½ cup. Pour the liquid over the pears, cover and chill.

Serves 4 to 6
Preparation time about 50 minutes

Hazelnut Heart Cookies

These decorative heart shaped cookies are as much fun to make as they are to eat. Similar to a Linzertorte, the sweet berry filling and sugar topping perfectly balance the nutty taste of the cookie. Raspberry jam is easily substituted for the three berry jam (blueberry, raspberry, and boysenberry) that is called for in this recipe.

1	**cup hazelnuts, toasted, skins removed**
⅔	**cup granulated sugar**
3	**cups all-purpose flour**
¼	**teaspoon salt**
¼	**teaspoon baking powder**
2	**eggs**
1	**cup unsalted butter (2 sticks), room temperature**
1	**teaspoon vanilla extract**
1	**teaspoon grated lemon rind**
1	**cup triple berry jam, or raspberry jam**
	Confectioners' sugar

Preheat the oven to 325°.

1. In the bowl of a food processor combine the hazelnuts and sugar. Pulse to form a coarse powder.
2. In a medium bowl combine the flour, salt, and baking powder. Set aside.
3. Use an electric mixer to beat the butter until fluffy.
4. Add the hazelnut mixture. Mix well. Add the eggs to the butter and beat again. Add the vanilla and grated lemon rind and mix well.
5. Add the dry ingredients to the mixture in 3 additions.
6. Remove the dough from the bowl and divide into four parts.
7. Form each part into a disk, cover with plastic wrap, and chill for at least 2 hours.
8. Remove one disk from the refrigerator. On a well floured surface, roll the dough out to about ⅛-inch thickness. Cut the dough with 2 heart shaped cookie cutters.

HELPFUL HINT:
Use a solid heart for the base of the cookie. Use a smaller heart cutter pressed into a large heart to form a window on the top cookie. The solid bottom and the top with the window form the sandwich cookie. The small hearts make extra cookies.

TECHNIQUE:
The cookies can be stored in an airtight container. Use wax paper in between each layer.

9. Place each cookie on an ungreased cookie sheet. Bake for about 10 minutes. Remove to a rack and cool.

10. In a saucepan heat the triple berry jam over medium high heat for about 5 minutes. Stir the jam constantly until it begins to thicken. Remove from the heat and cool.

11. Dust the top cookie (the heart window) and the smaller hearts with confectioners' sugar.

12. Assemble the cookies by placing a layer of jam on top of one solid heart leaving a ¼-inch border. Place the window cookie on top and press together gently.

Makes 20 large cookies and 20 small heart cookies
Preparation time about 1 hour and 30 minutes plus refrigeration

...erry Cake with Cream Cheese Frosting

This can... blends a sweet batter with the tartness of cream cheese. It is easily prepared and will serve well for a luncheon or summer dinner party.

2¾	**cups cake flour**
2½	**teaspoons baking powder**
2	**cups granulated sugar**
1	**3-ounce box strawberry flavored gelatin**
1	**cup margarine**
4	**egg yolks**
1	**cup milk**
1	**teaspoon strawberry extract**
6	**to 8 strawberries, puréed, about ½ cup**
4	**egg whites**

1	**cups heavy whipping cream**
1	**tablespoons powdered sugar**
½	**teaspoons vanilla extract**

½	**cup shortening**
2	**8-ounce packages cream cheese**
3	**cups confectioners' sugar**
2	**teaspoons vanilla extract**
8	**to 10 sliced strawberries (about ¾ cup)**

Preheat the oven to 350°.

1. Prepare three 8-inch round layer pans by first spraying with vegetable oil cooking spray and then dusting with flour.
2. In a medium bowl combine the flour and baking powder. Set aside.
3. Use an electric mixer to combine the sugar, gelatin, and margarine until fluffy.
4. Add the egg yolks one at a time. Mix well.
5. Add the flour mixture in 3 parts alternating with the milk. Stir in the strawberry extract and puréed strawberries.
6. Pour the batter into a large mixing bowl. Set aside.

SETTING THE SCENE:

Place one layer of cake on a cake plate. Top with a layer of whipped cream. Cover with sliced strawberries. Repeat with another layer of cake, whipped cream and strawberries. Top with the last layer of cake. Cover the sides and top of the cake with the cream cheese frosting. Serve a slice of the cake on a dessert plate with whole strawberries for garnish.

7. Beat the egg whites until stiff. Fold the egg whites into the batter.
8. Divide the batter into the 3 pans. Bake in the center rack of the oven for about 25 to 30 minutes or until a toothpick inserted into the middle of the cake comes out clean. Cool the cakes in the pan for 10 minutes. Continue cooling by removing each cake from the pan to a rack.
9. Use an electric mixer to combine the whipping cream, powdered sugar and vanilla. Whip until stiff. Set aside.
10. Use an electric mixer to combine the shortening, cream cheese, confectioners' sugar and vanilla to form the frosting.

Serves 10 to 12
Preparation time about 1 hour 30 minutes

Chocolate Mahogany Cake

This special cake has been served for every birthday, anniversary, graduation, and welcome visit in our family for the past 100 years. Follow each step in order to make sure that the cake comes out perfectly.

3	cups cake flour
1½	teaspoon baking soda
½	teaspoon salt
6	tablespoons cocoa powder
2	cups granulated sugar
¾	cup margarine
4	egg yolks
1½	cups buttermilk
1	teaspoon black walnut flavoring
4	egg whites

6	cups confectioners' sugar
¾	cup cocoa powder
¼	cup butter (½ stick), melted
⅓	teaspoon salt
½	cup brewed coffee, hot
2½	teaspoons black walnut flavoring
⅓	to ½ cup milk

Preheat the oven to 350°.

1. Prepare three 8-inch round layer pans by first spraying with vegetable oil spray and then dusting with flour.
2. In a medium bowl combine the flour, baking soda, salt, and cocoa and set aside.
3. Use an electric mixer to combine the sugar and margarine until fluffy.
4. Add the egg yolks one at a time. Mix well.
5. Add the flour mixture in 3 parts alternating with the buttermilk. Stir in the black walnut flavoring.
6. Pour the batter into a large mixing bowl. Set aside.
7. Beat the egg whites until stiff. Fold the egg whites into the batter.

TECHNIQUE:
Place one layer of cake on a cake plate. Top with a layer of icing. Repeat with all layers. Cover the sides and top of the cake with the icing. Serve a slice of the cake on a dessert plate that has been dusted with powdered sugar. Garnish with fresh raspberries.

8. Divide the batter into the three pans. Bake in the center rack of the oven for about 25 to 30 minutes or until a toothpick inserted into the middle of the cake comes out clean. Cool the cakes in the pan for 10 minutes. Continue cooling by removing each cake from the pan to a rack.
9. Use an electric mixer to combine the confectioners' sugar, cocoa, melted butter, and salt. Stir in the hot coffee and the black walnut flavoring.
10. Add just enough milk to reach the desired consistency.

Serves 10 to 12
Preparation time about 30 minutes plus baking

A Few Good Menus

A MONTH FULL OF SUPPER MENUS
Want some food for thought? At 4:00 P.M. each day, seventy-five percent of us do not know what we will cook for dinner. Here is another tidbit: about forty cents of every food dollar is spent on food eaten away from home. Did you know this year it is estimated that the typical U.S. consumer will spend about fifteen minutes a day preparing meals? What does this all add up to? We spend too much money on fast food mostly because we don't plan in advance. This in turn has an impact our stress level as well as the family's nutrition. Let's see if we can come up with a few solutions to counter this unwelcome food trend.

CONSTRUCT A MEAL PLAN
We are all so busy that we often forget to plan ahead for family meals. But most of us have the skills. At your workplace you prepare business tactics, meeting agendas, long-range strategy procedure, or sales schedules. At home you schedule car pool, after-school activities, PTA meetings, and homework lessons. Why not utilize the same skills to map out well-balanced weekday dinners? Here's how. Identify your favorite easy-to-prepare meals. Take a blank calendar and fill in each day with one meal. Place the easiest recipes onto your busiest days. Reserve more difficult meals and involved desserts for weekends. Try to vary the meals so that you avoid serving heavy foods two days in a row. By the same token, you won't want to eat chicken Tuesday through Thursday. Allow a "day off" for pizza night or dinner out with friends.

SPEND A FEW EXTRA MINUTES ON WEEKENDS
Put in place a weekend meal plan that allows you to do extra shopping and cooking when you have some spare time. Use extra portions to create easy meals during the week. Sunday's marinated flank steak becomes Monday's flank steak quesadilla. A roasted vegetable side dish becomes Wednesday's turkey hash with the simple addition of cubed cooked turkey or browned ground turkey. Get the idea? Here is another example. If you are cooking for friends on Saturday, make enough so that you have Sunday's dinner in hand. Turn leftover roasted pork tenderloin into barbeque pork sandwiches. Chop enough veggies on Saturday to use leftovers in Sunday's salad.

EVERYDAY CELEBRATIONS
In this section, I have identified some of the easy recipes in the book and placed them into doable weekly meal plans. Individualize your meal plan by identifying your favorite recipes and the days that you plan to cook at home. This tiny bit of preparation is all you need to enjoy a personal meal plan that will save you time and money while allowing you some stress-free quality moments at home with your friends and family. Just enough time to make any day an everyday celebration.

FOUR WEEKS OF EASY SUPPERS

WEEK 1

Easy Does It Monday:	Spicy Caesar Salad with Sliced Grilled Chicken Breasts
Hectic Tuesday:	Fresh Tilapia Fillets with Sautéed Bananas Baked Cauliflower
Chill Out Wednesday:	Grilled Pork Chops with Mango Salsa Oatmeal Chocolate Chip Cookies
Almost There Thursday:	Stuffed Chicken Breasts with Ham and Swiss Cheese
Fun Friday:	Pizza with Sun-Dried Tomatoes, Basil and Goat Cheese
Spare Time Saturday:	Ricotta Bread* Sweet Cucumber and Mandarin Orange Salad Meatballs with Eggplant Topped with Muenster Cheese
Sunday Supper:	Classic Beef Stew Key Lime Buttery Cake*

WEEK 2

Easy Does It Monday:	Super Sandwiches** (made with Ricotta Bread)
Hectic Tuesday:	Grilled Chicken Breast with Vegetables Key Lime Buttery Cake**
Chill Out Wednesday:	GLOP
Almost There Thursday:	Spiced Up Turkey Burgers Cajun Potato Spears
Fun Friday:	Salmon Cakes with Sauce Remoulade
Spare Time Saturday:	"Creamy" Asparagus Soup Baked Veal Chops with Red Wine Mushroom Cream Sauce
Sunday Supper:	Island Spiced Flank Steak* (make extra) Herb Glazed Roasted Tomatoes Loaded Chocolate Brownies*

WEEK 3

Easy Does It Monday:	Greek Style Salad with Garlic Lemon Dressing** (made with extra Island Spiced Flank Steak)
Hectic Tuesday:	Chicken Pepperoni Broccoli with Garlic and Lemon Loaded Chocolate Brownies**
Chill Out Wednesday:	Baked Eggplant Parmesan Classic Caesar Salad
Almost There Thursday:	Marinated Pork Tenderloin Baked Zucchini with Parmesan Cheese
Fun Friday:	Mushroom, Bacon and Jack Cheese Quesadilla
Spare Time Saturday:	Grilled Chicken* and Baby Back Ribs with Mustard "Cue" Southern Style Slaw Dilled Potato and Egg Salad
Sunday Supper:	Seared Tuna in Oriental Marinade* Roasted Herb Potatoes* Peanut Butter and White Chocolate Chip Cookies*

WEEK 4

Easy Does It Monday:	Salad Nicoise with Dijon Vinaigrette** (made with extra Seared Tuna in Oriental Marinade)
Hectic Tuesday:	Sweet Potato Hash* (made with extra Roasted Herb Potatoes and extra Grilled Chicken) Peanut Butter and White Chocolate Chip Cookies**
Chill Out Wednesday:	Poached Yellow Tail Snapper with Chopped Tomato and Parsley Ratatouille
Almost There Thursday:	Baked Ziti Fresh Vegetable Salad with Tarragon Vinaigrette
Fun Friday:	Sesame Beef Stir Fry Fried Spiced Rice
Spare Time Saturday:	Grilled Artichokes and Baby Portabella Mushroom Salad Linguini Carbonara
Sunday Supper:	Dilled Beef Stroganoff* (make extra for Monday!) Spinach with Caramelized Onions Key Lime Squares* (make extra for next week)

* Cook once
** Eat Twice

Dinner Party Menus

Tips For Party Tables

What happens when you throw all of the elements of formal and casual dining into the same pot? The result is an entertaining style that I call "casually fussy." A casually fussy approach to a dinner party invites you to use good china when serving homemade pizza to your jean-clad guests, or to serve elegant lobster burritos on a clay colored pottery platter to a more formally dressed group. The idea is to make your family, friends, or guests totally comfortable so that they can enjoy the wonderfully prepared and delightfully presented dishes. An important component is an inviting table. Here are a few ideas that you can use when giving a dinner party.

Mix and Match Placesettings

Thrift stores and garage sales are a great place to pick up mix-and-match table setting treasures. You may find an odd set of china or glassware at a great price. Perhaps the set has a piece or two missing. Even if there are six dinner and butter plates, only five bowls, and four cups and saucers, don't pass them up! Instead, blend your table settings by pairing the new purchase with the china that you have on hand.

There are several ways to accomplish this. One suggestion is to set a different china pattern at each seat. For example, use a gold embossed place setting at the host's place, and a colorful, patterned place setting for a guest. Continue setting the table with full place settings that include a dinner plate, cup and saucer, salad plate, and butter dish. Each place is set exactly like the next, except the china is mixed rather than matched.

A second suggestion for a fun table is to alternate between two or more sets of china with the various table setting pieces. For example, on a table for six, place the same dinner plates, and contrast with a different pattern for the salad bowls. Continue with six butter plates from a third china pattern. Make sure that the china colors blend well together and with the rest of your table decorations.

The secret to setting a beautiful and irresistible table is in your well though out creativity. There should be a pattern to each place setting that works on the table as a whole. If you are using cups and saucers, don't insert a mug. If you are using salad plates, then only use plates—no bowls. Get the idea? There is a definite order to the table, but you set the tone with the mixing and matching of patterns.

A casually fussy style of entertaining is a constant invitation to be creative. Explore new ways to serve food. Serve hot soup in a coffee cup or cold soup in a large balloon wine glass. Serve a saucy entrée (like Braised Lamb Shanks with Gramalata Garnish) in a shallow pasta dish. Use oversized coffee cups for a chilled chopped salad and offer your guests a drizzle of dressing from a cream pitcher. A tall glass vase makes an interesting presentation for bread sticks. Experiment with various dishes, bowls and containers while choosing the menu. Your guests will be delighted with your innovative presentation.

Centerpieces as the Focus of the Table

Although bountiful bundles of fresh flowers are the favorite objects to work with when creating centerpieces, many things can create interest on your table. A centerpiece does not have to be in the center of the table and it can even be two or more objects. As long as the pattern is balanced, the centerpiece can even wander all over the table, by using porcelain figurines with lace, ribbon or fabric to tie it all together. An array of Victorian doll statues, placed decoratively on top of crushed velvet fabric, serves as a romantic centerpiece. Six or more porcelain figurines, dressed in sporting themes and surrounded by baseballs or tennis balls, define an athletic theme.

Piles of fresh fruit and vegetables in baskets work very well as centerpieces. Or, stack them on platters, place them on fabric, paint them with spray paint or dust them with sugar. There is no end to the effects that you can achieve.

Look around the house for objects to turn your table into an interesting party theme. Alphabet blocks mixed with rolled up newspapers, or stuffed bears tied with old lace and ribbon, can make wonderful centerpieces, and set a whimsical party mood. For a summer party, I persuaded a young friend to part with her Barbie and Ken dolls. After a sincere promise to return them unscathed, Barbie and Ken, dressed in swimsuits, appeared atop my backyard table, seated on beach towels, underneath a festive umbrella. Lemonade anyone?

PLACE CARDS

Place cards are white folded cards, written with your absolute best penmanship, that tell your guests where they are to sit. However, when thinking in a casually fussy party approach to table setting, the place card becomes a part of the table decor, and is seldom just a folded card.

When they were younger, my children would draw a picture for each guest to put at their place setting. This practice evolved into themes for the holidays. Easter brought monogrammed eggs and Christmas offered personalized gingerbread men. I have used miniature pots filled with fresh herbs, for a summer party. Each guest's name was painted on a clay pot with a gold paint pen. Larger clay pots, in various sizes, were used to hold the centerpiece flowers, and clay platters were used to serve the food. Gold flatware pieces were the finishing touch for my casually fussy party. Clay pots for the casual—gold flatware for the fussy.

For sports themed parties, "autograph" a ball with your guest's name on it at his or her place. Miniature picture frames, with the guest's name printed where the picture should be, make fun place cards, as do napkins that have been tied with strands of wide ribbon with the guest's name written with a calligraphy pen.

THE ART OF THE SALT

For the past several years I have collected different types of salt and pepper shakers. These are useful and interesting additions to any dinner table. In all sizes and shapes, salt and pepper shakers are made from sterling silver, crystal, pewter, glass, porcelain, and more. Use more than one pair on a buffet table, and as many as one pair per place setting at a sit-down dinner table. I use so many porcelain figurine salt and pepper shakers on my Christmas table that my guests think they are tree ornaments.

On a formal table, you may want to offer individual salt dishes, often called salt cellars, and miniature spoons for each place setting. Pepper mills, whether electric, hand grind, or lighted, are a must when serving big, fresh salads. Or place several of them in the center of the table to create an interesting "pepper mill skyscraper" centerpiece.

FABRICS AND RIBBONS

When you think of tablecloths and napkins, think also of fabrics and ribbons, and use them interchangeably. Doing so, especially when working within a budget, can change the entire appearance of the table. Spruce up a plain white tablecloth by tying the corners with beautiful ribbon. Or take that same white table cloth and throw a colorful piece of fabric on top. Bunch it up, lay some flowers around, and you have a very interesting table.

A lace square placed below the dinner plate adds a romantic flavor to the place setting. If that same square is fiesta striped, a Mexican celebration is on the way. Flowered sheets work well as table cloths for a garden party. Lace napkins tied with rich red ribbon are fabulous for a tea party. Even a faux fur pelt can be draped over a buffet table when you are serving wild game. Again, the idea is to let your imagination and creativity shine.

FLOWERS AND CANDLES

Both are an absolute must on most party tables. When entertaining with a casually fussy flair, flowers don't have to be in vases. For example, tulips are wonderful in a pottery pitcher, and fragrant flowers like gardenias can float in small custard cups.

Candles and flowers lend themselves to varying heights on your table. Votive candles and floating flowers can sit alternately on inverted bowls draped with fabric or on pedestal plates. Large candles can sit on mirrored trays to double the brightness of the flames. Although not technically flowers, fresh herb sprigs stuffed in bud vases are fragrant, and can serve equally well amid floating flowers, or around the base of candles.

The casually fussy style of entertaining relies on all of the rules of the past, yet opens the door for today's host and hostess to work creatively within their budget. When fashioning an event to share with friends and family, you build on the freedom and inventiveness that this concept allows. Before you realize it, you will develop a passion for entertaining.

DINNER PARTY MENUS FOR 4 TO 6

FRIENDS FOR DINNER

The spectacular first course deserves to be displayed on great china. Plan ahead and have everything purchased and thawed before you begin to make the dish. The veal chops are easily prepared in advance and then quickly browned and baked. This can be done just before you serve the first course. The Panzanella salad is made just in advance of your guests' arrival and served at room temperature to enjoy all of the terrific flavors. The pumpkin brownies can be made the day before, chilled and then removed from the fridge to come to room temperature. Use an eclectic place setting for each guest.

Lobster Burrito with Cilantro Cream Sauce ✽ **Grilled Stuffed Veal Chops**
Panzanella ✽ **Pumpkin Brownies with Cream Cheese Frosting**

CANDLELIT DINNER

This is a great spring party plan. Place candles of various heights on a mirrored tray in the center of the table. Place other lit candles on the sideboard or counter top. Remember to use unscented candles so as not to detract from the aroma of your terrific meal. The soup, vegetable, and the dessert can be prepared the day before. The soup is warmed over medium heat. Bake the gratin 30 minutes before you plan to serve. It will keep warm for quite a while. Serve the soup in a shallow bowl on a plate sprinkled with fresh chopped mint. Prepare the lamb in advance and roast just as you present the soup. You will only need 15 to 20 minutes

for perfectly done chops. Bring the pudding to room temperature
and reheat the caramel sauce right before serving.

Sweet Pea Soup with Mint   **Herb Crusted Rack of Lamb**
Cauliflower Gratin   **Sticky Toffee Pudding with Caramel Sauce**

ENTERTAINING THE BOSS

Here is a stress-free dinner party meal plan that is guaranteed to show off your skills as both an easy-going cook and a relaxed host. Prepare the salad and place on individual plates in the refrigerator for up to several hours in advance. Make the dressing separately and drizzle onto the salad just before serving. Make the mushroom sauce for the steaks and keep warm. Grill the steaks just before you serve dinner so that they sizzle when you bring them to the table. The chilled asparagus platter is made in advance and placed on the table right from the fridge. The cheesecake dessert has been baked the day before. Set a simple table and serve the meal all at once to show your no-nonsense approach to easy entertaining.

Mixed Greens with Goat Cheese, Walnuts, and Chili Vinaigrette
Chilled Roasted Asparagus with Tomato Mayonnaise Salsa
Grilled Beef Tenderloin Steaks with Shiitake Mushroom Sauce
My Favorite Cheesecake

UPSCALE RUSTIC SUPPER

Use a colorful platter to serve the bruschetta. Place the long baguettes in a vase in the center of the table. Find a sun-colored shawl or orange blanket as a table cloth. Lay oversized sunflowers directly onto the table. Serve each guest a whole trout on a large buffet-size dish. Pass the platter of squash rings. Serve the free form dessert right from the oven and drop a spoon full of ice cream on top. Pass a pitcher of the warm sauce.

Bruschetta with Goat Cheese   **Vegetable Stuffed Whole Trout with Lemon Sauce**
Whole Wheat Baguettes   **Glazed Acorn Squash Rings**
Warm Apple Tart with Almond Crème and Caramel Sauce

NO REASON TO PARTY PARTY

You don't have to have a reason or a theme to have friends over for dinner. Impromptu parties are the best. Perhaps you find yourself faced with a rainy Saturday and plenty of time on your hands. Cook your favorite foods and pick up the phone to see who's hungry and in the mood to party. Here is an ambitious but fun menu that you can prepare in the afternoon and serve a few hours later.

Tortilla Soup   **Spicy Black Bean Cakes with Chili Cream Sauce**
Chicken Enchiladas with Black Bean Mole Sauce   **Gingerbread with Poached Pears**

CROWD SIZE ENTERTAINING
BUFFET BASICS

SUPPER BUFFETS

A buffet party is a style of entertaining that permits the guests to serve themselves from abundant patters of diverse and interesting food. By now you may have guessed that a buffet table doesn't have to be an actual table! A buffet is created wherever you please; on a stationery kitchen island or counter top. A dining room sideboard or a family room bar can make for excellent buffet space. An outside barbecue grill area or a living room coffee table all work equally well when you envision your party. There are two tips that make any section of your home a great place to set a buffet. First, make the buffet accessible so that your guests aren't stumbling over each other. Secondly, begin at the beginning. Build the meal with each dish and set the pace of the event.

You prefer that the buffet line flows well. Some hosts choose to set the buffet with duplicate food dishes on each side of the table. However, when the guests are invited to take a plate at one end of the table and then work his or her way down either side they may run into some trouble. Some guests will stroll around the entire table so as not to miss a dish. Others meet at the opposite end and have to turn around—plates in hand—to avoid running into each other. Ultimately we can avoid stumbling guests by organizing the buffet table.

Alert your guests to the proper starting location by placing all of the utensils, dishes, and napkins at the beginning of the buffet. You may want to wrap utensils in the napkins so they can be held easily. Place them in a large basket at the front of the buffet for easy identification.

The order of food platters on a buffet is designed to offer your guests the ability to choose their favorite foods in portions that they desire. You place the platters just as you would serve the meal. For supper buffet tables, the first course is the first platter. Soup or salad leads the food dishes. Serve fresh crisp salad greens in a chilled bowl. Salad dressings are placed next to the bowl so that every guests is able to view each available selection. Place a pepper mill nearby. Next in line are the bread or rolls and the butter dish. Rolls that are to be used for sandwiches with a meat entrée such as turkey breast or tenderloin are pre-sliced and kept covered in a basket or large bowl.

Following the bread basket is the entrée platter. You want your guests to know that they have hit the crescendo of the meal. The entrée platter should be lavish and well garnished in its presentation. Place a specialty sauce or rich gravy next to the entrée (not at the end of the buffet). Condiments are placed after a meat dish and may be served in interesting containers like mayonnaise from a candy dish or ketchup from a small pitcher. Place all of the side dishes after the main course. Scatter pairs of salt and pepper shakers at several points on the table.

More Buffets

A brunch buffet begins with pitchers of juice served in juice glasses, bowls of fresh fruit served in fruit dishes followed by dinner plates for the egg casserole or French toast. End the buffet with miniature muffins and pastries in napkin-lined baskets. Set the coffee service in a separate location to avoid confusion.

A dessert buffet, sometimes called a Viennese table, is truly an impressive addition to any party. It is done in lieu of setting the dessert on the same table as the rest of the meal. On this buffet, place each dessert in a separate area surrounded by everything required for service. Each section holds a dessert platter, serving utensil, eating utensils, napkins, plates. and any garnish or accompaniment. Balance the table by offering several desserts. For example, Peanut Butter Cup Cheesecake, served on a cake stand, is pre-sliced into wedges. Next to the cake stand are several dessert dishes, cocktail-sized napkins, forks, a cake server and perhaps a crystal shaker filled with confectioners' sugar. The next section offers Fresh Mixed Berries in a chilled crystal bowl. Smaller bowls, spoons, napkins, a slotted serving spoon and a pitcher of

Zabaglione Sauce sits close by. Across from the fruit is an elaborate baking dish steaming with Cinnamon Bread Pudding. Not far away are small cream soup bowls, a gravy boat filled with warm Bourbon Sauce, a small ladle for the sauce, a larger one for the pudding, and several more napkins. The far end of the table finds Chocolate Mahogany Cake sitting on a most unusual platter. The plates are piled high around this family favorite dessert. Adjoining the napkins (the cake can be very gooey), a cake server, and a small ladle is a beautiful bowl overflowing with whipped cream; the decadent ending to this dessert buffet.

BUFFET STATIONS

When space is limited, or to accommodate a large crowd, utilize buffet stations for a party. The first station is the party ice breaker. Chilled opened wine bottles and cold beer are arranged in a large ice-filled bucket at the center of a table. Place appetizer platters onto decorative napkins or fabric squares on the table with stacks of cocktail napkins readily available. As soon as most of the guests have arrived and the tidbits on the platters diminish, it is time to set the second station for the salad course. A low coffee table is the perfect place for a mini salad bar. Drape a small cloth or fabric square over part of the table. Set a chilled bowl of greens on top. Offer crocks of cheese, croutons and pitchers filled with various dressings. Small salad dishes, salad forks and more napkins are a must.

The kitchen makes an excellent place for the entrée station. Piping hot baking dishes sit on a clean counter top with crinkled fabric surrounding each one. The same fabric is used for dinner napkins and bread basket liners. The dining room table is perfect for the desserts. Light candles and lay fresh flowers among the platters.

Offer coffee and after-dinner cordials on a sideboard. To ensure that the buffet stations are well-manned by every guests, be sure that each dish offers bite-size pieces that are easy to eat. (The triple threat of a knife, fork, and lap-held plate definitely invite disaster.)

Buffet basics put your guests at ease while offering a wide variety of sensational flavors, enticing aromas, and savory textures. Use this style of entertaining for larger parties and for those occasions when the guests may not know each other well. A buffet party provides a magical vehicle that encourages people to mingle with each other and guarantees a successful event.

BUFFET MENUS FOR A SMALL CROWD
(Adjust the servings of each dish to fill your "crowd" requirement)

LADIES WHO LUNCH

Prepare all of the dishes in advance and set everything out on the table at the same time. The guests can nibble in between conversation. The sweet muffins and quick bread work as both the bread and dessert part of the menu. This is a great buffet meal plan for an afternoon meeting or surprise birthday party.

Fresh Fruit Salad with Raspberry Yogurt Sauce

Pasta Salad with Southwestern Vinaigrette ❧ **Grilled Lime Chicken Salad**

Apple Streusel Muffins ❧ **Banana Peanut Butter Chip Quick Bread**

Tips for Coffee, Mint Tea, and Lemonade

AFTER WORK KITCHEN BUFFET

Ask your favorite coworkers home on a Friday. Pull off the ties and take off the heels. Pull the chili out of the fridge—you made it the day before and it's even better reheated. Warm the spinach dip and serve a basket of baked chips. Warm up the corn muffins and ask a pal to toss the salad. Serve the chili right out of the pot and pass the Cheddar cheese around the kitchen table. A plate of cookies adds just enough sweetness for dessert.

Baked Spinach and Artichoke Dip ❧ **Chili Con Carne with Gusto**

Spinach, Apple, and Pecan Salad with Citrus Vinaigrette

Jalapeño Corn Muffins ❧ **Lemon Coconut Macaroons**

OUTDOOR ALFRESCO SUPPER

Use the freshest ingredients to enjoy this quickly prepared outdoor supper buffet meal. Choose a setting for your alfresco dinner party. An outdoor garden, backyard deck, or screened porch is a perfect place for a summer party. But don't stop there. An apartment rooftop, public park, or corporate lobby can be transformed to simulate outdoor dining. The secret is to surround the dining table with lots of fresh greenery. Enhance your outdoor setting by bringing in several large potted green plants. Incorporate small pots of flowering plants to give your dinner setting the feel of sitting in the midst of an intimate garden.

Tri-Color Tomatoes with Basil and Mozzarella Cheese

Grilled Florida Lobster Tail with Garlicky Tomato Sauce

Vermicelli with Olive Oil and Fresh Parsley ❧ **Sautéed Fruit with Walnut Shortbread**

BUFFET MEALS FOR A BIG CROWD

(Adjust the servings of each dish to fill your "crowd" requirement)

GETTING THE GANG TOGETHER

When preparing for a large party, don't forget to ask for help. Plan in advance. Take inventory on china and utensils. Make sure the bar is stocked. Make a shopping list for everything that you will need. Choose and prepare dishes that you can make in advance and cook at the last moment. Have a friend or pay a helper to assist in the actual cooking and cleanup. With all of the details taken care of, you are bound to enjoy your own party.

Roasted Peppers with Anchovies and Roasted Garlic Dip

Roasted Red Pepper, Garlic, and Eggplant Dip

Chopped Salad with Gorgonzola and Sun-Dried Tomato Thousand Island Dressing

Roasted Pork Tenderloin with Jack Daniels Whisky Pepper Corn Sauce

Salmon Livornese ❧ **Stuffed Baked Potatoes**

Strawberry Cake with Cream Cheese Frosting ❧ **Chocolate Mahogany Cake**

EVERYBODY'S GRAZING BUFFET

When the food is terrific you want to try a little taste of everything. That's grazing—just spending the evening eating a mouthful of this and that. Keep the platters of fun food coming and ask your grazing guests to help refill.

Bruschetta with Three Toppings ❧ **Garlicky Soft Shell Crabs**

Fresh Mussels Steamed in Garlic Tomato Broth

Vegetable Lasagna with Tomato and Sautéed Vegetable Sauce

Focaccia Bread ❧ **Mixed Fresh Berries served with Zabaglione Sauce**

SPORTS BAR PARTY

It's time for the big game and the big screen TV is fired up. Add some inspired dishes and terrific timing and you are set to be the winner with this terrific buffet meal plan.

Black Bean and Toasted Corn Salsa *❧* **Super Nachos Two Ways**
Buffalo Style Chicken Wings *❧* **Mexican Spiced Pizza** *❧* **Chicken Chili with Veggies**
Vegetable Party Platter with Tuna Sauce *❧* **Chocolate Cookie Cheesecake Bars**

NEW TRADITIONS FOR HOLIDAY PARTIES

HOME FOR THE HOLIDAYS

What is it about holidays that add to our overall stress level? Is it that we try to do too much in too short a time? There is a lot of pressure when baking Aunt Edna's pumpkin pie knowing that she will soon sit across the table from you to eat it. Perhaps we have reached an age when grabbing a basket for the annual Easter egg hunt has lost its appeal. Maybe—just once—we want to stay in rather than grill outdoors on a hot Labor Day.

Holidays should be about friends and family and fun gatherings. More than that, holidays are about blending cherished traditions into our fast-paced, time-constrained lifestyle. All the same, holidays present an opportunity to create new memories for the next generation.

Lets begin this year to establish workable, new holiday traditions that include great food, good friends, and less stress. We'll start with a little pre-planning.

PLAN THE OCCASION

Decide if your holiday at home will include a crowd or just a small group of close friends. Choose a buffet or sit-down party theme. Select a menu and take inventory of your place settings. Plan centerpieces and place cards. Pick up the phone and invite your guests. If asked, "Can I bring something?"—say yes. Allow your family to share in creating the new tradition dishes for your holiday meal. Blend a mixture of conventional favorites with new recipes or unusual ingredients. Update a dish with your own personal touches.

INCORPORATE TIME SAVERS

Remember the de-stressors—make a menu plan, write a grocery list, shop in advance, and prepare as many dishes as you can the day before the party. Blend store-bought goodies with homemade favorites. Design your table and centerpieces several days in advance. Every once in a while—STOP. Take a deep breath and smell the food. Enjoy the bustle of holiday preparations knowing that you are creating a new tradition.

HOLIDAY MENUS

ROMANTIC VALENTINE'S DAY DINNER

Light the candles, fill the vase with red roses, tie the napkins with a scrap of lace, and dust off the fine china. Luxuriate over a delicious meal that deserves to be savored one bite at a time. Bring on the chilled champagne!

Grilled Herb Shrimp *❧* **Braised Lamb Shanks with Gramalata Garnish**
Risotto with Wild Mushrooms *❧* **Fresh Lima Beans with Mint**
Hazelnut Heart Cookies

EASTER SUNDAY BRUNCH

You certainly don't have to wait until springtime to serve this easily made-in-advance brunch. There are several unique and unusual dishes to blend with the more traditional fare. Your guests will love the choices.

Hot Chocolate Rolls ❧ **Sour Cream Coffee Cake**

Smoked Trout and Brie Quesadilla with Dill Cream Guacamole

Plum Tomatoes with Basil ❧ **Fluffy Egg and Cheese Casserole**

Dicey Potato Casserole ❧ **Sautéed Ham Steaks and Candied Bacon**

FOURTH OF JULY PICNIC

A summer picnic is a ton of fun. The group works up a big appetite with all of the outdoor activities. A heavy checkered cloth on a picnic table is filled with platters of made-in-advance great dishes. Use paper products for easy clean up. Serve the chilled soup in paper cups and the grilled corn right from the husks.

Chilled Gazpacho Soup ❧ **Spicy Fried Chicken**

Deviled Eggs ❧ **Chilled Green Bean Salad with Mustard Shallot Vinaigrette**

Grilled Corn with Thyme Infused Butter ❧ **Apple Strawberry Cobbler**

LABOR DAY COOK-IN

Summer can be hot, hot, hot...way too hot to spend the evening in muggy heat. Who says that you can't cook in for a summer party? Use your trusted grill pan in place of the outdoor version to create some just-like-I-grilled-it-outside dishes.

Marinated Grilled Vegetables with Feta Cheese

Big Juicy Hamburgers with Grilled Onions ❧ **Rum Soaked Sweet Potatoes**

Peach Pie Y'All

HALLOWEEN OPEN HOUSE

With every little goblin that rings the doorbell comes a harried parent whose just trying to keep up. This open house menu is an invitation for everyone to drop by for a few minutes of relaxation. Serve the soups in covered tureens so that they stay hot. Place mugs and oversized coffee cups by each tureen. Offer slices of warm bread in baskets covered with festive napkins. Place a winking, lighted jack-o-lantern in the center of the table as a welcome to each guest. Don't forget to drop a handful of caramels into the trickster's pockets when they leave!

Curried Pumpkin Soup ❧ **Caramelized Onion Soup**

Black Bean Soup with Toasted Corn and Rosemary ❧ **Herb and Cheese Bread**

Quick Apple Cinnamon Bread ❧ **Chewy Caramels**

A REALLY FUSSY THANKSGIVING

Make copies of the recipes that you plan to include in your Thanksgiving dinner. If someone offers to bring a dish, don't hesitate to make a suggestion and offer your recipe. The extra help is much appreciated. Prepare the cinnamon rolls the night before and bake them for breakfast. With a full tummy you face the rest of the meal—most of which you have prepared in advance.

Best Cinnamon Rolls ❧ **Simple Salmon Spread**

Herb and Sherry Roasted Turkey with Savory Gravy ❧ **White Raisin Dressing for Poultry**

Roasted Garlic Mashed Potatoes ❧ **Corn Soufflé Casserole** ❧ **Yam Pudding**

Sautéed Green Beans and Caramelized Pearl Onions ❧ **Parker House Rolls**

Perfect Pumpkin Pie ❧ **Chocolate Pudding Pie**

CHRISTMAS EVE BUFFET SUPPER

Place the appetizers on the bar and greet guests with a festive cocktail. Serve the meal on a dining room sideboard and invite guests to fill their plates before they sit down to the table.

Warm Artichoke and Crab Dip ❊ **Chopped Chicken Liver Spread**

Roasted Vegetable Terrine

Rock Cornish Game Hens with Wild Rice Stuffing and Orange Cranberry Glaze

Broccoli Cheese Casserole ❊ **Cinnamon Bread Pudding with Bourbon Sauce**

NEW YEAR'S EVE FOUR COURSE DINNER

For a formal affair, a little helper in the kitchen is a must. Serve each course separately. The soup and its lavish garnish tastes as terrific as it looks. Present the stone crabs in a chilled bowl half filled with ice. The dinner plate is colorful with steamed fresh veggies, wedge of crisp potatoes and appealing roasted sea bass. Serve the torte just before midnight with a toast for the New Year.

Roasted Yellow Pepper Soup with Avocado Salsa and Sautéed Scallop Garnish

Cracked Stone Crabs with Dilled Mustard Sauce

Roasted Sea Bass with Red Wine Sauce

Julienne of Zucchini, Yellow Squash, and Carrots in Rosemary Butter

Pommes Anna ❊ **Flourless Chocolate Torte**

Index

Italic page numbers indicate menu suggestions.